the theory & practice of TEACHING

the theory & practice of TEACHING

EDITED BY
PETER JARVIS

KOGAN
PAGE

First published in 2002

Apart from any fair dealing for the purposes of research or private study, or criticism or review, as permitted under the Copyright, Designs and Patents Act 1988, this publication may only be reproduced, stored or transmitted, in any form or by any means, with the prior permission in writing of the publishers, or in the case of reprographic reproduction in accordance with the terms and licences issued by the CLA. Enquiries concerning reproduction outside these terms should be sent to the publishers at the undermentioned addresses:

Kogan Page Limited
120 Pentonville Road
London N1 9JN
UK

Stylus Publishing Inc.
22883 Quicksilver Drive
Sterling, VA 20166–2012
USA

© Individual contributors, 2002

The right of the individual contributors to be identified as the authors of this work has been asserted by them in accordance with the Copyright, Designs and Patents Act 1988.

British Library Cataloguing in Publication Data

A CIP record for this book is available from the British Library.

ISBN 0 7494 3416 4 (paperback)
ISBN 0 7494 3409 0 (hardback)

Typeset by Saxon Graphics Ltd, Derby
Printed and bound in Great Britain by Biddles Ltd, Guildford and King's Lynn
www.biddles.co.uk

Contents

PART THREE

Contributors

Dr Thomas Black is a senior lecturer in the School of Education Studies, University of Surrey and is responsible for the distance learning Masters degree in lifelong learning, applied professional studies and information technology. He has taught secondary school sciences in Nigeria and the UK, and been a lecturer in Education in Zambia, Northern Ireland and Surrey. His current research and development interests are in educational measurement, educational technology and quantitative research design.

Dr Bob Brownhill is a senior lecturer in the School of Educational Studies, University of Surrey. His current interests are in philosophy of ethics of teaching and learning.

Dr Josie Gregory is a lecturer in the School of Educational Studies, University of Surrey where she directs the Masters degree programme in Change Agent Skills and Strategies, an advanced training for organizational development consultants. Among her current interests are experiential learning and spirituality.

Dr Colin Griffin is an Associate Lecturer in the School of Educational Studies, University of Surrey. He has published books and articles on curriculum and policy, and is particularly interested in policy analysis of lifelong learning. His latest book is *Training to Teach in Further and Adult Education,* with David Gray and Tony Nasta.

Professor John Holford is Director of the Unit for Lifelong Learning and Director of Research in the School of Educational Studies, University of Surrey. He is a founder member of the Centre for Research in Lifelong Learning. His current research is in Education and Training for Citizenship and Governance, in which he is directing a six-nation research project. His other research interests have been into the social and historical analysis of lifelong learning and the learning society. He is author or editor of several books, and is Reviews Editor of the *International Journal of Lifelong Education.*

Professor Peter Jarvis is Professor of Continuing Education and currently convenor of the Centre for Research in Lifelong Learning, University of Surrey. He is a former Head of Department of Educational Studies. He is the founding editor of *The International Journal of Lifelong Education* and widely published. His most recent books include *The Practitioner-Researcher* (Jossey-Bass) and in 2001 Kogan Page has published his new books, *Learning in Later Life* and *Universities and Corporate Universities: The higher learning industry in global society.* Kogan Page has also published in 2001 two books that he has edited: *The Age of Learning* and the revised edition of *Twentieth Century Thinkers in Adult and Continuing Education.*

Dr Linda Merricks is senior lecturer in the School of Educational Studies and Director of Studies of the Centre for Continuing Education, University of Surrey. Her research interests include progression, credit and other curricula matters in continuing education, policy and practice in lifelong learning and learning partnerships.

Professor Gill Nicholls is Professor of Education at Kings College, University of London and Director of the King's Institute for Learning and Teaching. Her research areas are science education and professional development. She has significant publications in the area of teaching and learning, and science education. Her most recent book is *Professional Development in Higher Education: New perspectives and directions* (Kogan Page, 2000).

Dr Julia Preece is currently seconded to the University of Botswana; she has been a lecturer at the University of Surrey since 1998. Prior to that she was at Lancaster University where she was responsible for an action research project exploring exclusion and educational participation issues amongst social and cultural minority groups. Her current research interests are citizenship, lifelong learning, adult education and social exclusion.

Dr Paul Tosey is a senior lecturer in the School of Educational Studies, University of Surrey, and Director of the Unit for Teaching and Learning. He joined the School in 1991, and was responsible for validating and coordinating for five years the highly successful MSc in Change Agent Skills and Strategies. He has published on topics such as the learning organization and experiential learning processes. His current research is into the experience and unintended learning of participants in organizational change.

Preface

While much government emphasis has been placed on the learning society in recent years, it has not omitted consideration of teaching as well. A number of reports have included it in their considerations, especially the Dearing Report (1997), which is discussed in considerable detail in the opening of this book. But the traditional notion of teaching is also changing – no longer can it be conceived of as just standing in front of a class and talking, with the occasional use of the chalkboard. While it is acknowledged that the practice has not changed for some teachers, teaching itself is undergoing change. For instance, this book has deliberately focused on the interpersonal, more traditional side of teaching, with only one chapter on distance education. Had time and space permitted we would have included more chapters of teaching aids and on distance education.

Many books have been written about interpersonal teaching and so it might be asked whether we need another, but many of those are entirely practical. While this book is certainly not divorced from the considerations of practice, it is also concerned with many of the theoretical issues that underlie teaching. Consequently it is designed to help practitioners think about their practice as well as extend the techniques that they employ. This book provides a multi-discipline analysis of teaching, and contains three parts:

1. the first five chapters examine theoretical issues underlying teaching itself;
2. the following section examines teaching methods;
3. the final brief one looks at issues surrounding assessment of learning, since teachers often find this a problematic area.

This book is written primarily for teachers and lecturers in post-compulsory education, that is:

- higher education;
- further education;
- education for managers and professionals;
- adult education.

Since the book focuses on theoretical and practical issues of teaching, those who teach school children will also find it of interest. Others will also find this book particularly useful:

- those who teach and assess teachers, like many of the authors of this book, will hopefully find many of the concerns in this book relevant to their work;
- schoolteachers;
- planners and policy makers might also wish to consider the human concerns underlying this book, since we seek to show that teaching is a moral activity concerned with the nature and identity of the learners.

The authors of the following chapters were all members of the School of Educational Studies, although one has subsequently left the School for another university. Ever since its formation soon after the University of Surrey was established, the School has focused on post-compulsory education and it still remains one of the only Schools of Educational Studies where there is no schoolteacher preparation. Its main concerns now are both in the preparation of educators for all forms of post-compulsory education and also for the study of these sectors of education and learning. Members of the School are interested in all of these sectors, from policy to practice, and undertake teaching, research and consultancy in all of them. The School has a large doctoral programme, and runs Masters degrees on a face-to-face basis and also has the first international distance education Masters degree in post-compulsory education – one it started in the 1980s.

The authors of this book come from two Centres in the School – those of Research into Lifelong Learning and the Human Potential Research Group. This latter group has existed almost since the formation of the School, which was then a Centre for Adult Education, while the former group has emerged as a result in the changes in the educational scene over the past decade or so. The Human Potential Group runs a world-renowned Masters degree in Change Agent Skills while the Centre for Research in Lifelong Learning has been responsible for the distance learning Masters degree which has three strands: lifelong learning, applied professional studies, and information technology.

Among the publications that have come from this group of authors in recent times have been *The Theory and Practice of Learning* (Jarvis, Holford and Griffin, 1998); *International Perspectives on Lifelong Learning* (ed Holford, Jarvis and Griffin, 1998); *The Age of Learning* (ed Jarvis, 2001); *Twentieth Century Thinkers in Adult and Continuing Education* (second edition, ed Jarvis, 2001) and *Learning in Later Life* and *Universities and Corporate Universities* (both Jarvis, 2001). All of these books have been published by Kogan Page.

Reference

Dearing, R (Chair) (1997) *Higher Education in the Learning Society,* Department for Education and Employment, London

Chapter 1

Teaching, learning – the changing landscape

Gill Nicholls and Peter Jarvis

In an era that has been termed a 'consumer society' it is not surprising that the way that knowledge is delivered has become a focus of attention. Recent debates in post-compulsory education, both nationally and internationally, have focused teaching on raising its quality and maintaining high standards in learning and achievement. While there has been a lot of discussion in Britain on teaching, there has also been a rhetoric that teaching and research are of equal importance. Nevertheless, research seems to hold the centre stage in different contexts, but one report above all other has placed teaching at the centre. The Dearing Report (1997) has brought attention to bear on the nature and quality of teaching and learning in universities in terms of lifelong learning. Responses to Dearing such as *Higher Education for the 21st Century* (DfEE, 1998a), have spelt out the government's aims, and the need to create a better balance between teaching, research and scholarship (scholarship here is being take to mean attainment and achievement) in higher education. These aims are to be achieved:

> through the promotion of effective learning and teaching, and enhancing the professional skills and status of teachers, and that all institutions of higher education give high priority to developing and implementing learning and teaching strategies which focus on the promotion of students' learning. (Dearing, 1997, p19)

A direct consequence of these aims and commitments has been the creation of the Institute for Learning and Teaching (ILT) and compulsory induction courses for lecturers. While this book is not only about university teaching, we want to use Dearing here to highlight some of the tensions that this emphasis has highlighted in universities since these ideas create the need to reconsider the role of the lecturer in teaching and learning, the changing nature of student intake, curriculum and pedagogy, and the way they are affecting the way in which academics have to function.

There is now an increased demand for improving the quality of teaching in higher education institutions. The debate has another dimension in the face of increased pressure for research excellence from such external assessment procedures as the Research Assessment Exercise (RAE). With a Quality Assurance Agency and the RAE the dichotomy of research or teaching has yet again taken centre stage, a stage that now includes external regulation and imposed professional development as a means of raising teaching quality. Bearing these issues in mind now is an appropriate time to re-evaluate the role of professional development and what teaching learning and scholarship in higher education means. It is important to consider why and how we find ourselves in the present situation.

What has made the landscape change? Initially one might say that the learning society is a consuming society and from the time that higher education was forced to become an earner, as well as a recipient of government funding, it has become more entrepreneurial – seeking to hold its old markets as well as to create new ones. The quality of its provision, therefore, is of crucial importance and so, at one level, it has been necessary to focus on quality assurance. But since government still exercises considerable control over higher education it has been a major player in seeking to improve its provision and generate new approaches to professional development, basically through the recommendations of the Dearing Report.

Historical background to the Institute of Learning and Teaching (ILT)

Following the Dearing Report and the White Paper on Higher Education, the role of professional development has not only changed, but has been given new dimensions and directions. These include the requirement for new lecturers to enrol on induction courses and programmes, which are assessed in some form. Within this context there has been the introduction of continuing professional development plans that are closely linked to appraisal, promotion and professional standing. Much of the current debate focuses on the introduction of the ILT and the implications this will have on higher education institutions in the future.

What makes the present situation different is the impact of the recent reviews and reports on higher education including the influential National

Committee of Inquiry into Higher Education (NCIHE) chaired by Sir Ron Dearing, and commonly known as the Dearing Report. This made recommendations that were to have significant implications for the status of teaching and the notion of professional development in higher education. One of the main features of the report has been the inception of the ILT, and the notion of imposed or enforced professional development. The Dearing Report recommended the immediate establishment of a professional institution for learning and teaching. The main recommendations in the report were set out as follows:

> We recommend that institutions of higher education begin immediately to develop or seek access to programmes for teacher training of their staff, if they do not have them, and that all institutions seek national accreditation of such programmes from the Institute for Learning and Teaching in Higher Education. (Recommendation 13)

> We recommend that the representative bodies, in consultation with the funding bodies, should immediately establish a professional Institute for Learning and Teaching in Higher Education. The functions of the institute would be to accredit programmes of training for higher education teachers, to commission research and development in teaching and learning practices, and to stimulate innovation. (Recommendation 14)

Other key recommendations in the Dearing Report included Recommendation 6, which covered the prospective role of the ILT in respect to students with disabilities; it recommended that the learning needs of students with disabilities be taken into account in its research, programme of accreditation and advisory activities. Dearing also proposed that the institute should recognize levels of expertise in teaching by conferring various categories of membership: associate member, member and fellow.

Recommendation 13, by implication, suggests some form of 'enforced' development programme for new staff in the higher education community and the suggestion that existing staff might also seek such professional recognition. This is not to say that some institutions were not already involved in good practice and providing new staff with extensive induction programmes. However, the statement in the Dearing Report clearly gives professional development a different dimension, by implying that it is now expected and indeed a prerequisite for probation to be completed. Dearing suggested that:

> Over the medium term, it should become the normal requirement that all new, full-time academic staff with teaching responsibilities are required to achieve at least associate membership of the Institute for Learning and Teaching for successful completion of their probationary period. (Recommendation 48)

Within this new environment of expectation and seeming enforcement the Report also proposed that the ILT might recognize levels of expertise in teaching by conferring various categories of membership, as we noted above. This suggests that development is no longer a choice but a requirement, a requirement that is differentiated through demands and expectations.

The government's approval for such an institution was made clear in its response to the Dearing recommendations:

> The government sees the new Institute for Learning and Teaching in Higher Education to be established by the higher education sector as having a key role to play in enhancing the professional skills and status of teachers in higher education and in spreading good teaching more widely. The Government's long-term aim is to see all teachers in higher education carry a professional qualification. (DfEE, 1998a, pp19–23)

It saw the ILT as being established by the higher education sector and having a key role to play in enhancing the professional skills and status of teachers in higher education and spreading good practice more widely. The above statement also makes it clear that the government's long-term aim is to ensure that all academics involved with teaching and learning in higher education will carry a professional qualification. The nature of this qualification is as yet unresolved as the ILT is not at present in a position to operate a 'licence to practice', nor does the higher education community appear to want such a licence. The Dearing Report envisaged the successful completion of an accredited programme or pathway would be a normal requirement for successful completion of probation. This links into the concept of a 'licence to practice' as operated by many professional bodies. The recommendations did not stop with initial entry, but suggested that continual professional development (CPD) be monitored and regulated, so that 'higher education teaching needs to have higher status and be regarded as a profession of standing' (Para 14.18). The report went on to specify that:

> The Institute would provide the basis for a nationally recognized system of professional qualifications for high education teachers based on a probationary period, and followed up with an appropriate continuing professional development at later career stages. (Para 14.29)

Guidelines for regular commitment to CPD for all its categories of membership and procedures for verifying these activities in terms of demonstrable outcomes achieved would be specified later.

These recommendations indicate the nature of the anticipated change that will be required, or even demanded of the academic community. Within the context of this changing landscape of higher education challenges are being made to some of the fundamental concepts and notions of what it is to be an academic. These challenges are proving contentious from a number of perspectives. At first sight it appears that the long-standing view of the autonomous academic is being threatened, as is the main perceived focus of academics' work being research. The notion of achieving a level of competence that matches a licence to practice is not only daunting to those primarily concerned with research, but also conceived as an imposition to the academics' *raison d'être*. Such initial reaction led the consultation documents, following Dearing, to ask questions related to professional development and a licence to practice, among many other issues. The higher education community was asked to consider the following questions: what kind of relationship, if any should there be between the accreditation of programmes/pathways and any conferment of a licence to practice upon individual staff? Should accreditation eventually become mandatory for all teaching staff?

Institutional responses to these questions varied considerably. In the context of the changing landscape it is important to consider the implications of introducing imposed professional development to meet the criteria of a professional body. The criteria as suggested by the ILT raise issues about the academic as a professional, and their anticipated behaviour as a professional within a professional body.

However, it is necessary here to highlight the way these changes are taking place. Suggesting the academic community requires a professional body assumes that academics do not already engage with this level of professionalism. It also assumes that throughout the academic community there is more bad practice than good in the areas of teaching and learning, hence teaching and learning support needs monitoring in a formalized way, so that new academics should be able to demonstrate their competence, be accredited and rewarded by membership of the professional body. Whether Dearing was prepared to recognize that university teaching was already an established profession or understood the complex nature of teaching in the learning society are other matters; the former is beyond the scope of this book but the latter is a part of this book's rationale.

Government intervention

Britain is not alone in the types of interventions being suggested and implemented in terms of imposed training for lecturers and educators. The emphasis in the sector at present seems to be a greater push towards standards and competency-based methods of assessment of teachers. Often these assessments are based on student learning outcomes and standards of achievement.

One only has to look at a few of the British examples of demands for change led by government documents such as *Induction of New Teachers* (DfEE, 1998b) and *Implementing the Vision* (1999) of the Institute for Learning and Teaching, and Further Education National Training Organization (FENTO) standards (1999), to see the increased regulation of teaching and learning.

Any attempt by the sector to change the teaching and learning activities, of both students and teachers, cannot ignore these documents and proposed changes. Yet consideration must be given to the learning environment of the professional, in preparation for imposed and other changes. For the post-compulsory sector, this means considering how teaching is going to affect the role of learning for the lecturer, facilitator or trainer in the pursuit of new knowledge, and the teacher (who is often the same person) applying his or her theoretical knowledge to a teaching situation. As members of a teaching/learning community individuals are not only expected to practise an art or science, but also act as a 'professor' of knowledge (Garrett and Holmes, 1995, p49). It also needs to be recognized that the development and reaction to change are enhanced when the importance of the working environment is considered and that the development process must not be alienated from the context of practice. The context may vary across institutions but is influenced by formal and informal, internally or externally imposed structures and strategies, such as the ILT.

Significant dilemmas for the university teacher in the changing landscape

Practice, in this case teaching, does not happen in a vacuum, but occurs in a variety of social, political and ideological contexts. The practice of teaching in the post-compulsory sector and the role of learning for the professional educator are equally dependent on the whole educational context, particularly at a time when the post-compulsory sector is facing periods of rapid change.

The post-compulsory sector has undergone, and still is undergoing a series of complex changes that are affecting its organizational structures and practices. A significant element of these changes has been the continuing expansion of higher and further education (Elton, 1992; Westargaard, 1991). Expansion and massification have brought with them considerable implications, affecting staff and students alike (Hatline and Marshall, 1996; Rowland, 1996), particularly in relation to the amount of time available for teaching and learning. This sector now has a less homogeneous student population, which in turn has led to a diversification of course content and structure as a means of differentiated learning (Nixon, 1997) and teaching.

Concurrent with the changing nature of student intake, curriculum and pedagogy, are the changes in the staffing structures within the sector. Kogan *et al* (1994, pp62–63) suggest that: 'The cohesion afforded by traditional structures is likely to be eroded as status and other differentials increase, especially between staff with permanent appointments and those in temporary or part-time contracts': something which Dearing does recognize.

A consequence of the FENTO changes is that 'the occupation of university teacher no longer automatically offers autonomy and status' (Nixon, 1996, p7). Incumbent in this argument is that educators have increased tension within their role. These tensions are further encapsulated by the imposition of statutory requirements for teaching standards or competences in the area of teaching and learning, as recommended by ILT.

Another major dilemma is the relationship between teaching and research. The research–teaching nexus has been established as a well-founded area of discussion, but cannot be seen in isolation. While the perceived differences between researchers and teachers have been gaining pace within the academic community, as we noted above, the higher education system itself has been undergoing changes in the nature of student intake, curriculum and pedagogy. It is the final one of these upon which this book focuses.

Further complicating the situation of teaching and research, has been the change occurring in staffing structures in higher education. Kogan *et al* (1994, pp62–63) suggests that: 'The cohesion afforded by traditional structures is likely to be eroded as status and other differentials increase, especially between staff with permanent appointments and those in temporary or part-time contracts.' This differential is currently increasing, with top level academics having to produce high profile research, while the day-to-day work of teaching and research in universities is, as Ainsley (1994, p32) suggests: 'sustained by a growing army of insecurely employed contract staff who make up to a third of all academic employees'.

These changes have left academics in a dilemma:

- Do they concentrate on keeping up with new innovations in teaching and learning?
- Do they try to adapt to a changing student population?
- Do they keep up with their research?
- Do they try to do all of these?

Some academics in seeking to resolve this dilemma have looked to the higher education's reward structures and systems to gain insight and reassurance about which direction to go. The reward system reveals why so many academics place their research before teaching even if they feel passionately about their teaching. Research is rewarded, teaching is not!

Alongside the reward systems favouring research, research itself has become more specialized with evidence to show how the research being undertaken in universities has little or no connection with teaching. Thus the balance in the traditional role of the university teacher between research and teaching has grown further apart. Within the changing landscape the teaching–research dilemma still exists but with the introduction of lifelong learning demands, this dilemma is exacerbated.

Against this background there is an urgent need to consider the role of teaching and learning within the post-compulsory sector, something which this book endeavours to do – but it also seeks to expand the common conceptions of teaching that prevail in a great deal of higher education.

Implications for teaching and learning

The introduction of national frameworks for the accreditation of teachers in the field of post-compulsory and adult education must open up many questions related to the underpinning assumptions about teaching and learning in this area. The fact that government policy is to make post-compulsory education institutions in lifelong learning one is inherent in other reports, such as and the Green Paper, *The Learning Age* (DfEE, 1998c) and its subsequent documents. The government is clearly intent on changing the nature of the student clientele in these institutions but more mature adults do not come with the same expectations and experiences as young adults. Moreover, as fee-paying clients, they may well have higher expectations of the way in which they are taught. But they also come with different experiences and, often, considerable knowledge – perhaps being far more mature than those who teach them. Consequently, traditional didactic teaching methods are insufficient and higher education is being forced to learn from adult education about the methods that it has traditionally employed. Universities, however, have been particularly slow in seeking the assistance of those who have spent much of their academic lives teaching adults, something that Dearing also failed to recognize. Adults have been a neglected species in higher education (Boud *et al,* 1993; Knowles, 1984) but adult education has pioneered teaching techniques that have been oriented to adult learning and which have recognized the experience and expertise of the learners. Indeed, the training of adult educators began many years ago in the UK, with Eldson (1975) being a major advocate.

Any introduction of standards and competence tends to make teaching and learning focus on the areas imposed or needed to be demonstrated to gain the accreditation required to practise rather than the breadth of expertise that adult students demand. Such standards and competences might well increase the operational standards of a teacher but they will not necessarily increase the underpinning knowledge related to how students learn and the learning context, what might be called the academic competence of the individual. Alongside this argument rests the notion of an imposed curriculum. Increasingly there is a government agenda to impose a curriculum on the post-compulsory sector, requiring transferable skills, information technology skills, communication skills as well as specific numeracy and literacy skills.

Indeed, this emphasis, which we quite understand although we might not fully support, resurrects another debate about the difference between education and training. This is an outmoded discussion, but it finds new form in lifelong learning – especially as government has tended to focus mainly on its vocational element.

Non-vocational education is also part of the tradition of post-compulsory education with its emphasis on liberal education and the fully educated person. Traditionally, fully educated individuals were thought of as receiving the breadth of their education all together, since education was perceived of as something that was completed by the end of young adulthood. Now, with the idea of lifelong learning, there are an increasing number of older people who seek education – although not of a vocational nature. Third age education is increasing and institutions of lifelong learning have to recognize that many of their learners will be drawn from people at the end of their careers (as well as in the middle) and after their careers are over. These students bring even more experience and understanding to their learning, which makes even greater demands on the expertise of teachers.

This, coupled with the standards required for teaching, it might be said, changes the nature and context of teaching and learning, or is it that teachers will have to adapt their teaching styles to comply with the set standards which may or may not reflect the reality of the situation on the ground? We would like to argue that the creative teacher can still use a variety of teaching methods that assist the learner and that these well-established methods can be used to demonstrate competence and standards within the field of teaching and learning, but any form of professional accreditation needs to recognize the complexity of the process that might now be understood as teaching.

This book is deliberately selective and concentrates on face-to-face teaching. While Dearing rightly looks at the introduction of technology into teaching, we have included only one chapter here pointing to all the other aspects of teaching but, as mentioned in the Preface, we feel that it is important to look carefully at the theory and practice of teaching face-to-face.

References

Ainsley, P (1994) *Degrees of Difference: Higher education in the 1990s*, Lawrence & Wishart, London

Boud, D, Keogh, R and Walker, D (1993) *Using Experience for Learning,* SRHE and Open University Press, Buckingham

Dearing, R (Chair) (1997) *Higher Education in the Learning Society,* Department for Education and Employment, London

DfEE (1998a) *Higher Education for the 21st Century,* TSO, Norwich

DfEE (1998b) *Induction of New Teachers,* TSO, Norwich

DfEE (1998c) *The Learning Age,* TSO, Norwich

Eldson, K (1975) *Training for Adult Education,* Department of Adult Education, University of Nottingham in association with the National Institute of Adult Education, Nottingham

Elton, L (1992) Research, teaching and scholarship in an expanding higher education system, *Higher Education Quarterly,* **46**, pp 252–67

FENTO (1999) *FENTO Standards*, www.fento.co.uk

Garrett, D and Holmes, R (1995) Research and teaching: a symbiotic relationship, in *Research Teaching and Learning in Higher Education,* eds B Smith and S Brown, Kogan Page, London

Institute for Learning and Teaching (1999) *Implementing the Vision*, ILT, York

Knowles, M (1984) *The Adult Learner: A neglected species,* 3rd edn, Gulf, Houston, TX

Kogan, M, Moses, I and El-Khawas, E (1994) *Staffing Higher Education: Meeting new challenges*, Jessica Kinglsey Publishers, London

Hatline, J and Marshall, H W (1996) The relationship between research and teaching: a meta analysis, *Review of Educational Research,* **66**, pp 507–42

Nixon, J (1996) Professional Identity and the restructuring of higher education, *Studies in Higher Education,* **21** (1), pp 5–16

Nixon, J (1997) Regenerating professionalism within the academic workplace, in *The End of Professionalism? The restructuring of professional work,* eds J Broadbent, M Dietrich and J Roberts, Routledge, London, pp 86–103

Rowland, S (1996) Relationship between teaching and research, *Teaching in Higher Education,* **1** (1), pp 7–20

Westergaad, J (1991) Scholarship, research and teaching: a view from the social sciences, *Studies in Higher Education,* **66**, pp 507–42

Further reading

Elton, L (1977) Introduction, in *Staff Development in Higher Education,* eds L R B Elton and K Simmonds, Society for Research into Higher Education, Guildford

Elton, L (1995) Effects of Funding Council policies on teaching quality, in *Research Teaching and Learning in Higher Education,* eds B Smith and S Brown, Kogan Page, London

Chapter 2

Teaching in a changing world

Peter Jarvis

This book is about teaching in a learning society, in a completely different world to that in which the art and science of teaching emerged. Teaching itself has traditionally had a number of different meanings, as the *Concise Oxford English Dictionary* shows:

- To give systematic information to a person, or about a subject or skill.
- To practise this professionally.
- To enable a person to do something by instruction and training (to swim; to dance).
- To be an advocate for a moral principle (my parents taught me forgiveness).
- To communicate, instruct in a moral principle.
- To induce a person by example or punishment to do or not to do a thing (that will teach you to sit still; that will teach you not to laugh).
- To make a person disinclined to do a thing (I will teach you to interfere).

It may also be seen from these definitions that teaching has negative as well as positive connotations – indicating that sometimes people do not want to learn and have to be taught or that they will be punished if they do not learn. This is something that will occur again in the next chapter when we look at teaching styles. Yet, it also contains moral overtones and indications that it is generally regarded as a good thing. However, this diversity of function has been increased dramatically over the past few years because of the globalizing forces in society and the rapid changes in knowledge, resulting in both the knowledge society and the learning society. It is interesting that the concepts of teaching mentioned above do not explicitly specify learning but, perhaps, the most significant aspect of teaching is in helping others to learn.

This book seeks to analyse the nature of teaching in relation to the learning society. Its thesis is that the type of teaching will vary in relation to the status of the content (knowledge) being taught. We will examine first theories of the learning society from which we shall draw out a few points about the way that knowledge is changing. Finally, we will locate the changing nature of teaching in this context and by way of conclusion ask whether educational institutions are responding to the challenge.

The learning society

The learning society is both a confused and a confusing idea. Indeed, one of the phenomena that makes society a society is a sense of permanence and patterns of behaviour. In other words, members of society repeat certain fundamental processes, like language and behaviour patterns, and so non-learning is a feature of society (Jarvis, 1987). If learning either produces change or reflects it, then the nature of society is itself changing. This we know to be the case, since change is endemic. But not everything is changing; there is still a degree of stability and permanence. There is both learning and non-learning.

Coffield (2000, p28) actually suggests that all talk of '*the* learning society will have to be abandoned rather than refined' (emphasis in the original); he says that there are simply too many modern and postmodern readings of the term for any general agreement on one approach or model to be possible. He highlights 10 different approaches from the various research projects on which he reports (p8):

1. skills growth;
2. personal development;
3. social learning;
4. a learning market;
5. local learning societies;
6. social control;
7. self-evaluation;
8. centrality of learning;
9. a reformed system of education;
10. structural change.

A number of things emerge from these 10 approaches. First, they are not different models of a learning society but merely different aspects of the society being studied; secondly, therefore, they may be describing something of the fragmentation of contemporary postmodern society; thirdly, they have neither a sophisticated nor an agreed model of learning on which to base the analysis which prevents genuine comparison of the 14 projects that he reports. Since all the projects were conducted in the UK, I want to argue that it is still possible to talk about a learning society with each of these projects concentrating on but one aspect of the whole. Indeed, these models are actually Western cultural models and societies such as Hong Kong, which is very committed to the creation of a learning society and in which a tremendously high proportion of the adult population attend post-secondary education, provide other perspectives on the learning society.

On further examination of Coffield's 10 types of learning society we can see that even within a single society, the forces of change do not produce standardized responses, and nor should we expect this to happen since we have not postulated a deterministic model of society. Nevertheless, we can see that it is possible to classify his types into a smaller number of categories:

- *personal development* – personal development, self-evaluation, centrality of learning;
- *utopian* – social learning, structural change;
- *planned development* – social control, skills growth, reformed system of education, local learning societies;
- *market* – learning market.

From the above it is possible to argue that those aspects of the learning society that fall under personal development are the natural outcomes of learning. They are about the individual rather than the social, so that we do not need a learning society concept to understand them, although they will have some social outcomes. Nevertheless, when personal development issues involve planning and the control of that development, then they fall into the category of planned development – or strategy. The other three are about vision, strategy and market, and they are distinctly different from each other.

However, one aspect of a learning society not really touched upon in Coffield's report is that of learning in the risk society (Beck, 1992) – what Beck calls 'reflexive modernity'. Coffield (2000, p22) makes an implicit reference to this when he claims that the phrase, 'We're all learning all the time' is anodyne. The fact that we are being forced to learn all the time is actually the very basis of the learning society rather than an educative society, which underlies the other three approaches. Only those who have disengaged from society are not really being forced to learn a great deal, and even they are still exposed to some of the forces of change. Much of this is either unplanned or uncontrolled, or both, but it is an aspect which is central to contemporary society – for the learning society is also reflexive modernity (Jarvis, 2000). We see this form of learning as a crucial dimension of the learning society, but one that cannot be controlled, and this is important when we consider the complex nature of teaching in a society where all forms of learning are occurring in an uncontrolled and uncontrollable manner.

We suggest, therefore, that there are four dimensions to a learning society, which we will examine: vision, planning, reflexivity and market, starting with the vision.

Vision

Early writers about the learning society, Hutchins (1968, p133) for instance, started with an educational vision that everybody would have access to part-time adult education throughout the whole of their lives, but it would also be a society that had 'succeeded in transforming its values in such a way that learning, fulfilment, becoming human, had become its aims and that all its institutions would be directed to this end'. For him, the learning society would be the fulfilment of Athens, made possible not by slavery but by modern machinery.

It was the realization of the computer revolution that led Husen (1974) to very similar conclusions. He argued (p238) that *'educated ability* will be democracy's replacement for passed-on social prerogatives'. He recognized that the knowledge explosion would be fostered by a combination of computers and reprographics and he foresaw (p240) the possibility of *'equal opportunities* for all to receive as much education as they are thought capable of absorbing'. Despite Sweden's long history of adult education, Husen still regarded the learning society as being educational and based on an extension of the school system.

There are reflections here of Dewey's (1916, p51) claim that:

> It is commonplace to say that education should not cease when one leaves school. The point of this commonplace is that the purpose of school education is to insure the continuance of education by organizing the powers that insure growth. The inclination to learn from life itself and to make the conditions of life such that all will learn in the process of living is the finest product of schooling.

In a recent book on the learning society, Ranson (1994, p106) has suggested a similar picture:

> There is the need for the creation of the learning society as a constitutive condition of a new moral and political order. It is only when the values and processes of learning are placed at the centre of polity that the conditions can be established for all individuals to develop their capacities, and that institutions can respond openly and imaginatively to a period of change.

The vision of these authors, and others who have written on this topic, is of a 'good society' that is both democratic and egalitarian; one in which individuals can fulfil their own potential through education and learning throughout the whole of their lives – something for which they have been prepared in school.

Planning

There have been many policy documents published by European governments in recent years, all illustrating the strategies that they regard as important in the development of the learning society. It is unnecessary to make reference to many of them here, but they too recognize the significance of the knowledge economy.

In the introduction to the OECD report (1996, p13), the following appears:

> Success in realizing lifelong learning – from early childhood education to active learning retirement – will be an important factor in promoting employment, economic development, democracy and social cohesion in the years ahead.

In the European Union White Paper (1995, p18), a similar claim is made:

> The crucial problem of employment in a permanently changing economy compels the education and training system to change. The design of appropriate education and training strategies to address work and employment issues is, therefore, a crucial preoccupation.

In the British government report *The Learning Age* (DfEE, 1998, p13) it is clearly stated that the learning society is something to be created and that it will be educative in nature:

> In the Learning Age we will need a workforce with imagination and confidence, and the skills required will be diverse: teachers and trainers to help us acquire these skills. All of these occupations... demand different types of knowledge and understanding and the skills to apply them. That is what we mean by skills, and it is through learning – with the help of those who teach us – that we acquire them.

Despite the inclusion of some rhetoric about learning enriching our humanity and even our spirituality and the democratic society, the main emphasis of planning in all of these documents is that its end result will be the learner's employability.

Reflexivity

The risk society (Beck, 1992) is one in which the complexities of the contemporary world make decisions based on certainty impossible, and uncertainty is introduced into an instrumentally rational world. There are now hardly any points of decision in individual or social life that do not offer alternative viable solutions, but there are rarely any such incidents that have only one certain unequivocal answer. Every decision is a risk, which Beck (1994, p6) sees as underlying reflexivity:

> Let us call the autonomous, undesired and unseen, transition from industrial to risk society *reflexivity* (to differentiate it from and contrast it with reflection). Then 'reflexive modernization' means self-confrontation with the effects of risk society that cannot be dealt with and assimilated in the system of industrial society – as measured by the latter's institutionalized standards. The fact that this very constellation may later, in a second stage, in turn become the object of (public, political and scientific) reflection must not obscure the unreflected, quasi-autonomous mechanism of the transition: it is precisely abstraction which produces and gives reality to risk society. (Emphasis in the original.)

That society has emerged in the way that it has means that it takes risks when it implements 'solutions' to its problems because there is no necessarily proven answer. Consequently, there is always a need for it to confront itself about the outcomes of the decisions it makes, or fails to make. This is a reflexive society, one of the outcomes of which has been that people are forced to make decisions for themselves, often without having more than everyday technical knowledge to guide them. Individuals are forced to take risks, to learn and reflect upon their decisions, and so forth. They are also forced to adjust to the changes that occur in society as a result of whatever changes occur. As Beck (1994, p13) suggests, individuals 'must produce, stage and cobble together their biographies themselves'. People must decide for themselves, adjust to social changes and keep on learning, either by doing and reflecting upon the outcomes, or thinking and planning before the action takes place. In another sense, creative discoveries and new decisions made in the workplace are also individual learning. As Beck (1994, p16) claims, participation in work in reflexive societies 'in turn presupposes participation in education' – or at least in learning. One of the outcomes of reflexive modernization is that individuals are learning more often throughout the whole of their lives – both reflectively and non-reflectively. This is 'learning all the time' – it is not an anodyne statement but a necessary feature of reflexive modernity. In this sense a reflexive modern society must be a learning society, but the learning is individual and much of it is autonomous and occurs outside the institutionalized provision of learning opportunities.

Another aspect of this form of society is that upon reflection learners can be critical about what they have learnt. Traditionally, teachers taught truth propositions but now there is recognition that many decisions are made without there ever being evidence to prove that they are the correct decisions, and consequently learners should be encouraged to be critical.

Market

Contemporary society is also a consumer society and the history of consumerism can be traced back to the 18th century. Campbell (1987) traces it back to the romantic period in the 18th century, when pleasure became the crucial means of realizing that ideal truth and beauty which imagination had revealed and, significantly, this Romantic Movement 'assisted crucially at the birth of modern consumerism' (p206), so that a longing to enjoy those creations of the mind becomes the basis for consuming new phenomena. In other words, there can be no market economy unless there are consumers who want to purchase the products that are being produced. Advertising plays on imaginary pleasure – and learning becomes fun! While learning was equated with education in people's minds, they remembered their unpleasant experiences at school when it was no fun to learn, a barrier to further education was erected and it was one which every adult educator sought to overcome.

As we pointed out earlier, one of the advantages of the concept of learning is that it is a consumer term, whereas 'education' is a producer concept. Once learning became separated from education, then learning could become fun – and there is a sense in which this has become a more popular thing to do in the UK since the creation of the British Open University. Now people could learn all the things that they wanted to learn, and they did not have to go to school to do it. They can read books, watch the television, listen to the radio and go and talk with other people – if they want to. The Open University marketed a commodity, and other organizations have followed suit. Now it is possible to learn by purchasing multi-media personal computers and surfing the Web, watching television learning zone programmes, buying 'teach yourself' books and magazines and, even, purchasing self-directed learning courses.

There are tremendous implications of the learning society for our understanding of teaching since the social milieu in which we teach has changed, people of all ages are exposed to much more information and can, and do, learn a wide variety of things, so that, for instance, no longer can teachers be sure that they know more about their topics than do their students, and so on. There is a real sense in which the Internet has assumed an all-embracing role of information provider (teacher) for many.

One of the features of the learning society upon which we have not placed a great deal of emphasis yet is that it is one in which knowledge is no longer static. Since it appears to change with great rapidity, it is difficult to construe it any longer in terms of truth propositions to be learnt and memorized, but rather to be considered and utilized if it is appropriate.

The changing nature of knowledge

The nature of teaching might, therefore, change both with the nature of the knowledge being examined and the form of learning being encouraged. At the same time, since it is learning that is now being encouraged rather than teaching, it might first be necessary to redefine teaching away from the definitions provided in the *Concise Oxford Dictionary* – for instance, teaching might be regarded as an activity designed to foster human learning. But then it might be asked, is any activity designed to foster human learning the process of teaching? Are managers, for instance, who create a situation where any of their staff learn in the workplace, teachers? Clearly, as the nature and status of knowledge have changed, so teaching has changed – from demonstrating scientific truth through word or action. It is difficult to consider the idea that the nature of knowledge has changed and in order to illustrate this a little more we need to look at some different ways of understanding knowledge.

In *A Dictionary of Philosophy* (Flew, 1979) three types of knowledge are discussed: *knowledge that* (factual knowledge); *knowledge how* (practical); *knowledge of* (people and places). *Knowledge that* is knowledge based on argument or research, so that it is possible to claim that 'x' is a fact. *Knowledge how* is practical knowledge: I know how to do it. There is a sense in which this latter type of knowledge is also often confused with *knowledge that* since it becomes shorthand for *knowledge that this is how* it is done. *Knowledge that,* in both of the forms described here, can be taught in a traditional school, college or university setting since the knowledge is usually being mediated to the students through the lecture. By contrast, neither *knowledge how* nor *knowledge of* can be taught in this way, since neither can be mediated in the same manner.

Additionally, Scheffler (1965) has suggested that knowledge can be legitimated in at least three different ways: rationalistically, empirically and pragmatically.

Rationalist

This form of knowledge is legitimated by reason – it is *knowledge that*. Pure mathematics is often the example provided for knowledge of this type;

mathematicians need no objectives beyond the problem and no form of proof that is not to be found within its own logic. Philosophical knowledge is another form of knowledge that is legitimated in the same way. We can help students master the art of rational argument through their writing and in the way that we help them construct an argument, or a case.

Empirical

Empirical knowledge is also *knowledge that* but relies on the sense experiences; knowledge is true if it can be shown to relate to an empirical phenomenon. Thus, I know that there is something upon which I am sitting – I can feel it and I do not sink to the ground when I sit down. There is a chair here and I know that there is an object here by my sense experience, even though the *idea* of 'chair' is a construction of my experience – but the chair is part of the situation! We can have knowledge of a reality beyond ourselves through our senses. However, facts have no meaning in themselves, so that we always have to interpret facts and give them meaning. This was a relatively easy task when the meaning of facts was undisputed, but now it is much more complex because different schools of thought provide different interpretations of phenomena and so we become interpreters rather than legislators of different theories (Bauman, 1987). Competing interpretations hardly have the status of knowledge; rather they are theories and should always be treated in this way, and Foucault (1972) has shown that dominant theoretical interpretations are often those of the dominant elite, so that teachers should expect students to be critical especially when they are examining such theories.

Pragmatic

Pragmatic knowledge is *knowledge how;* it is also scientific knowledge since its validity rests on experimentation. If the experiment can be replicated, if the findings of the experiments fit the situation or achieve the desired results, then it is valid knowledge. The pragmatist also emphasizes the experimental nature of certain forms of experience: individuals try something out and find that it works, or it fails. For instance, young university lecturers can be told how to lecture but until they have actually done it they do not know that they can do it, and it is only after having done it many times that expertise in lecturing might begin to develop. They find out by doing it and achieving their desired aims. As Heller (1984) points out, this is also the nature of everyday experience and everyday knowledge – we learn by experiment. Lyotard (1984) has stressed that in postmodern society knowledge will be legitimated by its performativity; that is by whether it works. But another significant thing about pragmatic knowledge is that it is practical and tends not to be based on a single discipline, so that our teaching has to take a practical turn and, as we shall see later in the book, innovations in teaching practical and pragmatic knowledge lead us into problem-based learning, among other new teaching methods.

Teachers have to recognize the type of knowledge included in their lessons and adapt their teaching to the legitimate claims of the content – we should never claim too much for the knowledge we teach because we can be assured that our learners might soon question the claims that we make, especially since they have many other channels of information by which they can check what we claim. False claims for the validity of our content will expose us in an unfavourable light and lower our credibility with our learners.

The changing nature of teaching

The traditional image of the teacher is someone who tells students what to learn and encourages them to learn and rehearse what they have been taught. It has been they who have mediated knowledge to children and adult learners alike. Teachers were 'the fount of all wisdom' but now that has all changed. Teachers, for instance, now no longer:

- have a monopoly on transmitting knowledge;
- determine or legislate on matters of knowledge but they may be interpreters of different systems of knowledge;
- deal with truth but they certainly teach truths;
- teach with unchanging knowledge but now they deal with scientific knowledge that is transient;
- are confined to the classroom, but like the ancient teachers they may have to function where their learners are;
- teach only theoretical knowledge but now they also help learners acquire practical knowledge;
- can assume that their learners know nothing about the subjects that they teach but must learn to build on knowledge acquired by their learners from a wide variety of sources.

In addition, with the mode of delivery changing as the learning market develops, so it is no longer only an interpersonal activity – now it might be mediating knowledge through the written script and through the spoken word on audio tape and even on interactive electronic systems. As education seeks to respond to the demands of the market, so teaching is forced to change to produce in the most efficient means the learning packages that will be useful to the work situation, or the socio-cultural one, and so on.

Conclusion

Teaching is changing; it is being forced to change by the dominant globalizing forces of social change. Teachers are faced with playing new roles requiring many more and sometimes different skills. Indeed, many of the new techniques that have to be learnt are ones that adult educators have learnt in teaching adults over the years, but others are new for all educators.

The aim of this book is not to produce a 'how to' book (see Jarvis, 1995, *inter alia*) but to examine some of the approaches to teaching that are arising from an informed and critical perspective.

References

Bauman, Z (1987) *Legislators and Interpreters,* Polity, Cambridge

Beck, U (1992) *Risk Society,* Sage, London

Beck, U (1994) The reinvention of politics, in *Reflexive Modernization,* eds U Beck, A Giddens and S Lash, Polity, Cambridge

Campbell, C (1987) *The Romantic Ethic and the Spirit of Modern Consumerism,* Blackwell, Oxford

Coffield, F (ed) (2000) *Differing Visions of the Learning Society,* Policy Press, Bristol, and ESRC (Vol 1)

Department for Education and Employment (1998) *The Learning Age,* Department for Education and Employment, London

Dewey, J (1916) *Democracy and Education,* Free Press, New York

European Union (1995) *Teaching and Learning: Towards the learning society,* European Union, Brussels

Flew, A (1979) *A Dictionary of Philosophy,* Pan Books, London

Foucault, M (1972) *The Archaeology of Knowledge,* Routledge, London

Heller, A (1984) *Everyday Knowledge,* Routledge and Kegan Paul, London

Husen, T (1974) *The Learning Society,* Methuen, London

Hutchins, R M (1968) *The Learning Society,* Penguin, Harmondsworth

Jarvis, P (1987) *Adult Learning in the Social Context,* Croom Helm, Beckenham

Jarvis, P (1995) *Adult and Continuing Education: Theory and practice,* 2nd edn, Routledge, London

Jarvis, P (2000) Globalisation, the learning society and comparative education, *Comparative Education,* **36** (3) pp 343–55

Lyotard, J-F (1984) *The Postmodern Condition: A report on knowledge,* Manchester University Press, Manchester

Organization for Economic Cooperation and Development (1996) *Lifelong Learning for All,* OECD, Paris

Ranson, S (1994) *Towards the Learning Society,* Cassell, London

Scheffler, I (1965) *Conditions of Knowledge,* University of Chicago Press, Chicago

Chapter 3

Teaching styles and teaching methods

Peter Jarvis

Few people have written about the educative society, Kidd (1961) being a notable exception, and no one, as far as I can discover, has written about a teaching society – although the information society contains echoes of it. Teaching has traditionally been associated with the idea that there is a truth proposition (knowledge) or an accepted theory that can be disseminated through the agency of the teacher. But in late modernity the idea that there is a truth or an indisputable theory to be taught is now harder to accept, although there are many people who still hold to the idea that what they are taught is true. Foucault (see Sheridan, 1980) called this a 'will to truth'. Even so, the fact that there are a variety of teaching methods – didactic, Socratic and facilitative – indicates that teachers have recognized that there are an increasing variety of ways of approaching their task. Nevertheless, this provides teaching with a degree of flexibility that might have become increasingly utilized in the face of the epistemological changes referred to in the previous chapter (see Jarvis, 1995, for a discussion on this).

Over the years, however, there has always been the recognition that some teaching is teacher-centred and some student-centred, although the latter has not been practised in all forms of education as much as it might have been. This distinction has been most well marked in the education of adults, but even in traditional adult education a great deal of the teaching has been didactic. By contrast, student-centred methods presage the learners and their learning and appear more relevant to the idea of the learning society. This is also closer to the ideas about education that emerged in the education of adults, since one of the major differences between the education of children and that of adults is that children tend to be more dependent than adults on their teachers. Children might, but not necessarily will, be more inclined to accept what teachers tell them, so giving it something akin to the status of a truth, while the content of the lessons of teachers of older learners may not be given such status. Indeed, Entwistle (1981) cites Bennett's (1976) study in several places in his book to illustrate the fact that children need more direction in order to learn effectively and this frequently occurred in more formal classroom settings, but many adults criticize teachers for treating them too much like children. In addition, Galton *et al* (1980) discovered that primary school children were mainly given individual attention in the classroom when the teacher gave information or controlled behaviour.

Teaching methods are frequently taught in courses preparing teachers for both school and adult education, but less frequently is reference made to teaching style. Indeed, a number of books on teaching in higher education make no reference to teaching styles at all and even the number of the different teaching methods discussed is restricted (see Brown and Atkins, 1988). Yet it is suggested in this chapter that understanding teaching styles is just as important, perhaps even more important, than teaching methods in teaching, and that the education of teachers should focus more directly on teaching style. Indeed, the teacher's style can influence the form of learning that takes place as much, if not more, than the teaching method employed. Brookfield (1990, pp12–13), reflecting on his own teaching career, makes reference to this in relation to the fact that the techniques that he was taught in college and in the textbooks as 'good practice' just did not work in the classroom, so that he eventually reached the conclusion that many teachers have reached – that those techniques specified as basic for good practice are simply wrong and that they should not relentlessly be applied to practice.

Indeed, teaching style might also influence the learners, even motivate them, much more than do different teaching methods. Even so, there is sometimes a tendency to confuse teaching method and teaching style and merge them into a single phenomenon (see Entwistle, 1981), so the first section of this chapter examines the differences between them that we feel need to be drawn out and, thereafter, both are examined separately. The final section extends the discussion of the influence of style on learning, with reference to charismatic teaching.

Teaching methods and teaching styles

Methods focus on the techniques that teachers employ; they are ways of doing it – processes, techniques. There is a sense in which the word 'style' also refers to the way that things are done – its design and so on. Indeed, 'style' is a much more difficult word to define but it is used here in relation to the manner of 'expression' rather than the actual process of doing. Conti (1990, p80) refers to this in terms of the 'distinct qualities' displayed by a teacher. There is a sense in which the teacher's style helps determine the ethos, or the culture, of the situation in which the teaching takes place, although it must be recognized that as individual classes are situated in a school, college or university this also contributes to the ethos.

The distinction drawn between method and style is important here since teaching methods are about the science of teaching whereas teaching styles are about the art of teaching. Our concern in this book is to recognize the complexity of teaching – it is both an art and a science, but in the learning society the nature of science itself is being called into question. Teaching methods are about the technical processes of teaching while teaching styles are more about the teachers and the way that they conduct themselves during the teaching session, although Morrison and McIntyre (1973, p156) point out that personality tests have not been useful in predicting the way that teachers actually teach.

Naturally there is considerable overlap between style and method, since it is the same teacher who usually decides on the methods and who then conducts the teaching process, both of which contribute to the experience that learners have and from which they learn. Entwistle (1981), reporting on the work of Bennett (1976) and Solomon and Kendall (1979) in the United States, refers to this combination as 'classroom types'. Consequently, this heuristic distinction is made here only to enable us to understand more clearly the processes of teaching and learning.

Teaching methods

The 'science of pedagogics' is not an uncommon phrase amongst education-alists from continental Europe, and while we have never referred to educa-tion in quite this way in the United Kingdom, there has almost been a belief that once we know the aims and objectives of the lesson and the content to be taught, then the method is self-evident. Indeed many early curriculum studies do not actually include teaching methods at all (Taba, 1962; Tyler, 1949, *inter alia*) as part of their discussion of the curriculum.

The self-evidency of the teaching methods assumed that either teachers would be didactic or that they would use the most efficient methods to achieve their specified objectives. Teaching involved the transmission of knowledge/theory or the teaching of a skill – it was an instrumentally rational activity, the outcomes could be measured and the techniques employed could be assessed. This is the science of teaching. Underlying it are certain Enlightenment values – rationality, empirical measurement, universalism (in that the same methods and content could be taught to students of a specified age and level of experience in a course) and the pre-eminence of scientific knowledge. Later in the development of the study of education, more wide-ranging discussion occurred about the different types of technique, although many of these were still basically didactic.

This apparent scientific approach was emphasized in the United States at this time in a number of studies in instructional design (Gagné *et al*, 1974; West *et al*, 1991, *inter alia*). The aim of these works was to provide a rationally consistent basis for the design of certain forms of teaching, to construct systems where teachers were enabled to consider as many eventualities as possible about the programme of teaching that they were preparing. All teachers need to prepare their lessons diligently, and systems certainly help – it was the almost universalistic assumptions underlying this movement that correct preparation would achieve the desired outcomes that are more questionable.

But in the 1960s, as well as this approach to teaching, student-centred methods became more common in schools and colleges; something that had been much more widely practised in adult education for many years. This even led Rogers, C (1969, p103) to claim that teaching was an overrated activity, but then he was also a person-centred therapist, so that he fully endorsed student-centred methods and wrote about facilitation as a method of helping students learn. Indeed, since the 1970s, there has been a wide recognition of different teaching techniques, although even a best-selling book on teaching in further education such as Curzon (1997), which was first published in 1976, still has only a limited section on teaching methods. Other books coming from an education of adults background, however, have concentrated on the wider variety of different teaching methods available (Galbraith, 1990; Jarvis [1983] 1995; Rogers, J, 1971 [1989], *inter alia*).

The implications of a science of teaching are that the Enlightenment values mentioned above are valid, something that is questioned here. For instance, the idea that teaching is only designed to achieve specified ends raises questions about the validity of the end and the legitimacy of the means by which the ends are achieved. In other words – does the end justify the means? The idea that we can measure the end result of a lesson presupposes that the learners stop learning at the point of the assessment and that what they have learnt is measurable, but if they are reflective learners they may continue to learn for a long period after the lesson. Additionally, if they have been motivated by a lesson to continue to study the topic long after the lesson is over, when is that measured and is motivation quantifiable? The idea that there is always a best method to achieve ends assumes that 'there is only one way to skin a cat!' The assumption that once the method is right, any competent teacher can achieve the desired ends fails to take into consideration the difference of classes, cultures and teachers themselves. This approach:

- omits consideration of value rationality, as opposed to instrumental rationality;
- is instrumental and assumes that the achievement of the specified objectives is always a sign of good teaching;
- emphasizes outcomes and omits consideration of the unintended learning outcomes;
- is universalistic and downplays social, cultural and individual differences;
- assumes that learning is always measurable, and so on.

While there are many ways in which a scientific approach to teaching is important, too much emphasis on the science of teaching depersonalizes the teaching and learning process – something that we see occurring in some forms of distance education, and this does have certain ethical consequences (Jarvis, 1997, pp111–20).

A scientific approach to teaching and the wise use of different teaching methods are important factors in teaching, despite all of the above criticisms. Teaching is still, in part, a technical process. Assessing the competence of teachers to employ certain methods is perfectly justifiable. Indeed, teachers who cannot use a wide variety of teaching methods, who do not evaluate the success of their teaching methods, and so on, are unprofessional. But, as every teacher knows, two teachers using the same techniques to teach the same content will frequently do so in entirely different ways and the outcomes of their lesson will not be the same. Learners know that – they evaluate a teacher as someone who:

- makes it interesting;
- lets you find out for yourself;
- respects our ideas;
- is friendly, and so on.

Basically, these types of evaluation point to the significance of the teacher's style.

Teaching styles

In the light of the criticisms of the scientific approach to teaching raised above, there is a certain irony that Conti's (1990) discussion on identifying teaching styles focuses upon a quantitative approach to measuring style, based upon the respondents' philosophy of teaching reflected in a Likert-type self-evaluation questionnaire. There is an assumption that if we can measure the teachers' philosophy, personality and so on, we can know something about their teaching style. Indeed, Eble (1988, p64) has suggested that 'style is the image of character'. But Morrison and McIntyre (1973, p156) have argued that there does not seem to be a relationship between personality tests and the approach to teaching that different teachers assume. Yet teaching is still about helping others learn, a process in which teachers as individuals still play an important role – but play the role they do, for teaching is an art form as well as a science. Their philosophy may indeed be apparent from the style that they adopt.

Teachers manage their classrooms (Davies, 1971) and much has been written about management style, and there is clearly some overlap in the literature on style between the two occupations of managing and teaching. Perhaps the best known literature common to both is McGregor's (1960) distinction between Theory X and Theory Y. Theory X suggests that managers assume that those with whom they work dislike it so that they have to be controlled, coerced and directed in order to achieve the desired outcomes, whereas Theory Y concentrates on the way that managers focus on the human side of their employees and endeavour to develop them as people. Clearly both of these approaches are very relevant to teaching.

Another classic study on style is that of Lippitt and White (1958) who examined the leadership styles of youth leaders, highlighting a threefold typology: authoritarian, *laissez-faire* and democratic. They found that:

- authoritarian leaders create a sense of group dependence on the leader, that their presence held the group together and that in their absence no work was done;
- *laissez-faire* leaders achieve little work whether they were present or absent;
- democratic leaders achieve group cohesion and harmonious working relationships whether they were present or not.

Their finding relates to that of Galton *et al* (1980) who noted how teachers sought to control their classrooms through the use of language. Vygotsky (1978) also raised a significant point about teaching style when he argued that children's understanding was not only developed through their interaction with the physical world but also through their active encounters with others in relation to the world. In other words, the style of the teacher in that interaction helps develop children's understanding.

Other studies have suggested different approaches to examining teaching style, so that teachers are seen as having formal or informal approaches, friendly or distant, humorous or dry, confident or withdrawn, and so on.

Eble (1988, p64) suggests that: 'Without character, a teacher is more ill-equipped than if he (*sic*) had not mastered particle physics, Shakespeare's tragedies, or harmony and counterpoint.'

Fundamentally, the character of the teacher plays a fundamental role in teaching – teachers themselves are their best teaching aids. Emphasis on teaching methods tends to standardize teaching but emphasis on style highlights the individuality of teachers and allows for the recognition that every class is a unique event, with the teachers alone being the common element in the different classes that they teach. However, teaching is both an art and a science and so we can combine the two approaches: we can have authoritarian facilitators and democratic didactics, as well as authoritarian didacticism and democratic facilitators. Teachers can be friendly but didactic or friendly but Socratic, and so on. There is no limit to the combinations that can be put together – each class is a unique event: this is what the task of teaching is all about. But it is no easy role, as those of us who do it know only too well, for our teaching style also makes demands on us as individuals, as Parker (1998) beautifully illustrates. The first chapter of this book opens with a sub-heading: 'Teaching beyond technique', which tells its own story. He (1998, p10) reflects upon his own teaching:

> After three decades of trying to learn my craft, every class comes down to this: my students and I, face to face, engaged in an ancient and exacting exchange called education. The techniques I have mastered do not disappear but neither do they suffice. Face to face with my students, only one resource is at my immediate command: my identity, my selfhood, my sense of this 'I' who teaches – without which I have no sense of the 'Thou' who learns… *good teaching cannot be reduced to technique; good teaching comes from the identity and integrity of the teacher.* (Emphasis in the original.)

His book explores the art of teaching from the perspective of knowing who we, the teachers, are when we enter relationships with those who learn with us. In it he illustrates that teaching is a personal vocation to be of service to those whom we teach.

The charismatic teacher

In this late modern age, emphasis is increasingly being placed on leadership rather than management – on having that something that encourages and inspires others to reach greater heights than they ever thought possible. Exceptional teachers may do this with students of whatever age, from the very young to adults and even to older adults, although bureaucratic standardization (and fear of litigation, etc) tends to place limits on the outstanding individual teacher.

One of the best known accounts of charismatic teaching remains Kohl's (1967) wonderful story of how he worked with 36 children from Harlem, gained their confidence and inspired them to reach beyond themselves to learn and enjoy learning. His style was his own and he did things that only teachers who open themselves to their children could do. He also recorded (1967, p192) that there were other teachers in this very disadvantaged school whose style enabled them to reach the children and gain their trust:

> There were a few who knew and loved the children, who stayed at school heartbroken, year after year, watching the other teachers, being abused by the administration, seeing the children fail and nobody care. I became friendly with one such teacher – he had been at the school for twelve years and all the children there knew him. He knew them too, and was constantly besieged by visitors, kids passed out of the school system returning to talk and feel that some element of the world was constant and available.

Palmer and Kohl write not about their techniques but about a perspective on teaching that comes from seeking to be caring and understanding, having a personality and a style that made them individuals enabling them to reach their learners and gain their trust. For them style is not a performance, it is a way of living, being and interacting – of being a teacher.

In this sense, teaching is beyond method, beyond the standardization of the modern age, it is beyond the visits to the classroom and the paper chases that the bureaucratic authorities require when then they inspect a school or a department, however necessary those visits are assumed to be by those in authority. Teaching is fundamentally about a concerned human interaction.

Conclusion

Teaching methods and teaching styles reflect the art and science of teaching; they reflect the modern age of science but point beyond it to the validity of the art, the performance and to the reality of the uniqueness and humanity of teaching. To try to restrict teaching to its methods is to fail to understand the teaching and learning process; to try to restrict it to its art allows for the possibility of irresponsibility and unacceptable eccentricities. To understand the relationship of the one to the other is extremely difficult since each of us who teaches engages not only in a time-honoured process but one that is quite unique to the occasion when we are actually teaching. The more we understand ourselves, the more likely we are to understand those whom we are privileged to teach. For style is as important, if not more important, than method in the process of teaching and learning.

References

Bennett, S N (1976) *Teaching Styles and Pupil Progress,* Open Books, London

Brookfield, S D (1990) *The Skillful Teacher,* Jossey-Bass, San Francisco, CA

Brown, G and Atkins, M (1988) *Effective Teaching in Higher Education,* Methuen, London

Conti, G J (1990) Identifying your teaching style, in *Adult Learning Methods,* ed M W Galbraith, Robert Krieger, Malabar

Curzon, L B (1997) *Teaching in Further Education,* 5th edn, Cassell, London

Davies, I K (1971) *The Management of Learning,* McGraw-Hill, Maidenhead

Eble, K E (1988) *The Craft of Teaching,* 2nd edn, Jossey-Bass, San Francisco, CA

Entwistle, N (1981) *Styles of Learning and Teaching,* John Wiley, Chichester

Gagné, R M, Briggs, L J and Wager, W W (1974) *Principles of Instructional Design,* 4th edn, Harcourt, Brace and Jovanovich, Fort Worth, TX

Galbraith, M W (ed) (1990) *Adult Learning Methods,* Robert Krieger, Malabar

Galton, M, Simon, B and Croll, P (1980) *Inside the Primary Classroom,* Routledge and Kegan Paul, London

Jarvis, P (1995) *Adult and Continuing Education: Theory and practice,* 2nd edn, Routledge, London

Jarvis, P (1997) *Ethics and the Education of Adults in Late Modern Society,* NIACE, Leicester

Kidd, R (1961) *18–80 Continuing Education in Metropolitan Toronto,* Board of Education, Toronto

Kohl, H (1967) *36 Children,* Penguin, Harmondsworth

Lippitt, R and White, R K (1958) 'An experimental study of leadership and group life, in eds E E Maccoby *et al, Readings in Social Psychology,* 3rd edn, Holt, New York

McGregor, D (1960) *The Human Side of Enterprise,* McGraw-Hill, New York

Morrison, A and McIntyre, D (1973) *Teachers and Teaching,* 2nd edn, Penguin, Harmondsworth

Parker, P J (1998) *The Courage to Teach,* Jossey-Bass, San Francisco, CA

Rogers, C (1969) *Freedom to Learn,* Merrill, Columbus, OH; 3rd edn, Rogers, C and Freiburg, H J, published in 1994

Rogers, J (1971) *Adults in Education,* British Broadcasting Commission, London; 3rd edn (1989) published as *Adults Learning,* Open University Press, Buckingham

Sheridan, A (1980) *Michael Foucault: The will to truth,* Tavistock, London

Solomon, D and Kendall, A J (1979) *Children in Classrooms: An investigation of person-environment interaction,* Praeger, New York

Taba, H (1962) *Curriculum Development: Theory and practice,* Harcourt, Brace and World, New York

Tyler, R (1949) *Basic Principles of Curriculum and Instruction,* University of Chicago Press, Chicago, IL

Vygotsky, L S (1978) *Mind in Society,* Harvard University Press, Cambridge, MA

West, C K, Farmer, J A and Wolff, P M (1991) *Instructional Design: Implications from cognitive science,* Prentice Hall, Englewood Cliffs, NJ

Chapter 4

Ethics and education

Bob Brownhill and Peter Jarvis

Traditionally ethical approaches to education have been concerned with certain themes: the relationship between teachers and students, the moral status of the students, the aims of education, the methods of teaching, and epistemological questions related to the distinction between education and indoctrination. The basic moral principle is concerned with the teacher–student relationship, and brings out the moral status of the student. It is a principle derived from Kant (Paton, 1961) and states that people should be treated as an end in themselves rather than as a means to an end. We should therefore take account of the interests of individuals and try to provide opportunities that are suitable for their needs. This principle really points out that a person should be treated as an autonomous rational being or potentially as such a person. It also gives us an important aim for education, which should be to produce autonomous individuals who have the ability to appraise differing concepts and situations and act independently, without relying on the authority of others. It suggests that teachers should seek to develop students' independence, critical abilities, self-confidence, and rational approaches to living. There are other closely related aims, such as self-fulfilment and the sustenance of 'mental health' (Peters, 1966), which are, in a sense, aspects of becoming autonomous and self-directed learners. The methods used are those that are considered appropriate to help to provide the conditions for the achievement of these goals.

The morality of method and style

In the previous chapters we have examined the different approaches to teaching under the heading of method and style. We have argued that teaching style is as important as teaching methods. Here we want to develop this argument a little further in as much as we can see that certain authoritarian teaching styles, for instance, might deprive the learners of their independence of thought. We often come across students who seek to discover from their teachers what type of answer they want. Now, very clearly when we are teaching students how to answer examination questions, we might want to suggest certain techniques of structuring answers and so on, but the idea that there is always a correct answer, or always only one way to answer a question, is often completely wrong, a point to which we will return below. Authoritarianism restricts the manner in which students respond to questions but, even more significantly, it might lead to them thinking that they have to learn in a non-reflective manner and in so doing authoritarianism in education restricts the growth potential of the learners.

It might be argued that in certain situations teachers have to be authorities – and we would not query that. Schools and colleges need organization, rules and regulations in order to function smoothly, but the teaching-learning relationship is an interpersonal one and we would want to argue that at the heart of this relationship is the moral principle of concern. Elsewhere (Jarvis, 1997) we have argued that the only universal principle of goodness in this late modern world is that it is never wrong to be concerned for the 'other', whatever their age, gender, ethnicity and former behavioural record, and so on. But we know that in some situations women are treated differently to men in the expectations of the subjects they will study or their achievement levels in those subjects. We run the danger of treating older learners as if they are less able than younger ones. Black people are regarded as not having the same abilities and intellectual interests, and so on. Indeed, we showed in the previous chapter how the charismatic teacher can overcome all of the problems of deprived social situations and anti-school attitudes to inspire students to want to learn through the formal educational system – despite the fact that the system itself was not conducive to it. But then we do not teach mathematics or science; we teach *individuals* mathematics or science, and we need to know and understand students as human beings in our class.

This concern for the other should be self-evident in the teaching methods selected, the styles adopted and the endeavours the teachers make to relate to all their students as people. This principle should not only be found in the conduct of education but also in methods of assessment, the ways by which teachers communicate with their students when they assess written and oral work, and so on. Indeed, crudely marking a piece of work wrong is often immoral since it neither gives the learners a chance to explain how they reached the decisions they did nor for them to justify their work. Since we all identify ourselves in relation to the other, teachers can and might be responsible for young people identifying themselves as failures. This is also true in adult teaching where there is considerable evidence to show that if teachers assume that their learners will be successful, they are more likely to succeed. We have to help build the learners' identity into individuals who are confident and able.

Underlying this position is the fundamental argument that teaching and learning are moral processes; students are always the ends of the process rather than means to other ends – even to that of the teachers' own self-fulfilment and self-achievement, and the schools and colleges' position in the so-called 'league tables'. Indeed, the lack of concern for these latter elements should typify teaching in contrast to our concern for the students – but, paradoxically, in so doing one finds self-fulfilment in the success of the other, and the schools might actually score more highly in the league tables. Teaching should always be regarded as a moral occupation, and those who practise it need to have the courage to teach morally (Palmer, 1998). This same ethic is captured in one of the last books Freire (1998) wrote, and published posthumously. In this book he captures the concern of the adult educator to develop self-fulfilled moral agents through the human act of teaching, but this does not mean that teachers are not intellectually rigorous. It is no act of human kindness to give students a false sense of their own learning, or even what academia expects from them.

The quest for truth

A major aim of the process of education is to give students the tools to approach, appraise, and to decide on and between numerous truth claims both in the physical world and in the moral sphere, including politics and religion. This points to another important principle for teachers since they themselves should have a commitment to and concern for the truth. This concern is the basis for the distinction between education and indoctrination, with the suggestion that the teachers are not showing integrity if they stray from this principle, but it also suggests that indoctrinators are not treating their students as autonomous people who must be respected as such, and in the process of denying the moral base people should be treated as ends in themselves and not used for some other purpose, such as the nefarious desires of the indoctrinators.

The argument so far is a reflection of a particular model of teaching which Scheffler (1967) calls the 'Rule Model'. It is based in the writings of Kant but it is also a position adopted by writers on liberal education (Hare, 1966; Peters, 1966, *inter alia*). It places an emphasis on reason, with the argument that reason is a matter of abiding by rules and principles. Thus in the cognitive realm reason assesses the evidence, and consists of a careful weighing-up of evidence and arguments for and against a proposition, in the interests of arriving as close to the truth as possible. In the moral sphere, a rational person is one who is consistent in thought and in action abiding by impartial and generalizable principles that are freely chosen and binding. This includes the notion that one should show respect for other people who, like oneself, are rational, autonomous, moral lawmakers. In precisely the same way action is undertaken in the light of best evidence. The aim of teaching in respect of the 'Rule Model' is to develop the ability to make principled judgements and to act accordingly. It is about building autonomous and rational character guided by the tenets of science, morality and culture. This process of teaching will also develop the ability of students to become self-directed learners.

Hare (1966) has argued that it is the way the world is looked at that is important not the actual content of what is taught. Indeed, one might argue that in teaching subjects where there are few if any undisputed truths, one should look at the way in which the problems are dealt with as much as the answered reached. In the case of morality we should not be concerned with passing on specific moral principles but the ability to understand what morality is and a readiness to think and act in a moral way. People need to understand the language of morality. It is therefore not a particular morality, but morality itself that needs to be taught, so that learners think morally for themselves so that they can justify what they are saying and doing. This does not mean that we should not have our own beliefs or that they should not show in our teaching. Indeed, it is difficult in the teaching and learning process not to reveal some of our own predilections, but the aim is not to pass these on but to help the students appraise principles for themselves.

In a postmodern, or a late modern world, the traditional notions of truth and reality have been abandoned. The notion of truth has undergone profound change and there is considerable debate about the extent to which there is any truth at all. Similarly, the concept of reality has given way to the idea of multiple realities. Traditional writings about indoctrination seemed to assume that there was an absolute truth, and that there was a reality to be revealed. Amongst the reasons why the practice of indoctrination was condemned was because it was understood that indoctrinators were present-ing false truths. We can still see this, for instance, in the way that the funda-mentalist power groups in the southern states of the USA seek to forbid any scientific teaching of the origins of the universe in schools since it contra-venes their own limited interpretations of the Genesis stories of creation in the Bible.

Clearly the way in which the problems of truth are now approached invali-dates the traditional arguments about indoctrination, although other problems remain, such as using our own belief systems as examples, of trying to get students to accept predetermined goals, and so on. If teachers have mistaken beliefs, either because they are outdated or have been brought up in a milieu, religious or political, where certain claims are thought to be true, we might want to ask ourselves whether they are still indoctrinators. In a sense we might claim that they themselves are victims of institutional indoctrination where they are teaching the 'truths' of creation and that they are teaching the claims in good faith. However, neither 'good faith' nor absolute commitment to 'truths' by themselves can guarantee the correctness of any belief. But still the problem remains: can teachers be accused of being indoctrinators if their intention is not to indoctrinate but to teach truths? Of course it is notoriously difficult to know a person's intentions. Hare thinks that at least we can get a good indication if we watch what a teacher does, over a period of time. He states:

> The educator is waiting and hoping all the time for those whom he is educating to start thinking... The indoctrinator, on the other hand, is watching for signs of trouble, and ready to intervene to suppress it when it appears... At the end of it all, the educator will insensibly stop being an educator and find that he (*sic*) is talking to an equal, to an educated man like himself – a man who may disagree with everything he has ever said, and, unlike the indoctrinator, he will be pleased. (Hare, 1966, pp69–70)

Yet if there are no truths, only interpretations and multiple realities, all constructed by ourselves – what then? Traditionally, scientists and social scientists have looked for a criterion of truth which normally has been a theory's correspondence with reality with a concept of a stable reality independent of ourselves. But according to construct theorists, there can be no criterion of truth. The only basis for any claim for objectivity and rationality is that the theories, concepts, and explanations hang together, they are coherent, and not internally contradictory. They are therefore consistent and follow the rules of formal logic. We could also argue that they need a degree of credibility if they are to be accepted. This has to be as near as we can get to a criterion of 'truth'. People within a certain construct will attempt to get professional agreement for a way of looking at the phenomena under review. In practice this means that there has to be debate within the specialist communities that allows for personal interpretations to be examined by other specialists in the field in the hope of arriving at some consensual agreement. This is the attempt to be as objective as possible, as the specialist debate is a form of objectivity, for a theory within the specialist community has to stand on its own feet and meet criticisms, if it is to be acceptable and become part of the consensus. An obvious objection to all this is that it is not really objective at all but subjective or inter-subjective and, in fact, it relies entirely on the passions and commitments of the theory constructors with the possibility that the consensus is entirely illusory. Indeed, we only have to look at apartheid South Africa of a decade or so ago, to note how the morality of this terrible practice could be sustained by those in power agreeing amongst themselves that what they were doing was right.

This raises the issue that those who were able to justify to themselves what they were doing had to have power to impose their interpretation on the remainder of the population. Such power gives rise to the idea that powerful interpretations of those realities are the dominant ideologies, something that Foucault (1972) demonstrated when he examined the power of discourse. In using the historical example of South Africa, we have pitched this away from the UK or the USA, but the same dominant interpretations of social reality exist here as well, and are imposed on us by those in power, often assisted by the media, and so on. If we, as teachers, pass those interpretations on to our students uncritically then we might still be unwitting indoctrinators in the processes of teaching and learning.

This brings out another dimension with the constructivist approaches to reality and the possibility of multiple realities, for it means that each approach is fighting the others for its own mental existence. Within the specialist communities themselves there will be internal power struggles for theory dominance but there will also be external power struggles, for whereas internally the specialist communities will look at the world in a similar way, externally they can come into conflict with other communities who look at the world in a different way but, nevertheless, claim the same grounds for their interpretation and deconstruction. We see this in the internal schools of thought and practice in psychology, for instance, although we can find it in most other theoretical approaches to society and the practices that are based on them. Like the Church, faith and commitment not only bring about splits in doctrine but also heighten conflict by its commitments to the purity of its divided faiths.

The discussion raises numerous dilemmas for teachers: in practice their own freedom is increasingly curtailed by tighter restrictions on the curriculum and the adherence to apparent practices of quality control. How far then should we introduce our students to the idea of multiple realities and to their different dimensions? How far should we teach the concepts of multiple realities, different faiths and scepticism to all truth claims in a multicultured society that has many different faiths? How do teachers, who may themselves have beliefs in a certain faith, cope with the essential scepticism of postmodernism? The response is problematic, but some sort of answer is provided by the doyen of the postmodernists, Jacques Derrida, in his arguments about the end of the metanarrative:

> All that a deconstructive point of view tries to show, is that convention, institutions and consensus are stabilizations (sometimes stabilizations of great

duration, sometimes microstabilizations). This means that they are stabilizations of something essentially unstable and chaotic. Thus it becomes necessary
to stabilize precisely because stability is not natural; it is because there is instability that stabilization becomes necessary... If there was continual stability,
there would be no need of politics, and it is to the extent that stability is not
natural, essential or substantial that politics exists and ethics is possible. Chaos
is at once a risk and a choice and it is here that the possible and the impossible
cross each other. (Derrida, 1996, pp83–84)

Derrida goes on to argue about the undecidability of the decision, and that
even the most desirable of closures can only be temporary stabilizations
(Derrida, 1996, pp84–87). He is arguing that a theory provides a closure, a
decision, and taken together with other theories gives us a metanarrative,
that is a temporary stabilization of our thoughts about mental reality.
However, he, like the philosopher of science Karl Popper (1959), is arguing
that a closure is never complete, and that a dialogue needs to continue until
the closure is deconstructed and a new closure temporarily agreed on.

Hare has provided us with an additional answer to the teacher's dilemmas. He has argued that it is not the role of the teacher to teach certain truths
but to give the students an ability to appraise principles and concepts for
themselves, and likewise with science, teachers should not insist on certain
beliefs but give students a scientific outlook so that they can make their own
judgements.

Conclusions

Basically, we have been arguing here about the way that we teach our
students; it is about our being concerned for them and helping them to be
critical thinkers who are able to make up their own minds for themselves.
Clearly this changes our role and even makes it more difficult. This difference is perhaps best summed up in Bauman's (1987) book, *Legislators and
Interpreters*. In a bygone era, teachers were the legislators of knowledge and
now our role has changed to become interpreters of the variety of legitimate
understandings that exist. As we have argued, to try to suggest that one is
correct makes us legislators – and that becomes a role of questionable ethic
in the contemporary world, despite what specific curricula might suggest.
We might be tempted to ask whether the role of education has changed as a
result of these changes and we can only respond by pointing out that different forms of knowledge are changing, but the ethical questions do not
change.

But it might be asked, is education no more than producing a variety of
interpretations of the multiple realities of the society in which we live?

Interpretation without producing the reasons why different positions are held or are reasonable is not the teachers' role. We are responsible for providing the evidence why people hold conflicting beliefs and interpretations; we are looking at the processes people go through in order to reach their own decisions. Perhaps we need to place more emphasis on the reasons behind the decisions made, and then to let the learners make up their own minds about the validity of one position or another. Intellectual freedom is still the underlying ethic of our educational system, as it should be in all societies that claim to be democracies, and we should endeavour to ensure that this freedom is retained by helping our students think critically and independently in a late modern world in which we all drown in a sea of information. Indeed, Strike and Soltis (1985, p60) go as far as to suggest that 'we see in human history writ large a positive development of a more humane and more broadly shared point of view'. Perhaps this is making too big a claim for history and for moral teaching – but at least it is putting our teaching of ethics in the widest possible context.

References

Bauman, Z (1987) *Legislators and Interpreters*, Polity Press, Cambridge

Derrida, J (1996) Remarks on Deconstruction and Pragmatism, in *Deconstruction and Pragmatism,* ed C Mouffe, Routledge, London

Foucault, M (1972) *The Archaeology of Knowledge,* Routledge, London

Freire, P (1998) *Pedagogy of Freedom,* Rowman and Littlefield, Lanham, MD

Hare, R M (1966) Adolescents into adults, in *Aims in Education,* ed T H B Hollins, Manchester University Press, Manchester

Jarvis, P (1997) *Ethics and the Education of Adults in Late Modern Society,* NIACE, Leicester

Palmer, P (1998) *The Courage to Teach,* Jossey-Bass, San Francisco, CA

Paton, H (1961) *The Moral Law,* Hutchinson, London

Peters, R S (1966) *Ethics and Education,* George Allen and Unwin, London

Popper, K R (1959) *The Logic of Scientific Discovery,* Hutchinson, London

Scheffler, I (1967) Philosophical models of teaching, in *The Concept of Education,* ed R S Peters, Routledge, London

Strike, K A and Soltis, J F (1985) *The Ethics of Teaching,* Teachers College, Columbia University, New York

Chapter 5

Radical and feminist pedagogies

Julia Preece and Colin Griffin

Introduction

Radical pedagogy is a theoretical approach that specifically aims to empower oppressed groups or challenge traditional forms of social and political oppression. The nature of these aims is changing in the postmodern conditions of society. So whereas it might once have reflected, for example, a straightforwardly socialist analysis (Youngman, 1986), radical pedagogy today reflects, as does society itself, a much more complex picture. Consequently, writers are more likely nowadays to contextualize their analysis within the complexity and ambiguity of the postmodern condition rather than within any single critical tradition such as socialism or feminism (Lather, 1991; Mclaren, 1995). For writers such as these, the nature both of oppression and of the pedagogical response has changed. Increasingly radical pedagogy is constructed against a background of globalization, the risk society, the primacy of culture, and so on. In short, what counts as radical pedagogy may no longer be a matter simply of politics, but of critical consciousness or of a concept of social inclusion or citizenship itself: the issue of cultural power and hegemony has always been at the forefront of the analysis (Livingstone *et al*, 1987).

The implications of postmodernism and the learning society for teachers are considerable, since they call into question the traditional concepts of truth, knowledge and authority upon which classroom teaching has hitherto rested. The relativism of knowledge claims, the primacy of learning over teaching, the global possibilities of information technology, demographic changes in the population of learners, all have major consequences for the perceived role of the teacher. In this context, the changing role of the teacher from legislator to that of interpreter (Bauman, 1987) was introduced in Chapter 2. Critical reflexivity in the learning process means that the authority of the teacher is both challenged and reformulated around the learning process itself. This is what radical or critical pedagogy has traditionally implied. That is, it casts the teacher in the role of empowering learners to bring about social and political change. In the learning society, the role of the teacher in this respect is rendered even more problematic.

This chapter will outline some of the major accounts of radical pedagogy, and place it in the broader context of change that the idea of the learning society stands for. The radicalism of pedagogy may take many forms. Whereas once it seemed an exclusively political or ideological stance, nowadays it is as likely to be associated with the critical reflexivity of learning itself, or with particular kinds of teaching and learning methods. Critical pedagogy may, in other words, take individualistic or collective forms, and it may be concerned with content or method, or the relation between them. In terms of context, it has been used to challenge the perceived failings of the system of public schooling (Kanpol, 1994). More often, it is based on the transformative possibilities for adult education associated with major figures such as Antonio Gramsci or Paulo Freire (Coben, 1998; Mayo, 1999). For these reasons, it is more appropriate to speak of radical pedagogies in the plural, rather than to suggest a single tradition or meaning. Finally, in the context of the risk society (Beck, 1992), we need to extend the concept of critical or radical pedagogies to include the teaching and learning implications of social movements, citizenship, peace, environmental and other such concerns of the postmodern world.

This chapter provides an overall background view of critical and radical pedagogies, identifying common themes and introducing some of the most important writers, before concluding with an account of some feminist positions and a case study of critical pedagogy in the context of environmental education.

Background

As has already been stated, postmodern society influences how we perceive knowledge and the role of the teacher. In addition to the opportunities and challenges of technology, increasing student diversity has implications for how and what we teach. Formal teaching has traditionally been based on the notion of a teacher who imparts a particular syllabus to a class of passive participants who are expected to absorb and reproduce the contents of that syllabus at relevant moments beyond the classroom. Teaching methods in this vein use technology as a tool to enhance and vary the presentation of material, but not necessarily as a means of stimulating new forms of critique.

The experience of new kinds of student (migrant, mature, disabled and so on) in the traditional classroom has raised the question of whether the teaching environment addresses their practical needs. In some cases these concerns also extend to whether the teaching content acknowledges the experiential background of different students, particularly adult ones. The concept of a learning society does not seem to particularly engage with the teaching experience itself, though there are clearly ideological concepts of how a learning society should function. Coffield (2000) offers 10 models of learning *societies*. These range from models that focus on skills development to social control or individualism to a more reformatory model for structural change. There is nevertheless a contemporary tendency to see *the* learning society in terms of market value and vocationalism (DfEE, 1998).

Radical or alternative pedagogies attempt to move beyond these practical foci for society in that they question the very ideology behind teaching. To varying degrees they all challenge the normative social, political and ideological contexts for teaching and learning. The radical goal is usually to empower the learner and change the educational relationship between student and teacher in order to effect societal change.

There are several labels for such pedagogical approaches; the most common can be linked together in two broad groupings: social purpose education and popular education. These visions are promoted by organizations such as the WEA and many university continuing education departments (Taylor, 1997):

- conscientization;
- pedagogy for the oppressed;
- emancipatory learning;
- social action learning;
- education for social justice.

These have proved to be the practice basis for the labels in the above grouping, particularly since the 1970s, with a focus on community and non-formal education (Allman and Wallis, 1995; Foley, 1999; Kirkwood and Kirkwood, 1989):

- critical pedagogy;
- border pedagogy;
- postmodernism of resistance;
- postcolonial pedagogy;
- feminist pedagogy;
- engaged pedagogy.

These consist of social visions and practices that are most closely connected to postmodernism. Gore (1993) offers a useful distinction between those who write about such teaching from a philosophical or ideological perspective (such as Giroux, 1983, 1992; Mclaren, 1991) and those who offer practical or instrumental techniques (such as Freire, 1972, 1976; Shor, 1980), though all writers express an intention to link their ideas with both practice and ideology.

Although the above teaching approaches are not necessarily confined to the post-compulsory education sector their arguments lend themselves to teaching situations that are free from systems of conformity (which are more likely to be found in the school sector). Moreover, whilst Knowles (1990) is not classified here as someone belonging to the radical pedagogy tradition, there is a sense in which his notion of andragogy (teaching adults) and other adult educators (for example, Brookfield, 1987; Mezirow *et al*, 1990; Thompson, 1997) have influenced how the teacher–learner relationship might be seen as something other than a didactic, one-way process of information giving.

Whilst there are many, therefore, who would claim to belong, at least in part, to a radical concept of emancipatory education, this chapter is confined mainly to a selection of authors who represent radical education from an ideological perspective and those who offer practical ideas for achieving this goal. These are:

- Freire, Shor, Foley;
- Aronowitz, Giroux, Mclaren;
- feminist educators.

The writers represent various 'takes' on pedagogy, though there is considerable sharing of certain themes.

Some common features of radical pedagogies

Radical pedagogies challenge conventional classroom practice. This is perceived as a relationship where the teacher is the knower and the student is the recipient of new knowledge emanating from the teacher. In doing so the teacher perpetuates existing social structures and cultural/political worldviews towards different social groups. This means that students are encouraged to internalize dominant values about society – which is traditionally blind to gender or other differences. The focus of such teaching is on disseminating predefined knowledge whose truth is legitimated through texts, written by established authors with authority to 'know'.

Radical pedagogy teachers assume that conventional teaching perpetuates false consciousness and hegemony (internalized value systems which encourage people to believe in their subordinate position in relation to the *status quo*). This diminishes oppressed or marginalized people's ability to see how they are being manipulated to accept their oppression.

Radical pedagogies attempt to redress this level of awareness by drawing on theoretical perspectives such as Marxist notions of class and reproduction, and poststructuralist or postmodernist understandings of discourse and power relations. Both stances usually take a political position that through education people can use their own self-determination to give themselves individual or collective power and challenge the *status quo*.

The goal of this approach is to give voice to the unseen, unheard and oppressed and stimulate action for change. This is achieved through a process of criticality – teachers acknowledging their inheritance of being the oppressor but being willing to work with the oppressed. They must recognize their own social situatedness and privilege the concept of difference.

The classroom experience becomes a process of democratic dialogue – with the teacher problematizing the *status quo* and getting students to articulate and theorize what they already know from their own experience. In this context the teacher refuses to be the expert and tries to learn as much as the student – by listening, encouraging critical awareness of the socio-cultural positioning of ideas, beliefs, values. Experiences are shared amongst the peer group and there is an emphasis on exploring themes from daily life.

A postmodernism of resistance slant on these perspectives looks more closely at how oppression functions through power relationships. This includes exploring how certain kinds of truth and knowledge are legitimized by people who have power and authority. In this respect language is regarded as a medium for power and domination. For postmodernists truth, meaning and knowledge are relative and based on subjective experiences. Therefore the goal of radical pedagogy is to legitimate the experiences of the oppressed or marginalized by relating those experiences to wider social influences and by encouraging a theoretical perspective that explains how people give meaning to their world.

There are issues associated with these perceptions of the teacher–student relationship. Brookfield (1987) warns for instance that any attempt to change someone's existing worldview is vulnerable to simply another form of indoctrination. Similarly, even if teachers acknowledge their social situatedness, they inevitably possess their own views. Nevertheless the protagonists claim that continual self-critical awareness should guard against this.

Freire, Shor and Foley

Freire (1972, 1976, 1978) is generally regarded as the founder of an educational approach that challenges the oppressed to critique their relationship with their oppressors – based on reflection and action. His writings have influenced many generations of educators concerned with social justice. He coined the words 'conscientization' and 'praxis' (shared critical reflection amongst the oppressed resulting in raised awareness of their oppression followed by group action for change).

Many of Freire's philosophical and teaching approaches are reflected across the different strands of radical pedagogy. For Freire the educator's role is to challenge people's awareness of their situation by encouraging dialogue and developing a permanent critical attitude to their social situation. Freire's goal was to create a teacher–learner relationship that assumed a mutuality: 'A process of knowing with the people how they know things and the level of that knowledge' (1978, p25). In other words, recognizing that the learner has knowledge that needs to be legitimized. Freire wanted educators to tread the dual path of recognizing their social situation as members of the elite – and therefore potentially the oppressors – but also to steer the learning situation by problematizing what might otherwise be accepted as normal and encouraging open discussion: 'The task of the dialogical teacher... is to represent that universe to the people from whom he first received it – not as a lecture but as a problem' (1972, p81).

The principal aim of Freire's approach was for all learners to act 'together in unshakeable solidarity' (1972, p100). Freire was writing on behalf of Brazilian peasant farmers. His philosophy has underpinned much community education work around the world, though the notion of solidarity is sometimes interpreted more loosely.

Shor (1980) adapted Freire's philosophy within the industrial context of worker education. His focus was on making the link between the internalized psyche and external social relationships in order to enable workers to understand how they were being manipulated by the dominant middle-class culture. Shor therefore advocated a dialogic teacher–learner relationship where the classroom subject matter consisted of ordinary, daily life situations that would be critiqued by examining familiar situations 'in an unfamiliar way' (p93):

> The teacher surrenders the mystique of power and expertise – while using his or her conceptual understanding of reality to provoke critical consciousness in the students. (Shor, 1980, p84)

Shor attempted to promote a form of vocational education, which he called 'critical literacy' – a means of combining literacy and political awareness that would empower students to intervene in their own destiny. The teacher's role in this situation is primarily as 'initiator' of questions: 'Raising consciousness about the structured failure built into the system is a key task of the liberatory class' (1980, p68).

Griff Foley, another follower of Freire, almost 20 years later claims a teaching goal of working for 'emancipatory action'. By this he means: 'the unlearning of dominant oppressive ideologies and discourses and the learning of oppositional liberatory ones' (1999, p4). He emphasizes, however, that collective action is not easy to achieve. People's notion of liberation may be complex and contradictory, influenced by 'intrapersonal, interpersonal and broader social factors' (p4). He also picks up the postmodern influences that learners need to develop: 'a critical understanding of how power works in society' (p26). Nevertheless he supports the 'enabling conditions' for emancipatory learning which require shared experiences of oppression within a learning group, with the opportunity for reflection and critical thinking that extends the learner 'beyond her (*sic*) current understanding' (p105). Foley advocates the use of case study material based on people's everyday experiences that can then be critiqued and discussed in relation to their socio-political contexts. He emphasizes that emancipatory learning inevitably requires a critique of capitalism. This is because capitalist systems are seen as based on exploitation and oppression of (usually) the majority for the benefit of (usually) the few.

These positions continue to form the basis of much working-class education in the Western world. Their emphases, however, on unified responses to class oppression, with limited recognition of other social structures, mean that for some educators this position alone is untenable in today's more pluralistic, risk society. A more elaborate way of interpreting emancipation is required.

Aronowitz, Giroux and Mclaren

Gore (1993) claims that these three authors present ideological rather than practitioner perspectives on pedagogy. They are principally postmodernists and as such introduce some new vocabulary into the realm of radical pedagogies. Aronowitz and Giroux talk of critical pedagogy, border pedagogy and a postmodernism of resistance.

Aronowitz and Giroux (1991) start from a similar premise to that of Freire, Shor and Foley. They state that postmodern educators 'need to build upon the tacit knowledge derived from the cultural resources that students already possess' (p15). They see postmodernism as a position that enables them to talk about a world where knowledge is constantly changing and meaning is contingent upon interpretation. It provides a reference point to demonstrate the forever fluid and changing borders of one's identity or 'place in the world' (p70).

Aronowitz and Giroux, however, attempt to move beyond a purely post-modern discourse that simply affirms difference without exploring the power relationships that constitute difference and domination:

> Postmodernism fails to link the emphasis on difference with an oppositional politics in which the particularities of gender, race, class and ethnicity are seen as fundamental dimensions in the constitution of subjectivity and the politics of voice and agency. (1991, p80)

By this they mean that people derive their sense of self from the way they are positioned by others. The balance of power defining the sense of difference derives from the sense of authority or dominance of one voice over another. So difference can be seen in multiple ways, as can power and oppression.

It is this perspective which distinguishes the advocates of critical peda-gogy from the Freirean notion of collective and unified oppression and collective and unified emancipation. Critical pedagogy therefore, 'respects the notion of difference' (1991, p118) and the relations of power which constitute those differences. Knowledge that derives from the experiences of being different forms the basis of the classroom curriculum. Aronowitz and Giroux (1991) call this 'a pedagogy of voice' (p100). It explores how students give meaning to their personal experiences and how those meanings help to explain what happens in wider society. In this process it is acknowledged that there is no single position. Indeed, voices are 'multilayered, complex and contradictory' (1991, p100). But in order to move the marginalized beyond where they are, Aronowitz and Giroux argue they must not only interrogate their own experiences but must also use those voices to question critically the 'hegemonic discourses that make up the official curriculum' (1991, p128). It is at this point that critical pedagogy becomes 'border pedagogy' or a 'postmodernism of resistance'. Giroux (1992) explains that border peda-gogy goes beyond merely the development of a critical capacity to challenge. It examines more deeply how institutions, knowledge and social relations are 'inscribed in power' (p28). It is only by understanding fully the processes which cause discrimination and difference that we can begin to understand how to change the social fabric of society. So, from a process of dialogue and critical review of text (critical pedagogy) learners can move to a sense of self-determination and individual agency plus action (border pedagogy) – but on multiple levels which have different meanings for different learners.

Usher and Edwards (1994) provide a further interpretation of the emanci-patory potential for critical and border pedagogy. They suggest critical peda-gogy will 'enable learners to become citizens in a reconstituted pluralistic society' (p125), whilst border pedagogy will move citizens to 'become their own agents' in a more political way.

In keeping with some criticisms of Freire, Usher and Edwards suggest that the emancipatory potential of border pedagogy is more ideological than real. They confirm again the teaching danger of creating a unified, essentialist notion of oppression. They also point out that such dialogue assumes a classroom of absolute trust between all members and underplays the difficulties of rationalizing the potentially multiple meanings for difference. There remain, therefore, inherent tensions between the desire of the educator and those of the learners.

Mclaren (1991) introduces yet another term: 'postcolonial pedagogy'. As its name suggests, this is a pedagogy for anti-imperialism (p135) but with a particular emphasis on challenging those responsible for global capitalism. In many respects the goals are similar to those of Aronowitz and Giroux's postmodernism of resistance – to enable the voicing of multiple differences and resistances to the *status quo*, as defined by imperialists. The focus again is on 'the self anchored in experience' (p140). In this rendering of pedagogy, Mclaren spells out all the different aspects of teaching which contribute to either emancipatory or banking education (Freire, 1972) – the curriculum, learning location, institutions, teaching style, social practices and the knowledge-power relationships within the learning culture.

Mclaren has drawn upon a postmodern notion of difference (shifting identities and constructions of reality) but taken a strategic oppositional position rather more akin to that of Shor. Capitalism is the prescribed enemy but in a form which enables it to be reproduced to suit the historical moment. Consequently teachers of a postcolonial pedagogy must take this into account:

> The assumptions which guide their work must be analysed in relation to the historical and cultural specificity of its production in the context of classroom relations to reveal both its enabling and disabling effect. (Mclaren, 1991, p140)

In order to achieve this he proposes the construction of 'border identities'. These are narratives of the self which are critiqued collectively, resulting in deeper understanding of individual histories and their relationship to wider social and cultural contexts:

> Border identities are constructed out of empathy for others by means of a *passionate connection through difference*. This connection is furthered by a narrative imagination which enables connections to be made between our own stories and the stories of cultural others. (Mclaren, 1991, p140)

The focus on self, personal histories and an understanding of how dominant cultures manage, through relations of power, to reproduce domination are common themes with all these writers. Their differences probably lie in the extent to which they privilege certain forms of difference and engage with the idea that deeper understanding of the self in relation to society can foster individual or group empowerment or action for structural change. As these are often conceptual, rather than evidenced outcomes it is difficult to know how much the ideology effects actual change, beyond an intellectual level, through practice. The presence of a body of feminist literature within academia perhaps indicates that some structural change is achievable through dialogue and theorizing – though it is debatable whether the change is endemic throughout the institution.

Feminist positions

A separate strand of critical pedagogies emanates from feminist writers. Gore (1993) has identified distinct locations for this literature – either in schools of education or in women's studies courses. She suggests this location influences whether the issue of feminism or teaching style is forefronted. The curriculum of women's studies courses, for instance, is already a locus for the topic of gender. In schools of education, educational practice is a presumed focus of study – particularly for different social groups of women.

Within these two dimensions this means there are several different feminist positions, ranging from a more liberal, equal opportunities approach to teaching, to the more political position of poststructuralism. All argue for women's space in the curriculum and classroom. This means recognizing women role models in texts and women's theoretical perspectives as well as identifying ways in which women's voices are heard in classroom activities. Poststructuralist concepts have strongly influenced these feminist critical pedagogies, focusing the emphasis on validating differences *between* women and their multiple contexts. Gore stresses, however, that feminist literature on pedagogy is largely not self-critical of its own practice and tends to ignore other literature on pedagogy. There is a tendency to define the latter as patriarchal and not linked to women's oppression or a commitment to women's emancipation (Gore, 1993, p25).

In spite of these caveats a number of feminist writers have developed more explicit concepts of difference within pedagogy – particularly from gender and race perspectives. Disability within the women's movement is still an under-profiled arena (Morris, 1992). A particular feature of feminist pedagogy is its effort to challenge the patriarchal nature of academic teaching and curriculum. There is an additional focus in that much feminist teaching involves women teaching women. This places a new identity relationship between teacher and learner, which is explored by black writers (for example, Hill Collins, 1990; Hooks, 1994).

Hooks (1994) takes a black feminist perspective, which she calls 'engaged pedagogy'. Here the learner's experiences and life histories become a medium for enhancing the curriculum: 'Linking confessional narratives to academic discussions so as to show how experience can illuminate and enhance our understanding of academic material' (p20). Her emphasis, like other writers, is to privilege marginality as 'more than a site of deprivation'. The teaching goal is to shift the experience of marginality to a place for resistance. In other words, learners are encouraged to 'look beyond the limitations of their current condition' and find a way of using that experience to build a different kind of world (Galloway, 1999, p226).

There is a sense in which feminist literature gives greater credence to the concept of 'emotional knowledge' than some of the other writers. Hill Collins (1990), for instance, talks about the 'insider view' and 'situated knowledge' that are grounded in the black experience of being part of a spiritual community of African Americans as well as articulating the insider experience of racism. The difference for most women's studies courses and courses that adopt an explicitly feminist approach is that the teaching is frequently done by women in an environment of shared identity between teacher and learner. An example of this can be seen in community courses for adults where Muslim Pakistani women may be discussing curriculum content in environments that are specifically designed for their needs:

> They walk into the community centre, at that time there are no male classes, they are all women tutors and it's a real sense of community and belonging and sisterhood and they feel comfortable, they feel that they own that place and they belong there. (Fahana, in Preece and Houghton, 2000, p83)

Barr (1999) extends this notion of the relationship between emotion and knowledge. She emphasizes it is not up to the educator to decide what is really useful knowledge. She claims we 'need to reinvisage the notion of rationality in less exclusive ways – which do not separate emotion from intellect' (p12).

For Barr, then, feminist pedagogy includes a critique of narrow forms of rationality and a recognition of feeling as a source of knowledge – as well as the use of collective inquiry to create new knowledge and the recognition of one's social location within those experiences. So from Mclaren's exploration of the psyche, feminists move to a more explicit acknowledgement of 'emotion' as contributing to reason and knowledge and therefore as a part of power relationships.

Critical pedagogy and environmental education

We have seen in this chapter that some radical pedagogies may reflect ideologies of oppression which are, from a postmodernist perspective, rather essentialist and homogeneous. In other words, they inadequately address the issues such as diversity, complexity, reflexivity, risk and ambiguity that increasingly characterize contemporary society. For this reason, it is sometimes claimed that the emancipatory potential of radical pedagogies can be more ideological than real. Despite the frequent reference in such pedagogies to critical praxis as envisaged by Freire (1972), there remains the question of the teacher's role. In other words, where is there a practitioner perspective in all this?

In this section we turn to consider the implications for pedagogy and the teacher's role in relation to one of the universal concerns of postmodern or risk society, namely, environmental education.

In a review of critical theory and praxis in environmental education, Fien (1994) has argued that 'Critical theory provides an emancipatory framework for educational practice as it asserts that individuals and groups should be in control of their own lives and be able to determine their own destinies' (p21). Environmental education therefore reflects the apparent contradictions in the ways in which environmental issues are constructed:

> Why do children generally express positive attitudes to the environment but fail to see the link between their consumer habits and environmental quality? Why does their enthusiasm for the environment dissipate as they grow older? In what ways might our teaching practices contribute, at least in part, to the action paralysis of modern society? (Fien, 1994, pp21–22)

The answers to these questions depend upon distinguishing between three approaches to teaching about the environment:

1. Education *through* the environment, be it in a city street, a beach, a park, a farm, a forest or the school grounds, can be used to give reality, relevance and practical experience to learning. Increased awareness of aspects of the environment can be expected from any opportunities for direct contact with the environment. Opportunities to learn out-of-doors can also be used to develop important skills for data gathering, such as observation, sketching, photography, interviewing, and using scientific instruments, as well as social skills such as group work, cooperation and aesthetic appreciation. Environmental awareness and concern can also be fostered by linking learning to direct experiences in the environment and allowing learners to become captivated by the complexity and wonder of natural systems or immersed in the values conflict over particular environmental issues.

2. Education *about* the environment. Such feelings of concern are not enough, however, if living responsibly and sustainably in the environment is an educational goal. Concern needs to be translated into appropriate

behaviour patterns and actions but, for this to happen, it is essential for learners to understand how natural systems work and the impact of human activities upon them. This will include learning about political, philosophical, economic and socio-cultural factors as well as about the ecological ones that influence decisions about how to most responsibly use the environment. Knowledge about the environment is essential if all citizens are to participate in any informed debate aimed at resolving local, national and global environmental issues. There is much that many non-formal avenues of environmental education, as well as formal curriculum areas, including the arts as well as the natural and social sciences, can contribute to providing such knowledge.

3. Education *for* the environment. Education *for* the environment aims to promote a willingness and ability to adopt lifestyles that are compatible with the wise use of environmental resources. In so doing, it builds on education *in* and *about* the environment to help develop an informed concern and sense of responsibility for the environment through the development of an environmental ethic and the motivation and skills necessary to participate in environmental improvement. Education *for* the environment may be located within the socially-critical traditions in education because of its concern for social critique and reconstruction. (Fien, 1994, pp20–21)

All of these approaches to environmental education can result in good teaching practices in relation to methods, curriculum and so on. But whereas education *through* and *about* the environment represents traditional pedagogy, education *for* the environment is intended to identify what Freire (1972) meant by critical praxis:

> The issues raised by consciously teaching towards social transformation and ecological sustainability through education *for* the environment pose many challenges to traditional schooling and necessitate a reconsideration of the way critical thinking, environmental values, education and political literacy are addressed… Critical praxis involves the wide range of teaching strategies… including enquiry based learning, value exercises, ideology critique, community contact, and social action of various sorts. What distinguishes critical praxis from the use of these strategies individually is their integration into a focused programme for conscientization and empowerment. (Fien, 1994, pp47–48)

The above illustration is contexted in schooling, but, as it suggested, whereas children are generally positive towards environmental issues, they often fail in later life to link their lifestyles as consumers with environmental quality: their enthusiasm is 'dissipated' as they grow older.

Clearly, the emergence of new social movements, together with widespread disillusion with traditional ideological politics, is a prominent feature of the learning society. Much lifelong learning theory and policy lay stress on the potential of social movements, informal learning and civil society as themselves major sites of learning.

But it is doubtful whether learning in later life has engaged very much with these developments, or that teachers in post-compulsory education reflect them in their teaching practices. This has recently been observed in the context of adult education:

> The emergence of new social and urban movements since the 1960s has grown... in opposition to the 'old' movements of labour... Such movements have relied more on popular protest and direct action of a 'personal and politi-cal' kind in order to create social change. For example, the women's move-ment, the peace movement, the environmental movement, to name a few of the more important ones, have had a significant educative impact in the public sphere as well as in the private life of many individuals... We need to learn from these movements. However, adult education is often outside of them and fails to connect with the potential they offer for a collective and critical pedagogy of learning. (Crowther, 2000, p488)

If this is the case, radical or critical pedagogy, and critical praxis in education, would have to be relocated into social movements and not confined to the early years of schooling, if education *for* the environment is to become a reality.

The case of environmental education as radical pedagogy draws attention to the general issue of the *site* of such learning in postmodern conditions, or in the learning society itself. Radical pedagogies are increasingly located in the learning contexts of social movements or civil society as such, more perhaps than in the formal institutional sites of education, which were the site of the radical pedagogies of the past. This does not necessarily mean that the conditions of oppression have disappeared, but only that, in the learning society, the educational conditions of resistance have been transformed.

Conclusion

Debates about the learning society have created opportunities for experimen-tation in teaching and learning – both practically and ideologically. Radical educators argue, however, that teaching that effects real change towards more equality in society requires structural change. This means educational systems and the people within them need to problematize what seems normal. Within that the notion of how knowledge is perceived at all needs to be re-examined. This chapter has described and highlighted a range of radical pedagogies that purport to do this. The field is awash with terminology that at first seems to be articulating very similar positions. Such a perception is further complicated by the limited amount of cross-referencing between the different thematic strands. For example, we have seen the failure to connect environmental education in school and in later life. Nevertheless there are some subtle shifts in focus from the idea of a predominantly Marxist and unified class-consciousness to a recognition of plurality within the learning experience. An exploration of different radical pedagogies involves awareness of these shifts in meaning to a more specific focus on how the self is consti-tuted within those differences. From here individual as well as collective identities, social situatedness and emotion all need to be considered within pedagogies that strive for intellectual criticality coupled with radical change in society.

References

Allman, P and Wallis, J (1995) Challenging the postmodern condition: radical adult education for critical intelligence, in *Adult Learning, Critical Intelligence and Social Change*, eds M Mayo and J Thompson, NIACE, Leicester

Aronowitz, S and Giroux, H A (1991) *Postmodern Education, Politics, Culture and Social Criticism*, University of Minnesota Press, London

Barr, J (1999) *Liberating Knowledge: Research, feminism and adult education*, NIACE, Leicester

Bauman, Z (1987) *Legislators and Interpreters*, Polity Press, Cambridge

Beck, U (1992) *Risk Society: Towards a new modernity*, Sage Publications, London

Brookfield, S (1987) *Developing Critical Thinkers: Challenging adults to explore alternative ways of thinking and acting*, Jossey-Bass, San Francisco, CA

Coben, D (1998) *Radical Heroes: Gramsci, Freire and the politics of adult education*, Garland Publishing, London

Coffield, F (ed) (2000) *Differing Visions of a Learning Society*, ESRC/Policy Press, Bristol

Crowther, J (2000) Participation in adult and community education: a discourse of diminishing returns, *International Journal of Lifelong Education*, **18** (6), pp 479–92

Department for Education and Employment (DfEE) (1998) *The Learning Age: A renais-sance for a new Britain* (Green Paper CM 3790) The Stationery Office, Norwich

Fien, J (1994) Critical theory, critical pedagogy and critical praxis in environmental education, in *Action and Action Competence: Key concepts in critical pedagogy*, eds B B Jensen and K Schnack, Studies in Educational Theory and Curriculum, Volume 12, Royal Danish School of Educational Studies, Copenhagen

Foley, G (1999) *Learning in Social Action*, NIACE/Zed Books, Leicester

Freire, P (1972) *Pedagogy of the Oppressed*, Penguin, Harmondsworth

Freire, P (1976) *Education and the Practice of Freedom*, Writers and Readers Publishing Corporation, London

Freire, P (1978) *Pedagogy in Process*, Writers and Readers Publishing Corporation, London

Galloway, V (1999) Building a pedagogy of hope: the experience of the adult learning project, in *Popular Education and Social Movements in Scotland Today*, eds J Crowther, I Martin and M Shaw, Leicester, NIACE

Giroux, H A (1983) *Theory and Resistance in Education: A pedagogy for the opposition*, Heinemann, Oxford

Giroux, H A (1992) *Border Crossings*, Routledge, London

Gore, J (1993) *The Struggle for Pedagogies*, Routledge, London

Hill Collins, P (1990) *Black Feminist Thought*, Routledge, London

Hooks, B (1994) *Teaching to Transgress*, Routledge, London

Kanpol, B (1994) *Critical Pedagogy: An introduction*, Bergin & Garvey, Westport, CN

Kirkwood, G and Kirkwood, C (1989) *Living Adult Education: Freire in Scotland*, Open University Press, Buckingham

Knowles, M (1990) *The Adult Learner: A neglected species*, 4th edn, Gulf Publishing, Houston, TX

Lather, P (1991) *Getting Smart: Feminist research and pedagogy with/in the postmodern*, Routledge, London

Livingstone, D W *et al* (1987) *Critical Pedagogy and Cultural Power*, Macmillan, London

Mayo, P (1999) *Gramsci, Freire and Adult Education: Possibilities for transformative action*, Zed Books, London

Mclaren, P (1991) Post-colonial pedagogy: post-colonial desire and decolonised community, *Education and Society*, **9** (2) pp 135–58

Mclaren, P (1995) *Critical Pedagogy and Predatory Culture: Oppositional politics in a postmodern era*, Routledge, London

Mezirow, J *et al* (1990) *Fostering Critical Reflection in Adulthood*, Jossey-Bass, San Francisco, CA

Morris, J (1992) Personal and political: a feminist perspective on researching physical disability, *Disability, Handicap and Society*, **7** (2) pp 157–66

Preece, J and Houghton, A (2000) *Nurturing Social Capital in Excluded Communities: A kind of higher education*, Ashgate, Aldershot

Shor, I (1980) *Critical Teaching and Everyday Life*, South End Press, Boston

Taylor, R (1997) The search for a social purpose ethic in adult continuing education in the new Europe, *Studies in the Education of Adults*, **29** (1), pp 92–100

Thompson, J (1997) *Words in Edgeways: Radical learning for social change*, NIACE, Leicester

Usher, R and Edwards, R (1994) *Postmodern Education*, Routledge, London

Youngman, F (1986) *Adult Education and Socialist Pedagogy*, Croom Helm, Beckenham

Further reading

Mayo, M and Thompson, J (eds) (1995) *Adult Learning, Critical Intelligence and Social Change*, NIACE, Leicester

Chapter 6

Didacticism: lectures and lecturing

Colin Griffin

Of all the didactic methods of teaching, that of lecturing seems the most obvious. It puts the lecturer in complete control of the learning situation, and seems to cast the learner in an entirely passive role. On the face of it, there seems little scope for the lecture as an appropriate teaching method in the learning society, with its apparent rejection of traditional forms of knowledge and authority, and its focus upon active, learner-centred, self-directed and experiential learning. The authority of the lecturer depended upon subject knowledge and the face-to-face teaching and learning situation, whereas the learning society is one in which traditional forms of authority are questioned, and in which communications technology is making possible more and more teaching and learning at a distance.

Moreover, lecturing as a teaching method reflects very closely the kinds of institutions and roles associated with the formal education system. But this system is losing its traditional place amongst all the possible sites of learning in the learning society, which are claimed to be the family, the community, the workplace, social movements, and so on. Then there are the technical drawbacks of lecturing with which all who have lectured or been lectured to are aware of, such as short attention span, the inaudibility of the lecturer, dependence upon rote learning through note-taking, the absence of social interaction or effective feedback. In short, the formal lecture would seem to lack almost every prerequisite for effective learning in the learning society. It is apparently a one-way process in which the learner plays little part; there is little scope for reflexivity or for learners to make experiential connections. Above all, the formal lecture provides almost limitless scope for boredom, and also for the irritation that many feel at being 'lectured at' in any situation in life.

And yet lecturing remains a major teaching method in all sectors of the post-compulsory education system. 'Lecturer' continues to be the title of the professional role for many in the further, higher and adult sectors of education, and continues to distinguish the role and status of teachers in these sectors from teachers in schools. Student textbooks for prospective lecturers invariably contain theories and practical advice for doing it well and avoiding pitfalls. The fact that lecturing is a kind of drama played out in 'lecture theatres', and depends for some of its effectiveness upon the personal or charismatic qualities of the lecturer, also singles it out as a didactic method. Memories of educational experience often invoke anecdotes of enthusiasm or eccentricity that proved powerful stimulants to learning on the part of students. Unfortunately, such charisma is randomly distributed amongst lecturers as it is amongst everyone else, so it is a matter of chance whether or not our educational memories of lecturing are positive or not. Also, and perhaps unfortunately, such randomness does not lend itself readily to the processes of quality assurance and inspection. So there are aspects of lecturing that are not readily amenable to certain features of the present system, namely, those having to do with public accountability and student success rates in a universal system of formal accreditation. Too much about lecturing comes down to personal qualities that do not lend themselves to control and prediction.

And yet, students continue to value precisely the personal qualities of teachers, which is why mixed-mode teaching and learning systems, incorporating both distance and face-to-face opportunities, seem to prove attractive to many. Moreover, lecturers themselves might draw attention to the fact that a good lecture is more than a charismatic performance addressed to passive students. Lectures may serve as useful overviews of a topic, or to stimulate reflection on contradictions, anomalies or discrepancies, or to suggest further reading and research. In short, a good lecture fulfils support functions: it need not be confined to the conveying of information, but may incorporate a variety of interactive learning opportunities.

This chapter will explore some of these issues raised by teaching as a didactic method, by examining:

- the basis of *didacticism*, or the nature of authority and control in relation to the changing role of the lecturer; three types of authority will be identified, namely, social, subject and professional;
- the *pedagogical challenge*, or the critique of lecturing in relation to effective learning, which reflects issues of professional authority;
- the *postmodern challenge* posed by developments in the idea of the learning society, which reflects issues of social and subject authority;
- the *reconstruction* of the function of lectures and the role of the lecturer in what, for some time now, has been described as 'post-education society'.

Lecturing as didactic method

Lecturing and teaching are both activities invariably associated with the system of formal education. For some, the era of postmodernism is also the era of 'post-education society' (Evans, 1985). Formal education systems worldwide are said to have failed to bring about the kinds of economic, social and political changes they were once supposed to help achieve. New policies for lifelong learning are needed in order to bring education more closely into line with the world that is emerging. Many international organizations have produced policy proposals for lifelong learning or the learning society, according to which the role of education systems, although still vital, has to be put into much broader learning contexts (EC, 1996; OECD, 1996; UNESCO, 1996).

Didactic methods rely upon forms of authority that are now much more disputed than they were in the age of education, such as the authority of subject knowledge and the social authority of teachers over learners. Formal lectures remain, for example, a common public function of learned societies, such as the Royal Society or the Royal Society of Arts. In the education system itself, however, we can distinguish three types of authority which provide the didactic basis of this kind of teaching:

1. *Social authority*. It is possible to speak of being 'in authority' and being 'an authority'. The social authority of the lecturer is constituted by being in control of the *social* situation of the classroom or lecture theatre, for example maintaining discipline through a combination of charismatic, traditional and rational authority. Charismatic authority refers to the *personal* qualities of the lecturer. Traditional authority might be constituted by the *status* of the lecturer (in the case of younger learners, for example, this might be based upon age and generation). Rational authority is conveyed by the lecturer's instrumental *function* as a means to the end of passing examinations or gaining qualifications.

2. *Subject authority*. It is self-evident that lecturers should be regarded as authoritative in relation to the subject knowledge that they teach. As far as higher education is concerned, this generally entails that they should have some direct experience of *research* in their field, although the connection between being an active researcher and an effective lecturer is by no means straightforward. Nevertheless, a lecturer's reputation for having added to the field of knowledge usually constitutes some form of authority in those situations where this is relevant. Thus, it is argued that 'The *unique* contribution of the lecture... derives from the nexus between research and teaching... It is still possible to provide that personal perspective on knowledge, both on the process of constructing and validating knowledge and on interpreting the outcome' (Biggs, 1999, p99).

3. *Professional authority*. Whether or not teaching, and hence lecturing, constitutes a professional discipline is open to question: 'there is little sustained analysis of what it is that teachers might have in common with other professionals in terms of the nature of their work' (Squires, 1999, p23). Professionalism is constituted by the professional skills which the lecturer commands, and which are the object of training to teach and covered in textbooks written for trainees. They range from voice production to the ability to change bulbs in overhead projectors, from planning and structuring the lecture to preparing visual and other teaching aids to a professional standard. In the past, little or no professional training was required of lecturers, their subject authority being sufficient for their role. But in future all lecturers will be required to have *professional* qualifications to bring them into line with schoolteachers. Thus there are the FENTO (Further Education National Training Organization) standards for lecturers in further education, and the ILT (Institute for Learning and Teaching) membership requirements for lecturers in higher education.

Bearing in mind these three types of authority which lecturing represents, we can analyse the role of lecturer and functions of lecturing according to the forms of authority which didacticism reflects. As we shall see, *charismatic* authority, or that which relates to the unique personal qualities of the lecturer, seems to constitute a fourth type by virtue of its significance for this particular method.

The pedagogical challenge: what's the use of lectures?

The fact is, the pedagogical analysis of lectures and lecturing has been almost exclusively confined to the forms of professional authority that these invoke, with surprisingly little reference to the other forms of authority that were distinguished above.

The reason for this is that a technical or common sense knowledge of what it is to be a good or a bad lecturer has developed, and indeed is now being further extended by the demands of public accountability and competition for accreditation and formal qualifications for lecturing. The question, 'What's the use of lectures?' begs the question, 'What's the use of teaching?' and it is readily assumed that learning *entails* teaching. But this is precisely the issue that is raised by developments such as lifelong learning, the learning society, and the postmodern challenge to traditional beliefs about knowledge and authority and, indeed, to the idea of professionalism itself.

Being an effective lecturer, with an appropriate range of skills, therefore continues to constitute much of the content of the training of teachers for further, higher and adult education. Understandably, trainee teachers tend to lay particular stress on their need to develop effective classroom skills as part of their professional preparation. As a result, there has been a focus in professional training upon:

- *types* of learning theory (behaviourist, cognitive, social, experiential, and so on);
- *names* of learning theorists (Pavlov, Skinner, Thorndike, Gagné, Dewey, and so on);
- *professional* discourses of learning (objectives, outcomes, styles, support, assessment, and so on).

Unsurprisingly, trainee teachers have often failed to make connections between these, except in the most superficial way and unrelated to the actual learning of actual learners.

The pedagogical challenge to lecturing has been constructed in terms exclusively of whether or not lectures are effective in bringing about learning from the perspective of *scientific* knowledge and *professional* skills. In the 30 years since 1971, when Donald Bligh's book, *What's the Use of Lectures?* was first published, the general tone of textbooks has been defensive with regard to lectures and lecturing. The conclusion has been that there is still a place for the lecture amongst the repertoire of professional skills of lecturers, but that it needs to be put into more learner-centred, reflexive and experiential contexts wherever possible. Since lecturing continues to be a major function of professional lecturers, this is perhaps not surprising. Nor is it surprising that the book continues to exercise widespread influence and continues to be in print (Bligh, 1998).

We will now consider the professional or pedagogic 'post-Bligh' account of lectures in the three contexts where this is the main professional role: further, higher, and adult and continuing education.

Further education

The further education sector is nowadays extremely heterogeneous, accounting for a wide range of types of students and courses and including a proportion of degree and postgraduate provision. The lecture remains a significant teaching method throughout. A typical professional introduction to the method will therefore provide a typology of lectures, stressing those functions for which it is most appropriate, such as an introduction and overview of particular topic. The kinds of objectives that it can achieve are generally described as ranging from the cognitive through affective to attitudes and values. Presentational issues of planning, structure and strategy are discussed, along with issues of the environment, delivery, feedback, lecture notes, and handouts and evaluation (Curzon, 1997). Other textbooks put more emphasis on the lecture as a successful 'performance' and the need for 'mastery' of the material (Gray *et al*, 2000), but issues of planning, structuring and effective presentation styles and materials are universally stressed, together with practical advice about preparation and context.

Higher education

There is a much weaker tradition of professional training for lecturers in higher education, simply because the research function of the institutions and the profession of 'scholarship' itself have pushed the concept of professionalism here much more into the field of abstract and theoretical knowledge. Also the tradition of elite recruitment to the sector has perhaps led to assumptions about the intellectual autonomy of undergraduate learners, assumptions which with the onset of mass higher education systems seem less warranted than they once were. The assumption, typically, was that 'Explaining is at the heart of teaching in higher education just as its obverse, understanding, is at the heart of learning' (Brown, 1978, p2). The functions of lecturing in higher education are therefore explanation on the part of the lecturer and understanding on the part of students. As the author says:

> There are two major strategies that one can adopt for this purpose. The first is to help lecturers to develop their methods of preparing and giving lectures through ideas and activities that increase their awareness of the processes involved. The second is almost the inverse of the first: it is to help students develop *their* methods of learning from lectures through ideas and activities that increase their awareness of the processes. (Brown, 1978, p105)

Thus, in addition to issues of structure, planning and presentation, students' listening to lectures and note-taking may be supplemented by activities such as buzz groups and audio-visual aids.

Adult and continuing education

In the case of adult students, the straight lecture has generally seemed much less appropriate as a teaching method, and pedagogic or didactic approaches have usually been adapted to the students' adult learning needs. In general, therefore, the lecture has been traditionally associated with opportunities for participation such as discussion and questioning. The attempt to differentiate sharply between the pedagogy of schooling and the andragogy of adult education (Knowles, 1978) has reflected to some extent the disfavour into which lecturing once fell. However, the lecture remains a major method of teaching in adult and continuing education, modified by more interactive and adult-oriented strategies: 'it must still be recognized that it is a useful teaching tool, especially when it is well used, but only for the transmission of knowledge' (Jarvis, 1995, p120).

In all of these three sectors of education, the lecture is acknowledged to be still a major teaching method, and to have survived the criticism it faced since the 1970s: 'It exemplifies the process of "one-way communication" and, as such, has been criticised severely. And yet the lecture persists as a common mode of instruction in colleges of further education and else-where' (Curzon, 1997, p314); 'the lecture is still an important part of a teacher's "armoury"' (Gray *et al,* 2000, p94); 'Lecturing is perhaps the most frequently employed teaching technique despite all the criticisms that have been levelled against it at various times' (Jarvis, 1995, p117).

In this section, we have considered the functions of lecturing and the role of lecturers in terms of *pedagogy,* that is, as a didactic teaching *strategy.* Much of the pedagogy of lecturing has been conducted in the light of Bligh's influential book. This was based upon a scientific appraisal of the lecture method in relation to effective learning, and was no doubt influential because it focused clearly on techniques and strategies. It also seemed to provide a clear criterion of appropriateness for effective learning:

> The lecture is as effective as other methods to transmit information.
>
> Most lectures are not as effective as discussion to promote thought.
>
> Changing students' attitudes should not normally be the major object of a lecture.
>
> Lectures are relatively ineffective to teach values associated with subject matter.
>
> Lectures are relatively ineffective to inspire interest in a subject.
>
> Lectures are relatively ineffective for personal and social adjustment.
>
> Lectures are relatively ineffective to teach behavioural skills. (Bligh, 1998, p10)

This pedagogical critique of lecturing seems to leave the lecture with a very limited role in bringing about learning, if scientific evidence about its effectiveness is to be believed. This has constituted the criticism against which, as we have seen, many continue to defend the method.

But from a learning society perspective, the problem of the pedagogic challenge to lecturing is simply that we have lost any sense of the learner, learning needs and, indeed, of learning itself. Bligh's book does not refer to learning at all; Brown, in the context of higher education, says almost nothing about it. Learning features much more prominently in the context of further and adult and continuing education, as would be expected where personal growth and development are more prominent in relation to learning.

Thus, in the pedagogic challenge to lectures and lecturing, which reflects effectiveness, strategy and technique, learning is reduced to a function of instruction, explanation and understanding. This projects a relatively homogeneous account of learners and their learning needs. It also leads to the somewhat paradoxical conclusion that if the lecture can only be effective in conveying information, then in a world awash with information technologies, the question 'What's the use of lectures?' seems more rhetorical than ever. To say that lectures need to be supplemented by other, presumably quite different teaching methods, in order to be effective in a wider context than information, simply begs the question itself.

The idea of the learning society, and of lifelong learning, poses a much more fundamental challenge to lectures and lecturing. With the individual learner at the centre of the stage, with formal educational institutions losing their pre-eminence as the sites of learning, with the challenge to 'professionalism' itself, and with a much more inclusive concept of learning than merely explanation and understanding, a more basic question needs to be answered.

The postmodern challenge: what's the use of teaching?

We have seen that the pedagogical challenge to lectures and lecturing is based upon the professional form of authority. It reflects scientific evidence about the appropriateness of strategy and technique, reduces learning to matters of instruction, explanation and understanding, and projects a homogeneous view of learners and their learning needs. With the primacy of 'learning' over 'education' in the professional discourse, much wider issues now arise (Jarvis *et al*, 1998).

The learning society, which is associated with the postmodern view of the world, poses a much more fundamental challenge, not only with respect to didactic teaching methods such as lecturing, but to the whole relationship between teaching and learning (Jarvis, 2001).

In order to begin to understand the nature of this challenge, it is necessary to go back to the basis of didacticism in the typology of authority with which this chapter began, and understand postmodern perspectives as, in part, a series of challenges to traditional forms of authority. The distinction was made between *social, subject* and *professional* authority as the basis of the lecturer's didactic role. To this might be added *charismatic* authority, since many textbooks on teaching methods, such as those mentioned above, place some emphasis on the personal qualities of the lecturer as contributing to effective learning, or not.

In the previous section, it was suggested that the pedagogical critique of lecturing, or answers to the question 'What's the use of lectures?', has been conducted mainly in terms of professional authority, with regard to scientific evidence, strategies, techniques and methods. The general conclusion has been that the lecture, alongside and integrated with other and more interactive methods, continues to have its place in the teacher's classroom 'armoury' or repertoire. It is said to be particularly suitable for conveying information but not, on its own, much else. It is still defended as a justifiable teacher-centred method. Above all, lecturing seems to be inescapably linked with the classroom situation of formal educational institutions.

The learning society, stressing as it does the learner-centeredness of education, the significance of non-formal, informal, reflexive, experiential and developmental learning, poses a challenge to didacticism in general and lecturing in particular. In other words, the pedagogical critique seems to demonstrate that, apart from conveying information, the lecture is ill-suited to most kinds of learning associated with the learning society.

The learning society, as a postmodern phenomenon, is associated with challenges to traditional forms of knowledge and authority, as well as challenges to the adequacy of traditional structures of educational provision, with their roles and functions such as that of lecturing. It is the professional base reflecting the authority of the role that is brought into question, as the various functions of explanation, instruction, interpretation and legislation are called into question. It is not only lecturing, of course, but all forms of teaching as such which are having to be reformulated.

The issue of how far learning depends upon effective teaching has long been an open one. Learning theorists such as Carl Rogers (1969), Malcolm Knowles (1978), Allen Tough (1979) and Jack Mezirow (1991) have all argued that effective learning is self-actualizing, self-directed, self-planned and self-transformative. Didactic teaching merely reproduces traditional categories of knowledge and forms of authority, and consequently fails to result in 'real' learning.

In order to explore some of these points, the implications of the postmodern challenge will now be briefly described in relation to the various forms which lecturers' and teachers' authority take.

Social authority

As was suggested at the outset, this can take a variety of forms, but in the present context it refers to the traditional social status basis of the lecturer, which is that of the professional. The concept of the professional has, however, been rendered much more problematic in conditions of market economics and consumerism. The changes wrought by new forms of information and communications technology have eroded the traditional status of professionals based upon the monopolization of forms of knowledge and expertise. The fast-expanding possibilities for self-directed or self-planned learning projects, with all their implications for personal growth and development, have forced professionals such as teachers into the marketplace. In other words, the authority of the teacher rests much more now upon the capacity to sell knowledge as a commodity in the marketplace, rather than the traditional claim to monopolize knowledge itself. Public accountability and quality assurance, rather than traditional criteria of professionalism, now determine the professional role in the public sector. In short, the autonomy of the professional, which the lecturer's role once reflected, has been successfully challenged and considerably eroded in the postmodern conditions of society.

Subject authority

From a pedagogical perspective, the authority of the lecturer has been based upon a body of subject knowledge, and the idea that lectures should reflect expertise or 'mastery' of subject matter is one of the most important criteria for success. The concept of the curriculum reflected discrete subjects or forms of knowledge, and lecturers were expected to have mastery of one or more of them. In fact, the social authority or status of the lecturer was reflected in the title of 'lecturer in physics' or 'lecturer in history', or whatever. To some extent too, the status of the abstract knowledge itself also contributed to the subject authority of the lecturer. In any case, clearly lecturers are expected to be authorities or experts in their fields. What counts as knowledge in the learning society, however, is rather different from that conveyed by the traditional curriculum of 'subject knowledge'. The idea of knowledge as a rather static body of abstract truth is giving way to a much more relative and reflexive one:

> Now technological knowledge is changing minute by minute and second by second. With this rapid change, it is almost impossible to regard knowledge as a truth statement any longer. We are now talking about something that is relative. It can be changed again as soon as some new discovery is made that forces people to change their thinking. (Jarvis et al, 1998, p7)

Although such relativism will be differentially experienced between different subject areas, there is little doubt that the whole concept of the 'subject area' and 'subject knowledge' is becoming problematic, with inevitable consequences for the authority that lecturers and lecturing derive from it.

Professional authority

On the face of it, there is an increase in the degree of professionalism which lecturers are expected to display, with new forms of qualifications and licences to practise that have traditionally characterized professions other than that of teaching, such as law and medicine. The standards demanded by frequent inspection and quality audits are nowadays required to be much more transparent than they once were. In this sense, the professional authority of lecturers can be said to be gaining in prominence. But it has to be acknowledged that this access of professional authority is driven by market forces and public accountability, rather than by any increase in the social status of lecturers or any increasing recognition of the expertise or mastery of subject knowledge. It focuses very strongly upon teaching *methods* and *strategies*, and competence in dealing with the bureaucratic apparatus of control, as statutory curriculum principles are imposed not only upon the school sector but the whole of post-compulsory education. In fact, much of the professionalism of lecturers consists of the kinds of form-filling and record-keeping activities that would once have been regarded as essentially secretarial rather than professional. In other words, the new professional authority of lecturers can be regarded as little more than de-skilling in relation to traditional criteria of autonomous professional status: competence, rather than authority, constitutes the professionalism of the lecturer in the learning society.

Charismatic authority

This is an aspect of effective lectures and lecturers which is often stressed in the literature on training, so much so that it seems to constitute a fourth type. It is the authority that derives from the personal qualities of the lecturer, and can be traced in other professions, such as law. Charisma, in fact, could be regarded as a typical form which authority in postmodern society takes, with its focus upon the personal qualities and lives of individuals in sport, popular culture and popular media. It cannot be explored in depth here, but it is to be noted because it involves the old issue of whether good lecturers are 'born', or 'made' by effective training. The pedagogic critique of lecturing reflects an acknowledgment of its importance, but whether or not a good lecture is a kind of theatrical 'performance' has always been suspect, since it seems to defeat the purpose of training, especially in those cases of individuals who were apparently not 'born' to teach. Charismatic authority is important for effectiveness, and seems consistent with developments in the learning society, with its stress upon the uniqueness of the individual. However, its basis is anecdotal and experiential rather than anything more systematic.

We are now in a position to compare and contrast the pedagogic and the postmodern or learning society critique of lectures and lecturing:

- The pedagogical critique reflects a view of professional autonomy, whereas the postmodern reflects a view of the lecturer much more in relation to the demands of the market economy and public accountability.

- The pedagogical critique reflects a view of subject knowledge as a body of truths which lecturers 'master' and which constitutes their expertise, whereas the postmodern regards truth in more relative terms, much more experiential and reflexive.
- The pedagogic critique of lecturers and lecturing tended to base professional status on a combination of social and subject authority, whereas the postmodern perspective stresses the primacy of competence and accountability, and implies a de-skilling of the lecturer's role to some degree.
- The element of charismatic authority, according to the pedagogic view, was a desirable if unpredictable attribute of effective lecturing, whereas charisma in postmodern society stands for individualism, rather than the pedagogic tendency to homogenize learners and their learning needs.

The contrast between these critiques or perspectives on lectures, lecturers and lecturing permits us now to draw some conclusions about this particular form of didacticism in the learning society.

Reconstructing lectures and lecturing

Most commentators agree that lecturing remains one of the most important teaching methods in education, and that this is likely to remain the case. Those days are gone when it was fondly imagined that all learners were self-sufficient with respect to their learning needs and autonomous in meeting them. Gone too is the belief that there was no longer any role for teachers and teaching, didactic or not.

However, it is equally true that the learning society has brought with it major implications for these kinds of methods. Apart from the changes in the nature of authority that have been outlined above, there are new contexts in which lecturers and lectures must reconstitute their role and function. Here are some examples:

- The focus now is upon learning, rather than education: this means that learning, and not simply understanding, is the ultimate aim of all teaching methods, including that of lectures.
- The formal system of education, with its institutions, roles and functions, is no longer the main or only site of learning: the learning society comprises non-formal and informal learning on many different sites, such as family, community, social movements and in civil society generally.
- Learning in the learning society is an activity, perhaps work-based or problem solving, with strong emphases upon experience, reflection and personal growth in all of the sites where it takes place.

- The role of the state in the formal provision of education is retreating in the face of market forces and consumer-led styles of teaching and learning: teachers generally have to accommodate their methods to developments in consumerism and information and communications technology.
- The status and authority of lecturers, and teachers generally, will depend less upon traditional forms of professional autonomy and more upon competence in meeting the learning needs of learners as consumers, as well as meeting externally imposed quality assurance standards.
- Didactic teaching methods, including lecturing, will have to be adapted to a much less homogeneous body of learners and their learning needs to be effective; lectures will have to address individual learning needs and styles much more closely than in the past.
- Developments in information, communications and media technology mean that learners as consumers will have a much wider choice of learning methods than in the past: the face-to-face lecture will have to find its place amongst a range of open and distance learning alternatives.
- Traditional roles of teachers and lecturers will need to be much broader than those concerned with instruction, explanation, understanding and subject knowledge, to include a range of counselling, pastoral, mentoring and facilitative functions.

These are the kinds of conditions in the learning society that will shape the future of lectures and lecturing. On the face of it, the traditional lecture, with its imagery of passive, authoritative and rote learning of information, seems considerably challenged by the developments associated with the learning society. And yet, as has been seen, the lecture remains a major teaching method, for all its didacticism, and seems set to do so for the foreseeable future.

The future of lecturing and the lecture method depend on a reformulation of what is meant by didacticism, and the forms of authority with which this is associated and which have been outlined in this chapter. As we have seen, some of these forms of authority are unlikely to survive the learning society or postmodern challenge.

Paradoxically, the only form of authority that seems to be strengthened under postmodern conditions is charisma. Students choose face-to-face methods because they represent the human face of learning. Once the traditional forms of social and subject authority have been abandoned, then the individual and personal relations of learning may be reinstated. Thus, the learning processes of doubt, reflection, critical thinking, questioning, and the live interaction of discussion and question and answer, are made possible in ways that distance methods cannot achieve with the same degree of immediacy. Didacticism in the form of social control is abandoned in favour of the acceptance of the self-direction of learners and their individual learning needs.

No doubt, the form of the mass classroom lecture does not permit the kinds of experiential, reflective, critical or interactive learning which seems central to the learning society, but the role of lecturer seems likely to be merged with wider and more learner-centred roles. Thus lecturing becomes just one element in an armoury or portfolio of teacher roles in a learner support context. The nature of the lecture itself may approach much more closely the kind of presentation that is familiar in business and commerce, with its PowerPoint and data projection technology. Whether a presentation can be said to be the same thing as a lecture is doubtful, in the light of the broad range of functions which have been introduced in this chapter, and in particular with regard to the increasingly heterogeneous body of learners and their learning needs.

What seems beyond doubt, however, is that the didactic element of lectures and lecturing will need to be adapted to those real-life learning contexts of learners, which comprise the family, community, work and social movements sites of learning, and which the learning society recognizes as equally significant as the formal institutions of education itself.

Conclusion

This chapter has outlined some of the consequences for the roles and functions of lecturers and lectures in the learning society, which is an object of national and international education policies. Didactic teaching methods have been placed in a context of the kinds of authority with which they have been traditionally associated, and the challenge of postmodernism analysed in terms of its consequences for this particular method. As a result, it was suggested that there is no *necessary* contradiction between didactic methods and effective learning. However, such methods need to be repositioned against a global background of change in thinking about authority and knowledge. These changes lie behind the kinds of social and economic forces that are bringing the learning society into existence.

References

Biggs, J (1999) *Teaching for Quality Learning at University: What the student does*, Society for Research into Higher Education and Open University Press, Buckingham

Bligh, D (1998) *What's the Use of Lectures?*, 5th edn, Intellect, Exeter

Brown, G (1978) *Lecturing and Explaining*, Methuen, London

Curzon, L B (1997) *Teaching in Further Education: An outline of principles and practice*, 5th edn, Cassell, London

European Commission (EC) (1996) *Teaching and Learning: towards the learning society,* White Paper on Education and Training, EC, Brussels

Evans, N (1985) *Post-Education Society: Recognising adult as learners*, Croom Helm, Beckenham

Gray, D, Griffin, C and Nasta, T (2000) *Training to Teach in Further and Adult Education*, Stanley Thornes, Cheltenham

Jarvis, P (1995) *Adult and Continuing Education: Theory and practice*, 2nd edn, Routledge, London

Jarvis, P (ed) (2001) *The Age of Learning: Education and the knowledge society*, Kogan Page, London

Jarvis, P, Holford, J and Griffin, C (1998) *The Theory and Practice of Learning*, Kogan Page, London

Knowles, M (1978) *The Adult Learner: A neglected species,* 2nd edn, Gulf Publishing, Houston, TX

Mezirow, J (1991) *Transformative Dimensions of Adult Learning*, Jossey-Bass, San Francisco, CA

Organization for Economic Co-operation and Development (OECD) (1996) *Lifelong Learning for All*, OECD, Paris

Rogers, C (1969) *Freedom to Learn*, Merrill, Columbus, OH

Squires, G (1999) *Teaching as a Professional Discipline*, Falmer Press, London

Tough, A (1979) *The Adult's Learning Projects: A fresh approach to theory and practice in adult learning*, 2nd edn, Ontario Institute for Studies in Education, Toronto

United Nations Educational, Scientific and Cultural Organization (UNESCO) (1996) *Learning: The treasure within,* Report to UNESCO by the International Commission on Education for the 21st Century, UNESCO/TSO, London

Chapter 7

The Socratic method

Bob Brownhill

Trainee teachers have often been recommended to use the Socratic method of teaching, as it encourages students to think for themselves, become self-analytic, and brings the students into a dialogue concerned with a search for the truth. It also hones the teacher's ability to teach and lead through discussion students in groups. In fact there are two versions of the Socratic method, each of which entail different teaching approaches. The two approaches form an interesting contrast for the modern teacher and are both relevant today. The first appears in Plato's early dialogues and presumably represents the real Socrates. The second appears in the later dialogues, like *The Republic* and *The Laws* where Socrates becomes the mouthpiece for Plato's theories (Zeller, 1963). The first is non-autocratic, the second autocratic and authoritarian.

The non-autocratic approach

The early Socrates was presented as existing in a world of Sophist thinkers: a world of uncertainty about the truth, and therefore one of continual argument. Socrates always claimed that he knew nothing, and was therefore ignorant. His method of teaching was one of questioning, of attempting to formulate a definition of something and then trying to test its accuracy by a careful analysis of its meaning, what it entailed, and how it fitted in with other familiar concepts. By this sort of questioning the student would hopefully arrive at a better definition, a closer approximation to the truth. However, the task was open-ended. The truth was not finally revealed but could be developed further by continued self-questioning; Socrates was not prepared to give a final answer. The definition arrived at was the best that was available at the time. This method seems very relevant today in a post-modernist world where all truths are challenged and uncertainty reigns.

The authoritarian approach

Plato was appalled by the uncertainty created by the Sophist's epistemological stance. There was no truth, and we therefore could not know what major ethical concepts such as justice entailed. Definitions were accepted through the skills of the more persuasive debaters, whose main concern were to further their own or faction's interests. He saw the Sophist teachers as charlatans who offered the rhetorical skills to control versions of the truth for the payment of fees.

In order to counter this situation Plato introduced metaphysics, which if accepted would create epistemological certainty. We can characterize it as a two-world theory: a world of material things, like trees, buildings, and chairs, etc, things that we normally see around us, which were in a state of flux and continually changing but changing for the worse. He saw all these things as merely degenerate copies of their originals, which existed in another world of absolutes, forms or ideals, which unlike the world we saw around us, existed outside space and time and never changed so therefore had everlasting existence. It consisted of abstract notions of beauty, truth and justice but also abstract generalizations of the essential nature or essence of things that existed in the world of material things, such as 'treeness', 'build-ingness', 'chairness', etc. This everlasting world of absolutes was the source of knowledge. It was unlike the material world, which could only be a source of belief and opinion.

Both worlds could be accessed: the material world through our senses, which because of our own changing nature could only provide us with opinions or beliefs. The world of absolutes or forms was not accessible through any of our senses but in order to give it some sort of accessibility Plato provided us with a myth that indicated how we could gain contact with it. It was a myth of recollection: our soul had perceived the absolutes before it entered the body. We therefore had a memory of them, which could be triggered off by the right environment and by the right process of education. This metaphysical and mythological background provided the basis for the authoritarian approach of the Platonic Socrates, because the truth that might be known by the teacher and students led to a correct understanding. Although the metaphysical background is no longer available, the authoritarian approach is still relevant in some subject areas where the experts make a similar manoeuvre. I will explore this later in the chapter.

Features of the Socratic non-autocratic approach

It takes up an epistemological non-dogmatic approach to reality: a belief that the truth is not absolutely knowable but is tentative, with the suggestion that our approach to an understanding and explanations can be improved by careful thought and analysis. It indicates that through self-reflection students can develop self-awareness of their own values and interests and also the limitations of their own suggestions and judgements. The method is partially a method of trial and error: we attempt to formulate something approximating to the truth and then by questioning it we become self-critical and begin to break down or deconstruct the original answer, and replace it by a better, more comprehensive one, which copes with the criticism. The process continues so that through this method of reflection and self-criticism we provide a continuing better explanation, although we never know whether we have achieved or can achieve an ultimate explanation. The method, in fact, is very similar to that proposed by Popper (1959) in his *Logic of Scientific Discovery*. It means, as it did for Popper, that the truth is only tentative, and that we can never know the absolute truth, even though we may be committed to search for it.

The method is achieved by a process of dialogue with a number of students. The role of the teacher is important. In one sense the teacher is bound to be an authority figure (Jaques, 1998). In modern teaching the teacher is invested with some of the authority of the institution, as it defines the rules and requirements of courses offered, and may be compounded by the teacher being judge and assessor of the students participating in the dialogue. (Even in the case of Socrates, he is the person the students have decided to listen to, and think of as an expert even though he claims ignorance.) The teacher ultimately sets the agenda and the way of procedure, and has decided on the aim of the exercise and how it might be achieved.

We can, however, distinguish between being 'in authority', being 'an authority' and being authoritarian. Tutors are usually accepted as being 'in authority' and to a degree being 'an authority'. If either of these two roles is challenged there is always the possibility that the tutor will make an authoritarian response. The art of the Socratic teacher is concerned with avoiding this stance. It is a recognition that teaching takes up a moral stance for it is concerned with developing the students' moral awareness of themselves and others, and is ultimately concerned not so much with the immediate task in hand but with an attitude towards life. In order to achieve this, students need to acquire intellectual abilities but also communicative skills and an ability to relate to others. The teacher, in order to achieve this, adopts a hybrid position: the topic for discussion is initiated by the teacher. A contentious topic is chosen which is known to raise numerous viewpoints, stimulating and encouraging student response, a traditional role recognized by teacher and students and one of leadership, but recognizing that this can lead to over-dependence on the teacher where the student attempts to act as alter ego of the teacher and second-guess what the teacher may like or say (Jaques,1998, p124). A facilitator style is then adopted. This involves careful listening and a drawing out of students' own views rather than a display of the teacher's own knowledge. It entails a mutual responsibility in the development of the dialogue. It is therefore student-centred, where the teacher helps the student to express a viewpoint clearly, and then by self-reflection begin to question and challenge the answer that has been given. The teacher at first does the questioning and attempts to point out inconsistencies in the argument. The attempt is to stimulate self-awareness, self-reflection, and eventually self-questioning where the student takes over the initial role of the teacher and becomes autarchic, formulating and accepting responsibility for the stance and argument put forward. At the same time it leads to a clarification of the student's own position and the production of better structured arguments that are consistent and credible. Indeed it is a skill a good rhetorician needs in argument and debate (Billig, 1996).

This dialogical approach is not confined to one pupil but in practice takes place with a group of people. It is a mutual search amongst peers for answers, and includes an idea of progress with no certainty that progress is being made. In a modern world where we have given up the notion that a reality exists which is independent of ourselves, that is absolute and never changing, a reality that through research we can access, reveal, and verify (see Chapter 4). We are more likely to believe that our notions about reality are personal or social constructs or interpretations (Bauman, 1987). In such a case we have to abandon the old claim that a statement is true if it corresponds with reality. However, we do not have to abandon a claim that, to a degree, we can be rational and objective (see Chapter 4). The Socratic method enables students to become stronger in public debate, and more persuasive. The method and the moral approach that goes with it includes within it the moral aim of bringing about better citizens. However, unlike some modern advocates of discussion methods of teaching it is not allied with a participation in democracy (Brookfield and Preskill, 1999) but is anti-authoritarian and is critical of all claims, democratic or not.

The style of the teacher is very important (see Chapter 3). We can look at Socrates' own position. He claimed ignorance, which enabled the process of discussion to become a joint exploration of the topic, and in effect a mutual achievement. The attempt was to avoid being an authority figure, and to respect the contribution of others not only as human beings but their ideas, even though they were encouraged to see their own weaknesses. He showed humility, passion and commitment to the task, whilst being recognized as a person of great wisdom and integrity. It led to many admirers of his teaching ability and his method, and his influence up to the present day, as he still provides a worthwhile and fruitful approach for the modern teacher. Yet, as has been pointed out by some commentators (Zeller, 1963), the method on the face of it seems rather dry and analytical, so why the influence? It does seem to be because of Socrates' particular personality and style: his passion to find answers, his moral integrity, his humility, and charisma. Above all his anti-authoritarianism, which together with his absolute commitment to moral principles, led him to be condemned to death, and his emergence as a moral martyr against the iniquities of the state (all states).

The method then provides us with a number of ideas about how to lead students to self-reflection by self-analysis, the importance of creativity in groups, how to get discussions started by reference to the students' own experiences and interests, how to keep continued interest by fostering differ-ent ideas and challenges in the discussions, while managing to maintain some balance in the debate by avoiding the teacher leading and taking over the debate, by not humiliating students by an outright rejection of their views but bringing students to reflect on their own ideas and the ideas of others. The method is a moral approach and, as we have seen, aimed at bringing about good citizens by fostering the ability to argue a point, to crit-icize and challenge, and as the truth is not manifest, to persuade and gain allies. The art of the rhetorician was also important, but in the service of truth and justice, not just to win arguments (Ackrill, 1981).

Features of the Platonic authoritarian approach

As we have seen the specific authoritarian approach of the Platonic Socrates was tied in to Plato's metaphysics, with his concept of the absolute truth or ideals, which could be accessed by the teacher whose concern was to lead his students to a renewed recollection of them. The teacher was the expert and his function was to lead and assess the ability of his students to achieve a knowledge of these absolutes. However, Platonic metaphysics is no longer available for the modern teacher. It is just an interesting phenomenon in the history of thought. However, in some respects, the method used by this version of the Socratic method is still relevant to the modern teacher.

In the modern world there are different strategies available for the truth seeker. The instability of all truth claims could lead to a hit and miss approach, using different features from different metanarratives or interpre-tations. A problem with this approach is that it leads to a rapid breakdown in the consistency of the argument or point of view the teacher is trying to put over, and therefore becomes incoherent, a jumble of personal (subjective) beliefs. It leaves itself open to the analytical and critical method that will soon destroy it. What is needed is stability or certainty in knowledge that can replace the outdated approach of Plato and the Platonic Socrates.

In recent years an attempt was made to do just this by the philosopher of education, Paul Hirst (1973) with his theory of forms of knowledge created by 'linguistic inter-subjectivity'. He argued that certain approaches to examining reality had grown up with their own language, logic and method of testing. These forms of language had to be the basis of the curriculum. They were logically separate to each other and therefore could not be mixed. The task of the teacher was to introduce students to these forms, and get them to learn the language and logic of the different approaches, and only when this task was completed could students be said to be properly educated. The idea was derived from Wittgenstein's concepts in his *Philosophical Investigations* (1953) and his theory of the games people play. In a sense the student had to be drawn into the point of view of the metanarrative or interpretation of the form. Students needed to be taught to understand the specialized language and the concepts that were being used, and develop a belief in their ability to lead to an understanding of the reality of the linguistic inter-subjective concepts. Indeed if this were not achieved they would have no hope of becoming experts in literature, science, history, etc, or even properly participating in their activities. Of course this approach was supposed to apply to all schooling. It was authoritative in the sense that the teacher was thought to already know the language, logic and concepts of the forms of knowledge, but within them taught analytical and critical skills to the students with the belief that they may be eventually used by the more successful students to develop the academic disciplines.

A good example of the authoritative Socratic method can be seen in the furtherance of a similar methodology in different approaches to psychotherapy. The client has to be drawn into the metanarrative of the proposed therapy. The client needs to learn the language and the concepts that are going to be used, and actually develop faith in them as a provider of a therapeutic solution to problems. The client has to be led to recognize the therapy's empowering qualities, and develop personal ownership of the approach by participating in a dialogue with the teacher/therapist, and perhaps a group of other learners.

The client/student needs to gain ownership of the way of looking at the world. Ownership in this sense means an internalizing and therefore an acceptance of the specialized use of language and concepts, which explain the student/client's condition and hopefully will lead to a recognition of the problems faced and their possible solution. If all goes well the students/clients will eventually do this for themselves without the teacher/therapist having to facilitate it. A self-reflective understanding is created so that they can take control of their own lives. As can be seen the method is akin to the Platonic Socrates' approach where through the question and answer technique the student is led to a recollection of the forms. In this modern example Plato's metaphysics are replaced by the educational and therapeutic constructs that the teacher/therapist uses. The student/client uses the constructs that have been internalized to gain self-knowledge.

The ownership of the way of looking at the world empowers the student/client to understand and take action. However, it is worth noting that the word 'empower' is used in the passive sense. In this sense it means the students/clients are empowered to do something. This means that students/clients are given permission to use the language and concepts of the point of view, the metanarratives to which they have recently been introduced and converted. This notion of permission actually points to the already existing power structure within the discipline, which is controlled by the cognoscenti of the point of view, and plays down their role, when in fact the opposite is the case, for the students/clients have been taken over by the gurus, and look at reality from their point of view. Of course, they will only remain hooked on the approach if it is fruitful and brings benefits. Part of the teacher/therapist's task is to try and maintain the students/clients' belief in the way of looking at the world by showing how the belief system is actually beneficial. The approach, and the interpretations of the results of the system must be credible and fit into the students/clients' belief system, which, fortunately for the teacher/therapist, has already been programmed by the internalization of the approach. In an educational setting the educational gurus' power is enhanced by their control over progression in a discipline even at the highest level.

It can be seen that this authoritarian approach is very different to the non-autocratic. As the teacher has knowledge, students are manipulated so that they will look at the world through the teacher's epistemological spectacles. The teacher often does not show humility and is an explorer who leads as he or she has been there before. Yet the teacher can still be said to have moral integrity, and a passionate commitment to beliefs and principles. The attempt is to inculcate beliefs about reality and the process of education into students, backed up by the belief that the approach offered will be fruitful and lead them into further understanding of reality and themselves.

It is a commitment to a particular view of reality with a belief that it is true and historically has led to progress and probably will do so in the future. It heightens understanding and allows students to gain access to an intellectual world and develop within it. It empowers students to be more self-aware and self-reflective, but within the parameters of this restricted way of looking at the world. Indeed, it is sometimes argued that these restrictive ways, or modes of experience, are in fact the way we organize our intellectual life

(Oakeshott, 1933) and that Hirst's forms of knowledge are really forms of public experience by which we actually access the intellectual worlds of literature, mathematics, science, etc (O'Hear, 1981). It is also the case that new ways of looking at the world, and commitments to them, often lead to a greater understanding. Faith, or passionate commitments to different realities, also provide security and give psychological certainty, and to a degree can be considered good and even provide an ability to criticize and analyse within their parameters. They can also compete with and criticize other worldviews, but what they rarely do is turn in on themselves and deconstruct their very basis.

Conclusion

The question arises whether, within a postmodernist world of many realities where there is no certainty, faith, passion and commitment become the only realistic way forward? Does not the non-autocratic approach of the early Socrates lead to an extreme scepticism where all beliefs and principles are open to challenge and a process of deconstruction, and in fact heighten uncertainty and a belief that there is no way of understanding the chaotic world around us? Does it not also indicate that we lose control and power over the world in which we exist? It is worth remembering that the old Plato in *The Laws* advocated that non-believers should be put to death (Zeller, 1963). The answer to these two questions is in the affirmative, but that is the way of the world. The non-autocratic method has a positive side, for it recognizes and shows respect for people's individuality. It assumes that people have the capacity to take control of their own lives and become autonomous legislators, and in this sense is aimed at people becoming self-directed learners. It also suggests that people have the capacity to become true reflective learners, become self-aware and really recognize their own basic values, which gives them the possibility of altering them for the better. It also indicates the important moral notion that people should always respect the other as self-legislators. This is a necessary component of good citizenship but today we would say especially of a democratic society (Brookfield and Preskill, 1999).

A criticism of this argument is that it is too individualistic, a symptom of a postmodernist and modern competitive world, where everyone's claim is as good as any other. It apparently ignores the gel, the culture, which binds people together as a community. In the sphere of education it can and has been argued that high culture is a sophisticated way of organizing and developing our understanding of the world we live in. It is in fact the historical way, which has been proven to be successful, from Shakespeare to Einstein. In this sense it is bound to be elitist and authoritarian as students grasp the way great figures in our culture have looked at and understood the world. It is also a recognition that progress does not always come from individuals but is a joint effort over many generations. The authoritarian method also respects the other and believes that all can have the opportunity to participate in the great conversations of humankind. In the process students become reflective and self-aware as they contemplate on their own culture. It is a method aimed at introducing students into their culture so that ultimately their understanding enables them to become independent contributors to its heritage and perhaps to its expansion. Socrates, himself, accepted death rather than escape in order to protect the traditions and laws of the state in which he lived.

In reality different approaches to teaching have different functions. A non-autocratic approach may help to foster early independence and confidence in a student; a danger is that it leads to too great a reliance on the individual rather than on a team of learners. It is clearly of benefit in an individualistic and competitive society. It is also clear that in certain areas, for the benefit of the student and those around him or her, an authoritative approach is needed. For instance, in civil engineering a potential engineer will need to know something about the design of buildings, the stresses different materials can take, and safety margins. These cannot be left to the potential engineer's personal whim as other people's lives may be at stake. A similar argument can be used in the case of historians, philosophers, etc: to develop a subject properly they will need to know what has gone before and the different approaches people have used. The good teacher will adopt the approach, which will be helpful to the student in his or her development. It will vary depending on the function of the exercise and its appropriateness in the circumstances.

References

Ackrill, J L (1981) *Aristotle the Philosopher*, Oxford University Press, Oxford

Bauman, Z (1987) *Legislators and Interpreters,* Polity Press, Cambridge

Billig, M (1996) *Arguing and Thinking*, Cambridge University Press, Cambridge

Brookfield, S D and Preskill, S (1999) *Discussion as a Way of Teaching,* The Society for Research into Higher Education and Open University Press, Buckingham

Hirst, P H (1973) Liberal education and the nature of knowledge, in *The Philosophy of Education*, ed R S Peters, Oxford University Press, Oxford

Jaques, D (1998) *Learning in Groups,* Kogan Page, London

Oakeshott, M (1933) *Experience and Its Modes,* Cambridge University Press, Cambridge

O'Hear, A (1981) *Education, Society and Nature,* Routledge and Kegan Paul, London

Popper, K R (1959) *The Logic of Scientific Discovery*, Hutchinson, London

Wittgenstein, L (1953) *Philosophical Investigations*, Blackwell, Oxford

Zeller, E (1963) *Outlines of the History of Greek Philosophy,* L R Palmer, Routledge and Kegan Paul, London

Chapter 8

Facilitation and facilitator style

Josie Gregory

What happens to another person in your presence is a function of who you are and not what you know. (From Ram Dass, *The Only Dance There Is*)

In my relationship with persons I have found that it does not help, in the long run to act as though I were something I am not.

I find that I am more effective when I can listen acceptantly to myself, and can be myself. (Rogers, 1961, p39)

Facilitation is an ancient art; it had a place in spiritual and monastic traditions in the form of guides, spiritual masters and spiritual directors where it still flourishes. Facilitation is found in many forms of experiential and practical learning such as role modelling, apprenticing and reflective, empirical experimentation. In the 20th century facilitation re-emerged within progressive or radical education and expanded through the 'new' psychotherapeutic fields such as Gestalt, psychodrama, therapeutic art and dance and other humanistic personal development approaches. From here it permeated into the adult education field with experiential approaches to learning, particularly in personal and professional development.

The philosophical and psychological orientation, which I outline below, offers a rationale and description of the particular forms of knowledge facilitators engage with. Propositional and practical knowledge are more recognizable within traditional forms of education. This chapter attempts to integrate two other forms of knowledge, experiential and imaginal (Heron, 1992, 1999) as a necessary foundation to propositional and practical knowledge.

In this chapter I will offer a definition of educational facilitation, describe some of the main skills and attributes of a facilitator, discuss the training of facilitators and, finally, describe some implications for practice. The chapter is strongly influenced by Heron's (1989) extensive research and publication on facilitator styles.

Facilitation

Facilitation literally means 'easing'. Its art is in drawing out the wisdom already embedded and lying dormant in the psyche of the learner. One approach of humanistic education and pragmatic constructivism assumes that learning is a recovery of or remembering that which we already know. Some believe that this inner knowledge is lost in the plethora of what we are told we should know and from a tendency, it would seem, to forget what we know. Facilitation may thus be seen as reawakening our latent talents and store of unconscious wisdom. Helping learners realize their capacity to learn is the hallmark of the facilitator, moving education from a delivery of static knowledge to a dialogical relationship where knowledge is co-created. Rogers (1983, p120) stated:

> We are, in my view, faced with an entirely new situation in education where the goal of education, if we are to survive, is the facilitation of change and learning. The only man who is educated is the man who has learnt to learn: the man who has learnt how to adapt and change, the man who has realized that no knowledge is secure, that only the process of seeking knowledge gives a basis for security. Changingness, a reliance on process rather than upon static knowledge, is the only thing that makes any sense as a goal for education.

Facilitation is the educational skill of accessing the phenomenological world of the individual, textured in social and cultural variables and helping learners get in touch with their internal capacities to learn and to make sense of their experiences. The facilitator works with internal constructs and their external manifestation in behaviour, bringing these to conscious awareness so that they can be looked at anew and developed if useful, or unlearned if inhibiting. Facilitation seeks to understand the frame of reference of self and the other, to reflect on how knowledge is derived from experience through implicit and explicit theoretical lens.

Facilitators are people with the skills to create conditions within which other human beings can, so far as is possible, select and direct their own learning and development. A facilitator is a 'process guide who works with a group to assist it to achieve its self-defining purpose' (Hunter, 1999, p118). The facilitators' philosophy informs their approach and is manifested as a concern with the psychological growth of the person. Rogers, who was influenced by Dewey's (1916) progressive education, thought that some teachers would not have the promotion of psychological growth as their educational aim.

Facilitators value experience and make it the premise on which other types of learning, imaginal, propositional and practical occur. This is part of the andragogical tradition (Knowles, 1978, 1985), where experience 'is not just a pedagogical device but more significantly an affirmation of the ontological and ethical status of adults, in particular the mark of their radical difference from children' (Usher *et al,* 1997, p95). Adult educators accept the validity of experience for children as much as for adults and in this sense the splitting of learning models into andragogy and pedagogy is false. The description of how adults learn does not invalidate how children learn; rather it is a reflection of the concerns among adult educators that sprang up in the 1960s as part of creating 'liberating structure' to facilitate adults learning.

The internal homogeneity between progressive education, humanistic education and experiential learning lies in the belief in the active learner as one who has personal agency in that he or she is self-directing, intrinsically curious and motivated to learn. Harré (1983) states that being an agent means to conceive oneself as a being in possession of an ultimate power of decision and action. This notion can be illustrated by Heron's (1974, p1) definition of the educated person:

> An educated person is someone who is self-directing: that is, one who deter-mines and is internally committed to what he [*sic*] conceives to be worthwhile objectives, to acceptable means of achieving them, and to appropriate stan-dards of performance in achieving the objects by those means. Secondly, he is someone who is self-monitoring: he evaluates his own performance in the light of the standards he has set and becomes aware of the extent to which that performance fulfils, exceeds or falls short of those standards. Thirdly, he is someone who is self-correcting: he modifies his own performance, his stan-dards, and means, or his objectives as experience and reflection appear to his considered judgement to require.

This demonstrates self-agency, commitment to a goal or direction in life and ability to make judgements about one's own self-development needs. These are the motivational forces that are aspired to in facilitation practice. Equally, it is advocated that self-agency is developed with the support of a facilitator and a learning group. The energy and commitment that is put into creating a peer learning community (as discussed elsewhere in this volume) attests to the importance of developing the social self, as well as the transcendental and rational contingent self. This is contrary to Usher *et al's* account (1997, p93) that self-agency is part of the humanistic tradition of myopic individualism. Rather, self-agency embraces all forms of individual, social and cultural learning and all forms of knowledge as they are useful to the participant or group. To only operate within restricted models such as the 'training and efficiency', or self-directed learning model, or humanistic education or critical pedagogy, to the exclusion of the other perspectives is to do exactly what holistic education resists, that is splitting into 'good' and 'bad', or 'this but not that'. This splitting-off of the individual from the social and cultural milieu with education portrayed as individual liberation would certainly offer a negative imagery of learning as concerned with individual blocks and barriers and oppressive pedagogy (Usher *et al*, 1997, p94).

These ideological approaches to facilitation emerge out of a particular philosophical framework that espouses the self-directed nature of learning. These values guide and direct intentions that act as a blueprint for facilitator style and interventions as well as for learning outcomes. Heron actually identifies participant qualities towards which the practitioner interventions are aimed, which underpin both facilitator practice and participant ideals. The facilitator works towards:

1.   Self-direction and co-operation.
2.   Informed judgement and open communication.
3.   Self-development and social change.
4.   Emotional competence and interpersonal sensitivity.
5.   Self-awareness and social perception.
6.   Celebration of self and others. (Heron, 1990, pp15–16)

Facilitators act as guides helping participants explore their own self-knowledge, transpersonal (incorporating the spiritual and religious experiences of the person), and social knowledge. Traditional didacticism has its proper place in education where much knowledge is seen to be outside the individual and often exclusively delivered by people who know to those who do not. But it includes only two of the four modes of knowledge – practical and propositional knowing. Theoretical and practical knowledge of science, much of the humanities and technology, and so on, are not part of the internal wisdom of the person and to that extent the pedagogical model is valid. Expressive art is an exception as are some forms of practical knowledge, where there is often a significant degree of freedom for individual interpretation and creativity. It is, however, possible to work experientially with propositional knowledge, looking at its application in specific and contemporary contexts, and to that extent such learning can be facilitated. However, other qualities such as emotional competence and interpersonal sensitivity are often not even considered as part of the educational context.

Skills and attributes of the facilitator

Facilitators help others develop from the inside out and facilitation can be explored in terms of both being and doing – what the facilitator 'is' and what the facilitator 'does' or the passive and active aspects of presence and performance. It is difficult to separate these fully because they are inter-twined and interdependent. Presence means who the facilitators are – their essence, self-realization, awareness, attention, charisma, states of being, sub-personalities, and so on. Performance is action, what facilitators do – skills, interventions, intentions, style, techniques, and so on (Gregory, 2000). I will first explore what a facilitator is.

Presence is how facilitators use their energy and attention during face-to-face interaction with participants. It is their self-awareness, being centred and grounded in their current state of being and is a function of their self-development and self- management. Being centred means being physically and mentally balanced, adopting an aligned posture combined with a calm mental state, and focusing attention on the present (Tosey and Gregory, 2001). Being grounded means being emotionally competent, so that other people's distress will not throw the facilitators off balance. Nevis (1991, p2) defines presence as:

> the living embodiment of knowledge: the theories, the practices believed to be essential to bring about change in people are manifested, symbolized, or implied in the presence of the consultant.

And later:

> living out of values in such a way that in 'taking a stance', the intervener teaches these important concepts. That which is important to the client's learning is exuded through the consultant's way of being.

Nevis, who comes from a Gestalt orientation, makes a clear distinction between presence, personality and style. He suggests that a part of the facili-tators' task is to provide the kind of presence that may be lacking in the client system to enable learning to occur. Heron (1987, p59) provides a more esoteric view of the nature of presence as outlined in the following extract:

> These three things – commitment of soul, charisma and bearing – all go together to make up presence. The result is a transfiguration of human expres-sion in this world by potency in another world. It is *as if* the person is living, breathing, being and moving in two worlds at once; is in conscious command of their expression in physical space and in ka space at the same time. Hence the sense of a visitor, an entrant from the other world into this.

('Ka space' means the non-physical, non-subjective realm. Ka is derived from the Egyptian concept of the Ka soul, set free from the human body at death to enter the future world (Heron, 1987, p1).)

This view of presence is based on the notion that as individuals we are capable of mediating various types of energy/presence from another dimension (eg the spiritual or cosmic dimension) and simultaneously manifesting these energies in the here and now. This is an important admixture in the performance of the 'charismatic facilitator' (Heron, 1999) and includes physical presence in posture, facial expression, gaze, touch, sensory perception, gestures and relative position in relation to others. It includes intrasensory perception, that is, an apprehension of the other's phenomenological world. When combined with sensory perception this creates an empathic energy field that allows attunement, resonance and deeper communication between self and the other.

An important aspect of presence is self-esteem, which develops with the growth of competence, achievement and recognition. Many practitioners find their competence and achievement blocked by a negative self-concept. Our presence is determined by both our self-portrayal and what we believe ourselves to be. Authenticity, which might be defined as being true to self is closely related to self-esteem, as Carl Rogers, in the quotation at the beginning of this chapter, emphasized. Pretence is another enemy of authenticity and presence. He goes on to make similar points about self-acceptance and being oneself all the time.

Presence is related to our states of attention: it promotes learning through what might be called free attention. Normally in our lives our attention is held by internal states of anxiety, distress, pleasure or fascination and by external events from the spectacular and sensational to mundane personal interest. Being able to free our attention from the various distracting forces and direct attention to issues through aware and intentional choice is an essential skill in any facilitator role. This is all the more important in experiential settings where the potential for distraction and deflection is enormous. The following (adapted from Heron, 1990, cited in Mulligan, 1992, pp35–36) is one way of mapping a scale of facilitator states of attention:

1. Facilitator shows no interest or empathy in participant or subject matter – submerged in his or her own internal anxiety and concerns.
2. Facilitator is fascinated by the subject, his or her own distress, or the participant, to the exclusion of all else.
3. Facilitator's attention is distracted, goes off in directions irrelevant to work at hand.
4. Facilitator displaces his or her own distress, confusion or conflict on to student by attacking, withdrawing, blaming, denial, complaining, etc.
5. Control of attention energy: some attention for task in hand while remainder is buried, displaced, distracted, etc.
6. Full attention directed to task in hand encompassing both own and participant's, needs.

7. Attention for work in context, encompassing past and future, but immersed fully in task at hand.
8. Attention for work in context at the engaged participant level and also at the disidentified witness/monitoring level.

The later states of attention (6–8) are obviously likely to be more effective in facilitating the learner than the earlier ones.

Finally, presence as disclosure and self-presentation entails a recognition that while we are in the presence of other people, we are making constant disclosures about ourselves both verbally and non-verbally, intentionally and perhaps unintentionally. For instance, our general appearance, the way we initiate contact and maintain it, and the forms of communication we chose all give others information about us. Facilitators may or may not disclose something of their background, knowledge, attitudes, goals and personal needs. Disclosure may help or inhibit the learning process and the building of the relationship necessary for facilitative interventions to be effective. Being aware of the impact of our presentation on others and appropriately choosing what to disclose and how and when to disclose, all enhance facilitation.

Developing personal presence is a central attribute of the effective facilitator. Presence can be enhanced by a variety of methods, for example disidentification with personalized and narrow perspectives; cultivation of internal and external awareness by transcending perceptive barriers; developing personal functional capacities, increased self-knowledge, charismatic training and grounding in and preparation of your subject matter; and development of a positive self-concept, self-esteem, self-presentational capacities, or evocation of the higher 'self'. I list below some specific personal qualities that Heron (1999, p20) believes the facilitator needs to have:

- *Authority*: being able to hold and use authority (both positional and expert authority) without displacing your personal distress upon others.
- *Confrontation*: to confront supportively, work with projections and defence as emanates from the group.
- *Care*: ability to show compassion, are genuine and empathetic in your work.
- *Range of methods*: effectively deal with deep regression, catharsis and transpersonal aspects of group life, and have a wide repertoire of techniques and exercises for personal and interpersonal development.
- *Orientation*: you can provide clear conceptual maps as required.
- *Respect for persons*: you respect the autonomy of the person and the rights of individuals to choose when to change/grow.
- *Flexibility of style*: you move deftly and flexibly as the situation demands, between interventions in one dimension, between dimensions and

between modes so that the group dynamic and individual learning can flourish.

Not all the above qualities are necessary for all facilitators nor for all facilitated events. Much depends on the type of facilitation required, but they are all listed above to demonstrate the breadth and depth of facilitation skills. The proviso is always that the facilitator does not, ever, offer facilitation in areas of personal, interpersonal and transpersonal exploration in which they have not been trained, are not competent, or have not experienced for themselves as a client or participant. Even the most innocent facilitation of personal development will touch on emotional, spiritual and imaginal levels if one is working holistically. The skill of containment of emotional expression (Stapley, 1996), containment of fear of getting it wrong, or being vulnerable in front of others, all require a nurturing yet respectful detachment from the group agenda. Heron (1987, p9) highlights this point:

> The enemy of presence is anxiety. Actors often have a lot of fear before going onto the stage. It usually goes once they are out front, with the secure content of rehearsed lines which they can fill with presence. But extempore speech in everyday life may often generate a lot of subtle anxiety.

For some facilitators this hurdle can be overcome by rehearsal or by deep relaxation exercises, but for others some significant personal development work may need to be done before presence in the face-to-face situation can be consistently achieved. Hence emotional competence (Heron, 1992; Postle, 1993) is one of the central planks on which facilitator presence sits alongside other attributes presented here. Harrison (1995, p37) refers to emotional competence as 'being open about feelings, expressing vulnerability and uncertainty, supporting, caring and the like'.

The facilitator–participant relationship

Heron (1999, p1), one of the first modern developers and writers in this field, states that 'a facilitator is a person who has the role of empowering participants to learn in an experiential group'. This role is seen as legitimized by the participants, who voluntarily accept the facilitator in this role. Unsolicited facilitation is an infringement of the participants' right to self-determination, so that there is a presupposition of a formal contract between learner and facilitator that must be in place before facilitators can act.

Both parties in the relationship, the individual participant (or group) and the facilitator metaphorically, sit side-by-side rather than face-to-face; both look out onto the same world and have a conversation about what they are experiencing and how they are making sense of their experience. For such a relationship to be effective, a degree of openness and honesty, of shared vulnerability to disclose self and the ability to articulate such disclosures are essential. Even the use of the word 'participant' rather than 'learner' denotes the different relationship, that is that both teacher and learner are participating in learning with a balance of power that strives to be more equal than usually found in traditional education. Such a relationship is different from teaching. While both types of relationships have their place in education, learning is most effective when there is flexibility for different forms of knowledge to be engaged with using different methods of teaching and facilitative relationships as appropriate. In the latter, a human relationship is established between the facilitator and participant, both are equal in this relationship, one is contracted by the other to share their knowledge and general worldview, in so far as it is relevant, and both share of themselves emotionally, behaviourally, spiritually and cognitively. The principle of holistic education is central to both parties in facilitation. 'An holistic approach to the person embraces and affirms complexity, inclusion and diversity and resists reductionism' (Clarkson, 1989, p8).

Facilitation is associated with student-centred learning. The teacher–student relationship is also a contract, usually of the type where students sign up for a programme and expect to be offered some form of tuition and to have their work fairly assessed towards some academic award. Depending on the nature of the programme the teaching may be teacher-centred, or the programme may run by independent study, or all shades in between. There will be an implicit contract that is mostly unconscious and only experienced by one or both parties if the contract is deemed to be broken. Many students have learnt through their initial education to expect variation in the different types of relationships they have with teachers. It may seem like a lottery to students as they experience having little influence over whether teachers will like them or not. Such relationships seem emotionally driven and often unpredictable, others driven by results and high grades. The implicit contract is called the 'psychological contract' and is the main driving force under-pinning relationships (Gregory, 1996). While it is seldom labelled as such, to sit and listen to students tell of their treatment at the hands of lecturers' shows that the students are aware of a psychological contract, because it has been broken. As a result, students become disenchanted or desensitized. This desensitization does not mean that the psychological contract is not needed nor that it does not exist: it exists if people feel unheard, rejected and treated as objects, an 'I-it' rather than an 'I-thou' relationship (Buber, 1958). The effect of a broken psychological contract is that students do not believe that the teacher or lecturer has their interests as heart, so they withdraw a major part of themselves from the relationship, do not give of their best and their learning is impeded. The psychological contract is based on (often) unexpressed expectations that are not fulfilled. However, it is also based on espoused promises that are not carried through.

Researching the concept of facilitating interpersonal skills within the health profession I found that facilitators ignore the psychological contract at their peril (Gregory, 1996). This contract is seen as paramount when facilitating others to learn about themselves; Figure 8.1 shows what is required for the psychological contract to be in place. The hourglass is analogous to a top-down filtration, which needs to be initiated by facilitators, and it lays the foundation for a conducive learning environment. It also reflects a positive feedback loop when the qualities of good facilitation filtering through to participants via an explicit psychological contract are reflected back to the

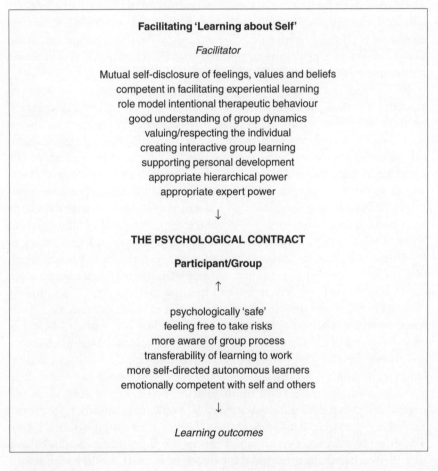

Facilitating 'Learning about Self'

Facilitator

Mutual self-disclosure of feelings, values and beliefs
competent in facilitating experiential learning
role model intentional therapeutic behaviour
good understanding of group dynamics
valuing/respecting the individual
creating interactive group learning
supporting personal development
appropriate hierarchical power
appropriate expert power

↓

THE PSYCHOLOGICAL CONTRACT

Participant/Group

↑

psychologically 'safe'
feeling free to take risks
more aware of group process
transferability of learning to work
more self-directed autonomous learners
emotionally competent with self and others

↓

Learning outcomes

Figure 8.1 Aspects of the psychological contract (Gregory, 1996)

facilitator from the participants. For example, having appropriate expert power will not automatically create psychological safety for the participants, but if facilitators feel psychologically grounded in themselves, with strong self-esteem and use their expert power appropriately, it is likely to create psychological safety. Consequently, facilitators need to be competent in all the attributes they want students to acquire through the educative experience. This is the essence of the psychological contract. In line with the philosophy of facilitation there are two other educational processes that are congruent with facilitation: collaborative assessment and cooperation with peers. Both of these are the subjects of other chapters in this volume.

As facilitators acknowledge that people are able to identify their own goals, they offer a way of negotiating how they may be met through some form of learning contract, which is made either formally or informally at the beginning of the learning experience. Equally, as goals are usually related to the participants' central needs or values their relevance is respected and given due consideration. Believing that the participants have all the resources and wisdom within them to meet their own needs and goals, facilitators are tentative about defining the 'correct path' that participants should take, preferring to act as a sounding board while the participants discuss options and make choices that best suit their particular worldview. To impose unsolicited solutions on a participant is considered degenerate, incompetent or unskilled (Heron, 1999). Yet, paradoxically, facilitators need to exercise diagnostic skills and offer these skills to participants so that they can confront distorted perceptions and limiting patterns of behaviour. A substantial part of the learning contract is the identification of learning needs and what needs to be unlearnt if the individual is to develop greater self-awareness and personal and professional competence. Often what needs to be examined are socially constructed perceptions of self that are experienced as inhibitive. Critical reflection using Bateson's (1973) levels of learning, Argyris' (1994) single and double loop learning with Paul Watzlawick's (1990) notion of first and second-order change are all seen as useful models to aid critical reflection.

Facilitation as a teaching and learning style

Having examined presence and performance and the facilitator–participant relationship, I now want to summarize and discuss some of the significant functions of the facilitator.

Rogers (1983) suggests that they enact the following broad role-sets:

- setting the initial mood or climate of a group's experience;
- eliciting and clarifying the purposes of individuals as well as the more general purposes of the group;

- regarding themselves as a flexible resource;
- responding to expressions they accept both intellectual as well as emotional attitudes, endeavouring to give each aspect the appropriate degree of emphasis that it has for the individual or group;
- taking the initiative in sharing him or herself with the group – feelings as well as thoughts – in ways that do not demand or impose but rather represent simply a personal sharing which participants may take or leave;
- in facilitating learning they endeavour to recognize and accept their own limitations.

Facilitators are often process facilitators, helping a work or learning group recognize the psychological agendas that might be impeding the group's effectiveness. They are not necessarily technical experts, and their process expertise rests on understanding the personal, interpersonal and group dynamics operating at social, psychological and existential levels of human relationships. Part of their expertise is to understand how individuals and groups learn and change.

When training facilitators we focus on 12 main themes (Mulligan, 1992, cited in Gregory, 2000); some I have already mentioned. I list them all here for the sake of completion. They are divided into four broad headings:

Headings	Themes
Practitioner:	presence, qualities, values and beliefs, knowledge and subject expertise.
Client:	diagnostic skills, assessment and evaluation of client outcome.
Interventions:	intentions, guiding models and theories, interventions, channels of communication.
Environment:	dynamics of relationship, organizational context.

Experience is a platform for learning; it is an integrated form of knowing. This does not mean that all experiences participants bring are unproblematic. Many earlier experiences that created difficulties for learning are brought to the new educational experience, consciously and unconsciously. These will have the effect of inhibiting learning, re-stimulating low self-esteem or, conversely, over-confidence, all of which will be brought to the surface. The former prevents self-directed learning while the latter focuses on some dimensions of the academic or commercial at the expense of the human or the spiritual, which Habermas (1974) calls distorted or constraining constructs. These constraints, developed as part of the socialization process, need to be critically assessed for their usefulness and validity as part of the emancipatory processes of adult education. Much of the training of facilitators focuses on helping trainees recognize in themselves the distressed patterns they bring to experiential learning from prior schooling and training and providing them with skills to help them unlearn the distorted and compulsive behaviours they bring to new learning. From this they are in a better position to facilitate the same processes in others.

Participants in facilitated experiential learning groups often seek a holistic learning experience that may focus on personal and/or professional issues. In order to achieve this, the facilitator of a workshop will intentionally ask for voluntary interactive participation and will offer some guidance or ground rules which may answer the question often asked of the group, 'What do you need to feel safe to work and learn here?'

The facilitator mode of working is both related to the learning contract and to the educational or social context. It is also in part dependent on the facilitator's own preferred style. Heron (1999) offered a model of facilitator style, discussed below.

The dimension of facilitator style

The model describes three political modes: hierarchy (autocratic or consultative), cooperation (negotiation or consultative) and autonomy (functional or contractual). They refer to the power relationship between facilitators and participants and address the questions about decision making in the group learning context. The six dimensions are:

1. The planning dimension – goal-oriented, aims, ends and means.
2. The meaning dimension – cognitive understanding of experience.
3. The confronting dimension – raising awareness to individual and group resistance.
4. The feeling dimension – addressing emotional competence and incompetence.
5. The structuring dimension – methodology of structuring experiences.
6. The valuing dimension – creating a support climate that celebrates individuals.

Combining each mode with each dimension provides a framework whereby facilitators might both plan and evaluate their own performance. This is the basis of Heron's analysis of facilitator styles. But they might also form the basis of guidelines for personal development, since they help facilitators reflect on their own identity, on the limitations of their own competences, on the types and techniques with which they can work, and so on.

Conclusions

In summary, the main factors influencing facilitation are the internal cultural environment or group context, the social and psychological contract, the wider culture, both institutional and environmental, the facilitator style and the model of facilitation. The reframing of experiential learning theory into theories of pragmatic constructivism and critical science addresses some of the postmodern critique about personal autonomy being disassociated from the social self. Within the educational theory and practice espoused here, the self is understood as socially constructed, personal and spiritual development having validity and essence in relationship – Buber's (1958) 'I-Thou' versus 'I-It'. It is the former construct through which people come together for the purpose of living and learning. All experiences are constrained as well as enhanced within the social and cultural milieu in which we act. The challenge in higher education and accredited programmes is to bring together theories of teaching and learning that take account of the individual and collective needs, the need for different forms of knowledge and how these might be facilitated, the institutional requirement for programme specifications and assessment within a philosophy that is ethical in its treatment of the person.

References

Argyris, C (1994) *On Organizational Learning,* Blackwell Business, Oxford

Bateson, G (1973) *Steps to an Ecology of Mind*, Paladin, Granada, London (new edition 2000)

Buber, M (1958) *I and Thou*, Scribner and Sons, New York

Clarkson, P (1989) *Gestalt Counselling in Action,* Sage, London

Dewey, J (1916) *Education and Democracy*, The Free Press, New York

Gregory, J (1996) *The Psycho-Social Education of Nurses,* Avery, Aldershot

Gregory, J (2000) *Facilitating Interventions: One-to-one* (Module 5, MSc in Change Agent Skills and Strategies), School of Educational Studies, University of Surrey, Guildford

Habermas, J (1974) *Theory and Practice,* Heinemann, Oxford

Harré, R (1983) *Personal Being,* Basil Blackwell, Oxford

Harrison, R (1995) *Consultant's Journey,* McGraw-Hill, Maidenhead

Heron, J (1974) *The Concept of a Peer Learning Community,* Human Potential Research Project, University of Surrey, Guildford

Heron, J (1987) *Confession of a Janus-Brain,* Endymion Press, London

Heron, J (1989) *The Facilitator's Handbook,* Kogan Page, London

Heron, J (1990) *Helping The Client: A creative practical guide,* Sage, London

Heron, J (1992) *Feeling and Personhood. Psychology in another key,* Sage, London

Heron, J (1999) *The Complete Facilitator's Handbook,* Kogan Page, London

Hunter, D (1999) *Handling Groups in Action,* Gower, Aldershot

Knowles, M (1978) *The Adult Learner – A neglected species*, 2nd edn, Gulf, Houston, TX

Knowles, M (1985) *Andragogy in Action,* Jossey-Bass, San Francisco, CA

Mulligan, J (1992) *Facilitating Interventions: One to one* (Module 5, Study Guide: MSc in Change Agent Skills and Strategies) University of Surrey, School of Educational Studies, Guildford

Nevis, E (1991) *A Gestalt Approach to Organizational Consultancy,* Gardener Press, New York

Postle, D (1993) Putting the heart back into learning, in *Using Experience for Learning,* eds Boud, D, Cohen, R and Walker, D, Society for Research into Higher Education & Open University Press, Buckingham, pp 33–45

Rogers, C (1961) *On Becoming a Person,* Houghton, Boston, MA

Rogers, C R (1983) *Freedom to Learn for the 1980s,* 2nd edn, Merrill, Columbus, OH

Stapley, L (1996) *The Personality of the Organisation: A psycho-dynamic explanation of culture and change,* Free Association Books, London

Tosey, P and Gregory, J (2001) *Dictionary of Personal Development,* Whurr Publications, London

Usher, R, Bryant, I and Johnston, R (1997) *Adult Education and the Postmodern Challenge,* Routledge, London

Watzlawick, P (1990) *Muenchhausen's Pigtail or Psychotherapy and Reality: Essays and lectures,* Norton and Company, New York

Chapter 9

Principles of experiential education

Josie Gregory

This chapter focuses on the theoretical principles of experiential teaching and learning, showing that it has its genesis in the philosophy of progressive and emancipatory adult education. The determination of some educators to value and account for adults' learning through life experiences has led to a growing literature on exactly how people learn what they learn through experience and from experience. The epistemological concerns raised in such studies can be found under such broad headings as emancipatory education and transformative learning (Mezirow, 1981, 1999); experiential learning in higher education (Boud *et al,* 1993; Weil and McGill, 1989); criticality (Brookfield, 2000) Habermas' (1974) critical social science; and personal and spiritual development (Heron, 1992; Rogers, 1983; Rowan, 1993; Postle, 1988, 1993). The debate spans many pedagogical issues within the education of adults, from teacher training to the lifelong learning agenda, and raises some tantalizing questions about how people learn from experience, to how experiential learning can be effectively facilitated. It also offers a critique on the educational environments that foster such learning. This chapter surveys some of the important principles of experiential teaching and learning with a view to highlighting some of the main contemporary ideological and practice issues. The main focus is the purpose of all learning, that is the acquisition of knowledge and how this might be acquired through aspects of experiential learning. A description and discussion of experiential teaching and learning methods themselves are covered elsewhere in this volume.

Context of experiential education

Experiential methods of teaching and learning have existed from ancient times. Meditation, awareness exercises, 'personality' profiles such as the

Enneagram, story telling, visualization and much more can be found associated with wisdom traditions such as Christian mysticism, Sufism, yoga and
Buddhism.

What is new is not so much the discovery of the methods themselves, but
issues of their acceptance in mainstream contemporary education. The
formal educational agenda in modern Western society has typically been
dominated by the acquisition of cognitive knowledge, and to a lesser extent
by vocational preparation, and sports education aside has either neglected or
actively repressed the education of body, emotion and spirit.

Exceptions tend to have stood out. There was a wave of radical and
counter-cultural thinking in the 1960s and 1970s, through figures like Carl
Rogers (1983), Heron (1974) and Knowles (1978). In fact, the modern
philosophical base that gave rise to experiential learning practice in higher
education since the 1970s has its origin in Dewey's (1938) progressive
education. Progressive education was adopted as a central tenet of humanistic psychology and the Human Potential Movement in the 1970s; and
continues to influence humanistic adult educators (Brookfield, 2000; Carr
and Kemmis, 1986). According to Dewey (1938, p20):

> We shape all knowledge by the way we know it (subjectively) (and) I take it that
> the fundamental unit of the newer philosophy is found in the idea that there is
> an intimate and necessary relation between the processes of actual experience
> and education. If this is true, then a positive and constructive development of
> its own basic idea depends upon having a correct idea of experience.

Yet radical or progressive educational ideas appear to have had little widespread
influence on formal education, despite the common rhetoric of educating 'the
whole person'. Their impact has been felt more in the personal development
workshops of the 'growth movement', and to some extent in areas of professional development. It is rare to find experiential learning underpinning a
curriculum, rather than being used as an occasional leavening or confined to
promulgating Kolb's (1984) experiential learning cycle. The idea that formal
(traditional) education might concern itself with the emotional and inner life
of the person remains a curious and potentially risky idea to many.

Traditional education, often termed 'education from above' (Jarvis, 1985)
is seen as more politically/socially controlling of learners and inhibitive to
individual creativity (Dewey, 1938) whereas progressive education is seen as
the 'education of equals' (Knowles, 1978). In fact Durkheim's definition of
traditional education (1972, cited in Williamson, 1979, p4) emphasizes the
sociological perspective:

> Education is the influence exercised by adult generations on those that are not
> yet ready for social life. Its object is to stimulate and develop in the child a
> certain number of physical, intellectual and moral states which are demanded

of him [*sic*] by the political society as a whole, and by the particular milieu for which he is specifically destined.

Contrary to the above and particularly when working with adult learners, Knowles originally asserted that the education of equals is based on the following four premises, although he added to these in subsequent works (Knowles, 1989):

- *Changes in self-concept:* as the person voluntarily moves, in terms of self-concept, from dependency to increased interdependency (in learning), he [*sic*] becomes psychologically adult. He then no longer wants to be controlled by others and displaces this in resentment and resistance.
- *The role of experience:* as the individual matures he accumulates an expanding reservoir of experiences that causes him to become an increasingly rich learning resource, and at the same time provides him with a broadening base to which to relate new experiences. To a child, experience is something that happens to him; to an adult his experience is who he is. So in any situation in which that experience is being devalued or ignored, this is not just a rejection of the experience, but of the person himself.
- *Readiness to learn:* adults are more ready to learn. It is not the case of learning what they 'ought to learn' as with children, but what they think they need to learn as relevant to their life, career and so on. The critical implication of this assumption is the importance of timing learning experiences to coincide with the learners' developmental tasks.
- *Orientation to learning:* adults tend to have a problem-centred orientation to learning. The reason for this is the timing of the learning to relevant here and now application. (Adapted from Knowles, 1978, pp58–59)

Such philosophical premises and educational values are best expressed through a curriculum that places experiential learning as pivotal to the educational process. For if personal experience and personal knowledge are valued and built on, the learning is more likely to mirror the three outcomes expressed above. Such outcomes have also formed the bases of many adult liberal educational programmes as well as continuing professional development.

Economic pressures of contemporary education appear to militate against experiential learning and personal development in the undergraduate and most postgraduate curricula, apart from some vocational degrees. Moves towards distance learning improve access for some, but they reduce face-to-face contact and the encounter of human beings to a minimum. Modularization of programmes, that grand rationalist project designed to maximize student choice, often means that 'learning communities' (see Chapter 12) are so transitory that students have little chance to bond, affiliate, and identify with their peers or their programmes (there is some hope that the costs of modularization for the 'student experience' are becoming more recognized). Funding for, and research into educational innovation is often restricted to technological developments. Increasing student numbers mean that large cohorts are the norm, and while these do not exclude the use of experiential methods they test the ingenuity and competence of educators to the limit. Professional development in 'large group teaching' continues to emphasize the lecture above all other methods. The idea of understanding and utilizing large group dynamics is rarely found outside organizational development methods such as 'future search' (Weisbord, 1987), the Tavistock Institute's 'Leicester conference', or (often educationally dubious) large group awareness training such as Werner Erhard's 'est' (Rawlinson, 1997).

Even so, a significant number of educators continue to believe in the value of experiential learning and holistic development. While these principles and practices, quite rightly, have to respond to contemporary critique (eg Burgoyne and Reynolds, 1997) they are also re-emergent, as in the UK Lifelong Learning agenda. For example, the theme of emotional competence (eg Postle, 1993) has been prominent in the educational agenda of the Human Potential movement for many years, without ever becoming a mainstream idea. But this is very close to the concept of emotional intelligence (Goleman, 1996), which has exploded onto the scene and is in danger of being seen as a panacea for all the psychological and economic ills of society. It seems that personal development is a strongly interdisciplinary field, a shared territory in which, for example, educators and organizational consultants embrace psychotherapeutic models of change, educational theories of learning, spiritual notions of human potential, and more. Whether one regards this as a welcome postmodern eclecticism or an ethically questionable slippage is, of course, another debate.

Principles of experiential education

Experiential methods usually relate to a cluster of educational principles. At times they may be regarded as stand-alone components that can be slotted into any educational process, and as such represent a valuable resource for educators. They are more likely to be potent, however, in an integrated approach to curriculum design in which experiential learning and personal development are the core, rather than the periphery.

Experiential learning is a complex process involving theory and practice, action and reflection. Boud *et al* (1993, p1) say:

> Most of what is written about learning is from the perspective of teachers or researchers who assume that there is a body of knowledge to be taught and learned. What is missing is the role and relevance of learning from experience

no matter where it occurs. Learning involves much more than an interaction with an extant body of knowledge; learning is all around us, it shapes and helps create our lives – who we are, what we do. It involves dealing with complex and intractable problems, it requires personal commitment, it utilizes interaction with others, it engages our emotions and feelings, all of which are inseparable from the influence of context and culture.

They go on to list five propositions about learning from experience (Boud *et al*, pp8–16):

- Experience is the foundation of, and the stimulus for, learning.
- Learners actively construct their experience.
- Learning is a holistic process.
- Learning is socially and culturally constructed.
- Learning is influenced by the socio-emotional context in which it occurs.

These propositions are very similar to Rogers' (1983) principles and were very likely developed out of his work. Rogers emphasized that education should be 'person-centred'. He coined the phrase 'person-centred counselling' and spread the concept to education. The assumptions underlying experiential learning that Rogers (1983, pp278–79) identified were:

1. Human beings have a natural potentiality for learning.
2. Significant learning takes place when the subject matter is perceived by the student to have relevance for his [*sic*] own purposes.
3. Much significant learning is acquired through doing.
4. Learning is facilitated when the student participates responsibly in the learning process.
5. Self-initiated learning, involving the whole person of the learner, feelings as well as intellect, is the most pervasive and lasting.
6. Creativity in learning is best facilitated when self-criticism and self-evaluation are primary, and evaluation by others is of secondary importance.
7. The most socially useful learning in the modern world is the learning of the process of learning, a continuing openness to experience, an incorporation into oneself of the process of change.

This list of assumptions of the characteristics of the adult learner, while humanistically based, is almost identical to Mezirow's description of adult learners in contemporary cultures. Mezirow's (1999) transformation theory sits within postmodern cultural relativism and some of his assumptions underpinning a comprehensive learning theory will be discussed later in this chapter.

From the above list of assumptions it can be seen that experience is central to learning, therefore any educational process that claims to foster the creation and assessment of experiences will need to fulfil this criterion. It can also be seen that this type of learning bridges the fields of personal and professional development and academic education, in that by its holistic nature experiential learning actively embraces all four functions of thinking, feeling, intuition and sensing which humans have of being in contact with the world, and acquiring knowledge. Heron (1992, pp14–15) expands on these four modes of functioning in the following way:

1. Affective – embracing feelings and emotions.
2. Imaginal – comprising intuition and imagery.
3. Conceptual – including reflection and discrimination.
4. Practical – involving intention and action.

These four modes are placed here to illustrate the holistic nature of humanistic learning theory, which can be applied to learning processes whether in a therapeutic, educational or social and health care setting. Experiential education, Dewey's (1938, p28) 'educative experiences', implies engaging all modes of functioning if learning is to be an integrative experience for the individual. As Heron (1989, p13) states:

> Experiential knowledge is knowledge gained through action and practice. This kind of learning is by encounter, by direct acquaintance, by entering into some state of being. It is manifest through the process of being there, face-to-face, with the person, at the event, in the experience. This is the feeling, resonance level of learning.

There is also Kolb's definition of learning as 'the process whereby knowledge is created through the transformation of experience' (1984, p38).

The reason for the choice of experiential methods as a way of manifesting the philosophy of adult learning can be summed up in Heron's (1999, p1) description of group experiential learning:

> By an experiential group, I mean one in which learning takes place through an active and aware involvement of the whole person, as a spiritual, energetically and physically endowed being encompassing feeling and emotion, intuition and imaging, reflection and discrimination, intention and action.

Certainly if experiential learning as described by Heron is to be holistic as well as expanding knowledge it needs to move through the face-to-face encounter to the other levels: the imaginal, conceptual and practical. To map such knowledge progression Heron (1999) has developed a useful model, which he calls a manifold or multi-modal learning. This has four dimensions, the experiential, the imaginal, the propositional/conceptual and the practical. These four dimensions form a pyramid or hierarchy with the affective/experiential dimension at the base and the imaginal, the propositional and the practical levels following upward. Thus the model suggests that experience is the primary form of knowing; that our experience is typically translated next into presentational knowing (using images, metaphors, fantasies); that conceptual or propositional knowing is a further stage; and that altogether these create the possibility of practical knowing, that is of using knowledge in action.

The current emphasis on the 'education of the affect', developing emotional competence or intelligence, means having the ability to 'manage one's own emotions awarely in terms of the basic skills of control, expression, catharsis and transmutation' Heron (1992, p131). This raises questions for some educators about the nature of the boundary between education and psychotherapy. For the purposes of this discussion, I believe that the boundary is by no means rigid if one adopts a humanistic perspective and if one defines psychotherapy as a non-clinical, growth-oriented activity, 'an intentional and committed process of personal development' (Rowan, 1993, p98).

Further principles of experiential education are those of self-directedness, empowerment and autonomy. These have been criticized (eg Burgoyne and Reynolds, 1997) for representing an individualized, psychologistic, non-political perspective, although this does not negate their concern to counter education that is other-directed, disempowering and alienating (see Habermas, 1974). Self-directedness is the principle that learners, rather than teachers or trainers, take charge of their own learning. It also refers to the process by which learners diagnose their needs, define learning goals, identify resources and methods, and assess their progress. Key writers contributing to the concept of self-directed learning are Stephen Brookfield, Cyril Houle, Malcolm Knowles and Allen Tough (see Jarvis et al, 1998, pp77–87).

Empowerment has become something of a slogan, especially in the business world where talk of 'empowering' people entails the idea that some external authority is capable of enabling others to become 'empowered'. Rather like learning, empowerment may be spoken of as if it were a universal good. Christine Hogan, a humanistic educator and facilitator from Australia, has written about empowerment from a personal development perspective. She cites a definition of empowerment by Hamelink:

> a process in which people achieve the capacity to control decisions affecting their lives. Empowerment enables people to define themselves and to construct their own identities and can be the outcome of an intentional strategy which is neither initiated externally by empowering agents nor solicited by disempowered people. (Hamelink, 1994, pp132–33, cited in Hogan, 2000, p12)

Finally in this review of principles, the experiential approach will often entail a notion of power sharing or reflect a form of 'peer principle'. In Heron's

(1999) model of facilitator styles, the peer principle implies mutual aid and support between autonomous people who are at the same level, politically. In adult education, particularly in professional and personal development and experiential group work, combining peer learning with benevolent hierarchy allows participants to see each other as a rich learning resource and not become solely reliant on the facilitator. This is an essential prerequisite for a peer learning community.

Application: forms of knowledge acquisition

Dewey's educational philosophy comes alive with the use of Kolb's (1984) and Heron's (1989) experiential learning cycles. Both cycles require the learner to move through an inquiry process of experience, reflection, generalization (or conceptualization) and testing (or practice) (after Kolb, 1984). Both models advocate learning with others for the purpose of the encounter, assistance with reflection and feedback on practice. This educational process is considered facilitative in that it follows the definition of a helping relationship where both the self and peers have the intention of promoting the growth, development, maturity, improved functioning, improved coping of life of each other (Gregory, 1996).

Learning is holistic if it offers opportunities for engagement of all seven capacities the individual (Mulligan, 1993) brings to experience for the purpose of acquiring knowledge. These are thinking, imaging, feeling, memory, intuition, sensing and will. Curriculum design and development that focuses exclusively on the cognitive and/or practical levels of knowledge will not succeed in providing 'whole person' education, just the same as those who focus on offering emotional and imaginal experiences without engaging the other functions will not succeed either, regardless of what they espouse. However, different capacities will be in the foreground depending on the type of learning involved and a model of these relationships is offered here. The four modes of knowing are:

The world of presence:	Experiential knowing
The world of appearance:	Presentational knowing
The world of essence:	Propositional knowing
The world of existence:	Practical knowing

In summary form, according to Heron (1992, pp157–60) there is:

- Experiential knowing, dealing with the *world of presence,* where imaginal and affective modes play an important part, with the affective the dominant parent. This is the worldview of the mystic and visionary. Presence refers to the unique impact of that particular being, its distinct signature.

On its own this could be seen as the subjective reality of the individual that includes visionary experiences, and process-engaged participatory perception sometimes of an archetypal form (p158). However, it also allows for a suspension of prejudged beliefs and knowledge so experimenters (learners) can create their own categories and interpretation to their experience.

- Presentational knowing focusing on the *world of appearance,* where the imaginal and conceptual modes conjoin with the conceptual mode being the stronger parent. 'The world view of the artist, poet, phenomenologist and discriminating observer' (p159).

The imaginal mode of intuition and imagery is primary where interaction with reflection and discrimination yields discernment about patterns and phenomena and their interconnections (p159). Here phenomenological concerns are relational, forming patterns and moving between Buber's (1958) 'I-it' to the 'I-Thou' forms of knowledge. If facilitated accurately it will flow from grounded experience and offer independent analysis of events. Learning is situated and contextualized.

- Propositional knowing as the *world of essence* where reflection and intention pair as the conceptual and practical modes. The worldview of the inquiring intellect. The conceptual or intention mode is the dominant parent. This worldview stems mainly from reflection and discrimination, and is focused on the essences of, or universal ideals, which we use in various combinations to define the nature of things (p158).

This combination can be viewed as scientific and technical and if isolated from the previous two modes could be labelled 'scientism' (Habermas, 1974). In combination however, it becomes a powerful means of critically examining underlying assumptions, personal and cultural.

- Practical knowing; the *world of existence.* The practical and affective modes engender the world of existence. The worldview of the doer. Intention and action are primary, and together with emotion and feeling, create a lived world of enterprise and endeavour, in which deeds encounter what exists (p159).

This combination can be seen as the creation and fostering of social structures and interpersonal relationships when the heart and will work in unison. It can also be the technical or practice world essential for action research type experimentation necessary to live responsibly in relation to our environment. Again if this combination excludes the propositional and imaginal, it could be considered conceptually superficial and dull.

In experiential education, working with the internal world of participants we need to be alert to consistencies between the above modes or their discontinuities. At any one time one of the modes will be in the foreground while the others will be tacit, falling into the background. According to Heron (1992) an integrated fourfold, simultaneous multi-world view is the characteristic of the educated person.

So far in this chapter learning has been viewed as individualistic through the explanation of the internal capacities of the individual, and the imposition of a holistic frame of reference that is both humanistic and therapeutic (Rogers, 1967; Rowan, 1998) yet I have also said that experiential learning is essentially emancipatory within progressive education. Emancipatory implies a need to feel liberated, but liberated from what? One form of liberation advocated by Mezirow (1999, p2) is 'to create new experiences deliberately to expose our mindless frames of references that rely on past forms of interpretation and action, or previously established distinctions and categories without questioning their underlying assumptions'. Mindful learning on the other hand implies an openness to make sense of new experiences using new categorization on that experience and using more than one perspective in interpretation.

Habermas, when developing his theory of critical social science in opposition to 'scientism' spoke of three 'knowledge-constitutive interests: the technical, the practical and the emancipatory (Carr and Kemmis, 1986, p135), the first of which is mainly instrumental, scientific knowledge and fits loosely with Heron's propositional knowledge, 'a knowing what and why'. Practical knowledge is viewed as an iterative hermeneutic process, a dialogical process, where shared meaning through language develops into an interpretive science, 'a knowing what, how and when' and is similar to Heron's practical knowledge. The cornerstone of emancipatory knowledge is based on Habermas's proposition that there is:

> a basic human interest in rational autonomy and freedom which issues in a demand for the intellectual and material conditions in which non-alienated communication and interaction can occur. This emancipatory interest requires going beyond any narrow concern with subjective meaning in order to acquire an emancipatory knowledge of the objective framework within which communication and social action occur. It is with this emancipatory knowledge that critical social science is essentially concerned. (Carr and Kemmis, 1986, pp135–36)

My experience of practising experiential education over the last 15 years has convinced me that learning from and by experience needs to have this critical reflective science in order to have educational value. The emancipatory emphasis is about moving beyond imposed restraints about how we acquire knowledge, constraints that are both internal and external that deal with the experience and the interpretation of experience. Equally it is about taking the cultural and social fabric of society into our reflective frames when we seek to learn by and from experience.

Psychotherapeutic education often focuses on the former subjective emphasis while Habermas, Mezirow and followers of critical social science (Carr and Kemmis, 1986) insist on using the latter as a theoretical lens within which the binding of the subjective with the interpersonal and environmental realities are all accounted for in understanding what impinges on the individual's sense of self. This form of emancipation interest Habermas calls 'critical sciences'. The medium used is power. Power within educational relationships occupies the minds of postmodern thinkers. The debate about which knowledge is valid in society, who holds this knowledge, who is best to impart knowledge and assess the legitimacy of another's knowledge, are central to critical social sciences and transformative theory. Usher and Edwards (1994, p223) ask: 'if emancipation and knowledge are chimeras deployed in the exercise of an omnipresent power, what point is there in challenging dominant practices?' Most education imparts established knowledge without a critique of its relevance or an examination of the underlying assumptions. Usher and Edward's belief is that experiential learning comes closer to postmodern thinking than other forms of teaching such as classroom instruction. However, this is predicated on experiential teaching and learning giving equal if not stronger emphasis to the critical reflection of the experience as much as the experience itself. Here is where the essential question of who facilitates experiential learning arises and how is it different from teaching. Teachers who only impart established knowledge are not experiential facilitators; equally educational and organizational trainers who offer tasks and experiences to learners for the purpose of showing them one right way of doing things, or one right way of behaving in a social and organizational setting (such as 'good team work'), may be doing an excellent job, but they are not experiential facilitators. The characteristics of facilitators will be discussed further in the following chapter. For now, the important distinction is that experiential facilitators are expected to be competent critical reflectors who can hold lightly a multi-perspectival view, will be experienced in working at the different levels of critique, subjective, social and cultural and who do not believe in one truth outside the individual, they live with uncertainty as the norm, wishing only to critically examine beliefs to liberate self and others from the oppressive bondage of imposed interpretative structures.

The experiential learning cycle offers opportunities for the student to voluntarily enter an experience, an encounter, for the purpose of understanding something about him or herself and something about the context and content he or she is engaged with. A typical experience offered as experiential learning is a psychosocial experience such as learning about group dynamics. This is done by asking the group to engage with some form of group work where the task is to understand what goes on in groups at a social, psychological and existential level. Frequent exposure to this type of experience allows students to learn an enormous amount about their behaviour, feelings and thinking in group settings, which is atheoretical at this point. Using the experiential learning cycle, they can move through the encounter to varying degrees of deep personal reflection about their own intrapsychic world. This often results in students sharing with each other previous family group dynamics and work team dynamics that appear to be similar or very different to the present experience. This phase is often experienced as deconstructive of old polarized interpretations and how to behave in the world. It is sometimes accompanied by a sense of instability, which needs competent facilitation. From this encounter they move to conceptualizing about group theories and testing new ways of relating to others in the group, ways that are more congruent with the present than the past. The reflective stage often expands from self-reflection and self-understanding to the social and cultural environment based on the belief that humans are relational and learned behaviour has strong historical and ecological influences. There is therefore a concern to check what behaviours are distorted and constrained by social conditions beyond the individual's control.

Mezirow (1981, p6) writes of 'the emancipatory process of becoming critically aware of how and why the structure of psycho-cultural assumptions has come to constrain the way we see ourselves and relationships'. Habermas advocates that such social constraints must be made transparent and if seen to be affecting the individual's right to freedom and rational autonomy, that a theory be found to explain how the constraints are distorting, with the intention of eliminating them. By distilling the historical processes, which have caused subjective meanings to become systematically distorted, the person can work towards liberation. The method for doing this is by critique, through a process of 'relentless criticism of all existing conditions' (Marx, cited in Carr and Kemmis, 1986, p138), including the power base of learning and educational and social knowledge. Experiential learning in group settings allows for this critique of personal and group forms of established ways of thinking to be witnesses, critiqued and dissolved so that new constructions are co-created which are grounded in the shared experience rather than ideology or compulsive distorted interpretations of others.

Conclusion

Learning through and from experience requires the recognition of what is subjective, what is social and what is ideology being lived out by the individual and by the group. The emancipatory process needs to address all three levels. Rogers' belief that man is goal-oriented and seeks ways of meeting these goals may seem to be negating the social environment and its constraints. There is a criticism of humanistic psychology that it is too individualistic, believing that the power to change and create one's own reality resides in the individual. Habermas (cited in Carr and Kemmis, 1986, p138) however, argues that:

> Social groups are prevented from achieving a correct understanding of their situation because, under the sway of ideological systems of ideas, they have passively accepted an illusionary account of reality that prevents them from recognizing and pursuing their common interests and goals.

Through an understanding of how ideological forces generate inaccurate self-understanding such frames of references are stripped of their power to influence and people are free to ground their knowledge in the collective experiences and needs. Humanistic education under the heading of pragmatic constructivism and aligned to postmodern critique is very concerned with the social and the political dimension; it always has been, hence its identity with progressive and emancipatory education, with its hallmark that people do not 'move from a false belief to a true one but from an unexamined to a critically examined belief' (Mezirow, 1999, p3).

References

Boud, D, Cohen, R and Walker, D (1993) *Using Experience for Learning,* SRHE and Open University Press, Buckingham

Brookfield, S (2000) Contesting criticality: epistemological and practical contradictions in critical reflection, *2000 AERC Conference Proceedings,* http://www.edst.educ.ubc.ca/aerc 2000/brookfield1-web.htm

Buber, M (1958) *I and Thou,* Charles Scribner Sons, New York

Burgoyne, J and Reynolds, M (eds) (1997*) Management Learning: Integrating perspectives in theory and practice,* Sage, London

Carr, W and Kemmis, S (1986) *Becoming Critical: Education, knowledge and action research,* Falmer Press, London

Dewey, J (1938) *Experience and Education,* Macmillan, New York

Goleman, D (1996) *Emotional Intelligence,* Bloomsbury, London

Gregory, J (1996) *The Psycho-Social Education of Nurses,* Avery, Aldershot

Habermas, J (1974) *Theory and Practice,* Heinemann, Oxford

Heron, J (1974) *The Concept of a Peer Learning Community,* University of Surrey, Human Potential Research Project, Guildford

Heron, J (1989) *The Facilitators' Handbook,* Kogan Page, London

Heron, J (1992) *Feeling and Personhood. Psychology in another key,* Sage, London, http://zeus.sirt.pisa.it/icci/partknow.htm

Heron, J (1999) *The Complete Facilitator's Handbook,* Kogan Page, London

Hogan, C (2000) *Facilitating Empowerment,* Kogan Page, London

Jarvis, P (1985) *The Sociology of Adult and Continuing Education,* Croom Helm, Beckenham

Jarvis, P, Holford, J and Griffin, C (1998) *The Theory and Practice of Learning,* Kogan Page, London

Knowles, M (1978) *The Adult Learner – A neglected species,* 2nd edn, Gulf, Houston, TX

Knowles, M (1989) *The Making of an Adult Educator,* Jossey-Bass, San Francisco, CA

Kolb, D A (1984) *Experiential Learning – Experience as the source of learning and development,* Prentice-Hall, London

Mezirow, J (1981) A critical theory of adult learning and education, *Adult Education,* **32** (1), pp 3–27

Mezirow, J (1999) Transformation theory – postmodern issues, *1999 AERC Conference Proceedings*, http://www.edst.educ.ubc.ca/aerc/1999/99mezirow.htm

Mulligan, J (1993) Activating internal processes in experiential learning, in *Using Experience for Learning*, eds D Boud, R Cohen and D Walker, The Society for Research into Higher Education and The Open University Press, Buckingham

Postle, D (1988) *The Mind Gymnasium,* Macmillan/Papermac, London, digital edition available in 2001 at: http://www.mind-gymnasium.com/

Postle, D (1993) Putting the heart back into learning, Chapter 2 in *Using Experience for Learning,* eds D Boud, R Cohen and D Walker, The Society for Research into Higher Education and The Open University Press, Buckingham

Rawlinson, A (1997) *The Book of Enlightened Masters,* Open Court, Chicago, IL

Rogers, C R (1967) *On Becoming a Person,* Constable, London

Rogers C R (1983) *Freedom to Learn for the 80s,* 2nd edn, Merrill, Columbus, OH

Rowan, J (1993) *The Transpersonal: Psychotherapy and counselling,* Routledge, London

Rowan, J (1998) *The Reality Game,* 2nd edn, Routledge, London

Usher, R and Edwards, R (1994) *Postmodernism and Education,* Routledge, London

Weil, S and McGill, I (1989) *Making Sense of Experiential Learning: Diversity in theory and practice,* The Society for the Research into Higher Education and Open University Press, Buckingham

Weisbord, M R (1987) *Productive Workplaces: Organizing and managing for dignity, meaning and community,* Jossey-Bass, San Francisco, CA

Williamson, B (1979) *Education, Social Structure and Development,* Macmillan, London

Chapter 10

Experiential methods of teaching and learning

Paul Tosey

In this chapter I survey a wide range of experiential methods, categorized in the following way:

- attention: methods intended to enhance states of being and awareness;
- creative thinking and accelerated learning;
- the gymnasium principle: enactment, simulation and expression;
- encounter: increasing self-awareness;
- group work;
- the imaginal: using imagination and intuition for inner exploration.

These categories are neither definitive nor mutually exclusive. For example, encounter methods to increase self-awareness often take place in groups. Nor is the survey by any means exhaustive of experiential methods that are, or may be, used in education. The chapter's purpose is primarily to indicate the vast array of experiential methods and processes available. The selection here reflects a cross-fertilization between fields such as management development, adult learning, and counselling and psychotherapy, and is based on a recent survey of concepts and methods relating to personal development (Tosey and Gregory, 2001).

For reasons of space I have not included in this survey a wide range of 'reflective practices' or methods that support experiential learning and which are essential in any experientially based curriculum. These include action learning, the use of critical incidents, and the use of learning contracts. Neither have I included the principles of problem-based learning (see Chapter 11) nor work-related learning (Tosey and McNair, 2000), both of which are fundamentally experiential.

Attention: enhancing states of being and awareness

Personal development will often lead to enhanced sensory awareness and emotional sensitivity (see Stevens, 1971). Awareness was, and remains, a central feature of the 'curriculum' of ancient disciplines such as t'ai chi chuan (a form of graceful, rhythmic, meditative exercise originating in China), yoga and Zen Buddhism. In contemporary personal development, Gestalt in particular (eg Clarkson, 1989) emphasizes the value of present-time, sensory awareness, what we sense and feel in the 'here and now'. In Gestalt it is suggested that people spend much of their existence thinking about the past or the future.

The idea that 'mindfulness' in everyday awareness can transform our experience is a frequent theme. Rowan (1998, pp61ff) advocates the development of a particular form of awareness or consciousness, less focused than usual, and a whole-body rather than intellectual awareness. He likens this to Freud's 'free-floating attention' and calls it 'listening with the fourth ear'. In Neuro-Linguistic Programming (NLP) (Bandler and Grinder, 1975) a related distinction is found between a defocused, expanded peripheral vision and foveal (focused) vision.

These and related disciplines also attend to the development of states of being and presence. This may extend to interest in 'altered' states of consciousness, for example the trance modes or states of attention found in Autogenics and in some methods of accelerated learning (see below). Modalities such as NLP take the view that everyday consciousness consists of varying states, and that it may be misleading to mark out some as extraordinary through the label 'altered'.

In the self-help technique of co-counselling (see the Web site of Co-counselling International: http://www.dpets.demon.co.uk/cciuk/index.html), attention means deep listening to the cues and insinuations of what another is saying and doing. It may involve all the five senses: kinaesthetic, auditory, visual, tactile, and olfactory. Giving full attention means that the counsellor listens attentively without interrupting and without non-verbal interference apart from a steady gaze, setting aside their own interpretations, concentrating on the client's story and their needs, and letting go of any need to take action.

There are copious methods of developing states of relaxation (in which the person is free of unnecessary emotional and physical tension), particularly in programmes concerned with stress reduction. Many self-help sources exist, such as the enduringly popular *Relaxation and Stress Reduction Workbook* (Davis *et al*, 2000). Methods include Autogenics ('self-generating'), which is based on self-hypnosis. Using simple mental exercises, according to the British Autogenic Society Web site (http://www.autogenic-therapy.org.uk/), the person attains a 'passive concentration', a state of 'alert but detached awareness', which is considered helpful for stress management and many stress-related conditions.

Most meditation practices are claimed to be calming and to lead to an internal silence, so that new insights and understandings develop. In education, meditation can be used as anything from a single activity to an underpinning of an entire curriculum (as in transcendental meditation). Contemporary Western interest in meditation has been prompted by exploration of Eastern religions, though is often practised mainly for stress management and relaxation (eg Bodian, 1999).

In Zen, and Buddhism generally, meditation begins by awareness of breathing, observing our own mental events non-judgementally. The quality and rhythm of breathing is significant in many other modes of development. Breathing is a primal experience. Rowan notes (1993, p192) that breathing works on physical, emotional, intellectual and spiritual levels. It has a significant role in voice work, as well as therapeutic modes involving regression (see Hendricks,1995).

Bodily awareness may be enhanced through movement (see below) and through massage, forms of which exist throughout the world. Applications range from the use of touch for health and relaxation to specialized methods of healing (such as Shiatsu and acupressure) and therapeutic and developmental modes of bodywork. These specialized forms require the practitioner to be properly trained. Touch is a universally important human experience, as well as one around which many taboos exist. Using touch is common in humanistic approaches and personal development workshops. For example, an icebreaker may encourage people to make some form of physical contact and energizing activities may involve brief massage. But where touch is not explicitly a working medium, and not explicit in the educational contract, practitioners need to take care so that touch is not experienced as invasive, sexual, or otherwise an inappropriate use of the facilitator's power.

Creative thinking

Many methods of creative thinking are related to the idea that the two hemispheres of the brain have different functions (see Ornstein, 1972; Sperry, 1964). The typical associations are that the left-brain is logical, sequential, rational, analytical and objective; the right brain is intuitive, holistic, synthesizing and subjective.

Recent researchers (for example, McCrone, 1998, 1999) have seriously challenged the somewhat simplistic and romantic nature of the distinction. If treated as a metaphor rather than as a matter of scientific truth, the left brain-right brain model is a useful, aid to 'thinking about thinking' even if it does not explain the workings of the brain.

Brainstorming is a creative problem-solving process whereby a person or group generates ideas without censoring or evaluating them (see Buzan, 2000), akin therefore to the psychoanalytic practice of free association. The principle is that by 'turning off' the judging, censoring part of the mind (typically the 'left brain') people can freely produce creative, nonsensical ideas which they might otherwise dismiss as irrelevant or stupid. Often these provide useful connections or new ways of perceiving a problem. A brainstorming session may last a set length of time (eg 10 minutes), or until the flow of ideas has dried up. Participants then move on to exploring and evaluating the brainstormed ideas.

Mind mapping is a note-taking and note-making technique, also associated with Buzan, who argues that notes based on spontaneous patterns developed around a central topic or theme are much more conducive to recall than those prepared in the traditional (within Western societies) linear form. Pattern notes (mind maps), utilizing key words, images and colour have, suggests Buzan, the benefit of engaging both sides of the brain.

'Lateral thinking' is a related practice devised by de Bono (1990). This refers to non-linear, non-logical thinking, the purpose of which is to make creative associations.

Synectics is a creative problem-solving methodology developed by Gordon (1961). It makes use of metaphor and analogy to break free from constraining assumptions or mind-sets – essentially, by making the strange familiar, or by making the familiar strange. He believed that the emotional and irrational components of creative behaviour are more important than the intellectual, but need to be understood and used as tools in order to increase creative output. Synectics is used in business, education, and other settings (for example, Nolan, 1989).

Rehearsal

Actual or mental, imagined rehearsal of a performance is another form of creative method ('live' rehearsal of interpersonal skills is addressed under 'enactment'). Mental rehearsal relates to our ability to practise a process or activity in our minds (Dilts, 1998). In NLP, it is used to strengthen or improve behavioural performance, cognitive thinking patterns and internal states. When applied to behavioural performance, mental rehearsal involves creating internal representations, in the form of images, sounds and feelings, of some behaviour or performance we desire to enact or improve. Mental rehearsal – a slight misnomer, as the rehearsal is by no means purely cognitive – is used extensively in sports psychology. It is reckoned by some that mental rehearsal can be as effective as actual practice.

Visualization is a mental process using 'the mind's eye' as a way of accessing imagery and internal information. It deals with inner events through visual rather than verbal thought and may be done consciously (remembering or imagining) or unconsciously (dreaming). Visualization is relevant to mental rehearsal and also to the imaginal realm (see section below). The assumptions behind such techniques as 'creative visualization' (Gawain, 1995) and 'imagework' (Glouberman, 1989) are that it is possible to bring about what people want to create in their lives.

Also relevant here is the notion of positive thinking. Peale (1953) was one of the first to write about this and he expounded the view that it is more constructive to focus on the positive (what we want) than on the negative (what we wish to avoid). This principle has been used in personal development applications (eg in the NLP practice of imagining personal goals or outcomes). Goleman (1996, pp86–87) comments on the importance of hope and the real effects of one's expectations, but if overdone, positive thinking can become unrealistic.

Accelerated learning

Meier (2000) refers to a variety of methods that claim to engage faster or more efficient learning, such as speed reading.

'Brain gym' is a systematized form of educational kinesiology developed initially to help people with learning difficulties, but available generally to enhance learning, creativity and enjoyment. Its emphasis is on the relationship between body movement and brain functioning. Bodily coordination and integration are significant not only physically but also mentally, and brain gym uses movement to enhance neural pathways.

Suggestopedia is a process that enables the learning of (for example) language through unconscious processing. Hooper-Hensen (1992, p197) says, 'Suggestopedia is the creation of a doctor and psychiatrist, Georgi Lozanov from the University of Sofia, Bulgaria. The method was developed in the 1960s, begun as an experiment to induce enhanced memorization in schools.' Hooper-Hensen notes that the term 'suggestopedia' is misleading, and has unwanted connotations. Lozanov now uses the term 'desuggestive learning', and eschews the use of any form of hypnosis. The Society for Effective Affective Learning (SEAL) was founded in 1983 to promote Lozanov's work.

The gymnasium principle: enactment, play and expression

Much personal development is based on the gymnasium principle (Postle, 1988), where the programme or workshop provides a safe practice ground for trying out behaviours and skills, and for expressing emotion. There are multitudinous exercises of this kind in sources on life skills training, interpersonal skills development, and counselling (see, for example, Heron's six category analysis – discussed by Gregory in Chapter 9). A similar approach may be taken to interpersonal skills in areas of assertiveness, listening, interviewing, negotiating, and so on.

Enactment

A key figure here is J L Moreno (1889–1974), the originator of psychodrama (an 'action method of group psychotherapy'; Holmes and Karp, 1991, p7). He is recognized as a pioneer of humanistic, existential therapeutic practice. Psychodrama is a method of dramatic (re)enactment of human encounters. It is used as a therapeutic modality and as a working method in personal development workshops.

The principal emphasis of role-play, which is derived from psychodrama, is on behavioural performance in simulated, training-type settings, where participants take specified roles to rehearse or act out an interaction; to practise particular skills (eg assertiveness); to explore interactions from others' perspectives and experience; and to explore options for handling a given scenario. Thus it may lead to attitudinal and/or behavioural change, as well as promote self-awareness. A current practical guide is Bolton *et al* (1997). In practice, people often feel uncomfortable with role-play's performative aspects and apparent artificiality but it is a powerful tool for experiential learning that needs careful preparation and sensitive facilitation.

Behavioural change and skills development may be assisted by coaching, a notion imported from sport. Coaching is usually, and primarily, a process in which a facilitator – often an external trainer or consultant – assists a manager to perform better (see Whitmore, 1996). Coaching will often concentrate on skills and behaviour but also involves reflective, verbal sessions. A variant of this type of coaching is the Zen-influenced, inner game approach (Gallwey, 1999).

The emotional dimension of enactment is emphasized more in methods such as co-counselling, where the focus is on the cathartic release of distress in order to reach insight. Co-counselling has many exercise formats that enable the person to 'act into' emotions or types of behaviour.

Simulation

Games and simulations are significant forms of experiential learning method. In play people are most likely to be spontaneous, uninhibited and expressive. An example of a personal development game is the Transformation Game, developed at Findhorn, the spiritual community based in Scotland. It is a board game format designed to promote self-awareness both through the content and through the interactions with other players.

Simulations generally place participants in specified roles within a simulated action arena in order to experience the dynamics of a 'real' situation within an educational setting. Simulations can range from individual activities to full-scale events simulating organizations, communities and so on. Many simulations also make use of computer technology. A variant on this theme is outward-bound training. This differs in that the experience is contrived but not simulated. It takes participants out of the classroom and, typically, into rural, adventure settings where activities such as abseiling, orienteering and outdoor survival become the source for learning (see for example Snow, 1997). Outward-bound training is often used as a team development format, as issues of interpersonal relating are heightened by dependence on other people for success and even survival (Huczynski, 1983). The need for physical and psychological safety is very important in these situations and effective facilitation should provide for these aspects during the experience, as well as for extensive debriefing through which participants can reflect on their experiential learning.

Creative expression

Experiential methods often involve creative expression, or make use of art forms or media (painting, drawing, music and sculpting), common in specific modes of development like Psychosynthesis (Assagioli, 1975).

Creative writing (Hunt and Sampson, 1998), including biography, poetry, short stories, and so on, is a valuable medium for self-expression. In experiential workshops, exercises such as writing one's own obituary encourage individuals to review their life and gain a different perspective on the present. Torbert (Torbert and Fisher, 1992) has used autobiographical writing as a personal and management or leadership development tool.

Story telling is used in education and in therapy (Gersie and King, 1990). More recently, story telling has been introduced into organizations as a way of acknowledging, capturing and working expressively with people's experience of work. Story telling is a traditional form of communication with many possible functions – entertainment, myth-making, oral history, and more. The notion of the 'teaching story' is particularly associated with the Sufis. Idries Shah has introduced this form to the West, and has published several volumes of stories about the Mullah Nasrudin, the Sufi 'wise fool' (eg Shah, 1973).

Dance and movement of many kinds are a prime form of experiential method. Movement is utilized in numerous modes of development (eg

NLP), and also has many specific forms and practices (eg the Alexander technique, Dance movement therapy, Feldenkrais, eurhythmy). An example that is conducive to general educational use is circle dance, which seeks to give people in groups a sense of pleasure and purpose in 'moving together', reflecting solidarity in their community. In contemporary applications, teams can debrief dancing together as models of how they operate at work – are they all, for example, 'dancing to the same tune'? The metaphor of 'being in step with each other' is also powerful.

Voice work is another expressive mode. It is essentially a whole-body and whole-person activity, as voice production depends on breathing, posture and movement, is directly linked to emotional expression, and has a spiritual dimension too. Some practitioners have a background in music or singing, and draw on traditions from around the world, including Tibet and Mongolia. Others have had a primary interest in the psychological and emotional significance of voice, and experience an enhanced ability to sing as a delightful added benefit.

Encounter and self-awareness

This approach concentrates on using encounter between people, and methods that generate information about the self, to enhance self-awareness. Educating oneself or learning to relate to others on an emotional level has to involve some self-awareness, which is a dimension of most methods, particularly those in the previous category of 'enactment'. However, encounter is in 'real time' – between people being themselves, rather than performing a role or enacting an exercise. This distinction is not hard and fast; psychodrama, for instance, also embraces encounter.

Self-awareness refers to our own nature and behaviour, and seeing ourselves as others see us. The extent to which people can be self-aware is philosophical, but social psychologists and others have also debated the subject. In personal development there is no ultimate definition of self-awareness. It encapsulates what is expressed by, for example, the exhortation inscribed above the Delphic oracle ('know thyself') and by Robert Burns' poem, 'To a Louse' ('O wad some Power the giftie gie us To see oursels as ithers see us!').

The human encounter

Buber (1958) identified the polarities of 'I-Thou' and 'I-It' as the two forms of meeting that human beings can experience in relation to each other and the world in general. An 'I-Thou' meeting is characterized by a genuine interest in the other person, valuing the 'otherness' of the person whose humanity is perceived as being an end rather than a means to an end. In an 'I-It' meeting, the other person is seen as an object and is utilized primarily as a means to an end. In reality, we experience a rhythmic alteration between the two. Interpersonal dialogue is a therapeutic approach developed by Richard Hycner (1993) and others that is based on Buber's concept of 'I-Thou', which is also the basis of 'Enlightenment intensives'. Rowan (1993, pp148–49) regards the latter as having the potential for discovery of the 'real self'.

Elements of encounter that we take for granted in everyday life may be placed, as it were, under the microscope in educational settings. For example, Heron worked with 'the phenomenology of the gaze'. In this he considered eye-contact through the mutual gaze to be a primal experience, a deeply significant human encounter.

Encounter also typically involves disclosure, sharing with others aspects of our internal world. Disclosure can have many forms, such as self-assessing attitudes and competence before soliciting feedback from others in self and peer assessment (Chapter 7) or sharing our own worldview and experience with others. The aim of disclosure is usually to be transparent (Jourard, 1971), better understood and authentic.

Research shows that people need to feel a strong sense of trust and be in an environment of empathy and understanding to self-disclose (Gregory, 1996). Workshops often involve trust exercises. These require, and thereby aim to build, a sufficient level of trust between participants to enable disclosure and honesty. A well-known trust exercise is the blind walk. In pairs, one partner is blindfolded and the other is the guide who must assist the blindfolded person to explore their world safely.

The Johari Window, which was developed by Luft and Ingram (1967) and named by conflating their first names, Joe and Harry, is a two-by-two matrix with dimensions of self-disclosure, and seeking feedback. This creates four sections or panes (the public arena, the hidden arena, the blind spot, and the unknown arena). The internal sectional dividers are such that the window panes can open further depending on the degree of disclosure and amount of feedback.

Sensitivity training

This started in 1946 at the New Britain Teacher's College Connecticut (see for example Back, 1972). It was designed to explore the use of small groups as a vehicle for personal and social change. The goal of sensitivity training is change through self-expression, rather than self-expression for its own sake. As in encounter, the experience tends to be emotionally intensive.

'Encounter group' (Schutz, 1971) and 'basic encounter', operating on person-centred principles and developed by Carl Rogers (Bozarth, 1986), are two specific forms of this. Schutz's practice of 'open encounter', originated at the Esalen Institute at Big Sur, California in the 1960s, works by facilitating encounters between participants in the here and now. It is often associated with a confrontational style – encouraging people to voice their irritation, anger, disappointment and so on with others in the room to become authentic. Encounter groups are, according to Schutz and others, capable of achieving great intimacy and releasing joy, but they can be anxiety-provoking and potentially destructive to those who feel insecure.

Another variety is the 'T-group', which stands for 'training group'. The T-group method is used for personal and/or team development and was a core method of organization development in the 1960s. According to Aronson (1994, p183):

> the first T-Group was an accident that happened when participants in a work-shop conducted by Kurt Lewin asked to sit in on the observers' debriefing sessions. The result was a lively and exciting debate, and the practice continued.

Participants are supported in exploring their interpersonal relationships, and the facilitator may intervene in group process or interpersonal conflict, but does not structure or lead the group. Often a T-group will have no task other than to study its own process.

Feedback for self-awareness

Encounter methods aim to enhance participants' self-awareness through drawing attention to their behaviour and their impact on others. It is also promoted through a very wide range of feedback formats, which do not necessarily involve the type of encounter described above. But they may be used as a basis for discussion between the respondent and a facilitator or peers. These include methods as diverse as the Enneagram (Palmer, 1995), the Myers-Briggs Type Indicator (Briggs-Myers and Myers, 1980), and myriad other forms of profiling, including psychometric testing.

In management, 360° feedback has been in vogue for some years. The positive intention of this is to ensure that managers are sensitive to their impact upon, and the views of, those other than their boss. Used well this can be a powerful developmental experience, both effective and ethical. Used as a mechanistic process without regard to relational and human dimensions, it can result in 360° fallout. A quick search on the Internet reveals many sites offering computer or web-based 360° feedback programs or services; worryingly, the emphasis typically seems to be on the efficiency of the technology and rarely on the personal and interpersonal dimensions.

It is worth emphasizing that in the original, cybernetic sense, 'negative' feedback is not bad, nor is 'positive' feedback good. In the interpersonal domain, however, we usually expect that negative feedback will be unpleasant. Various sources list guidelines or rules for giving and receiving feedback (such as that it is specific, timely and actionable). Handled unskilfully, feedback may do more harm than good (for example, the person who interjects with 'let me give you some feedback'... and launches into unsolicited criticism).

Group work

Experiential learning often takes place in a group format. There is not space here to outline the knowledge base that any facilitator of groups should have to hand, but see Jaques (2000). Suffice it to say that there are many theories and models of group dynamics, and related training. An educator using a group format should be familiar with some models of group dynamics (eg Bion, 1961), group roles, group stages or phases (eg Tuckman and Jensen, 1977) and the need for ground rules (a process of contracting), discussed elsewhere in this volume.

Included below are a few techniques that might be used in any educational group. However, just about all the methods and activities described here can be used in group work, and the techniques described below only scratch the surface of the formats and processes available in group work.

A 'check-in' is a period of time at the beginning of a group session for participants to arrive and prepare for the group's task. This allows participants to 'park' issues that are on their minds; to declare what is 'on top' for them (ie uppermost in their awareness); or to share news and to focus on the here and now.

An 'ice-breaker' is an exercise designed to 'break the ice', in other words to help participants overcome the anxiety and social difficulty at the beginning of the event. For example, participants may be asked to spend a few minutes in pairs telling each other something about themselves. Depending on the nature of the event, the 'ice' may be seen as something to avoid or to break through as swiftly as possible, or perhaps as a vehicle for drawing attention to group dynamics.

'Energizers' are exercises that raise or increase the level of arousal. These are usually physical activities employed to change the level of attention and arousal in a workshop. An example is where participants stand in a circle giving themselves a brief massage by brushing themselves down with their hands, as if brushing off anxiety or tension, starting with the head and moving downwards to the feet.

A 'buzz group' is a small group convened in the middle of a workshop or lecture to discuss and respond to workshop or lecture content. This changes attention and format; the 'buzz' comes from the sound of several groups in discussion.

A 'fishbowl' typically involves a selection of participants in some activity in the centre of the room, with other participants observing or witnessing in an outer circle. Those engaging in the activity are the 'goldfish'. This format has the advantage that those looking in on the goldfish can also engage in the activity. First, they can observe and be charged with giving feedback to participants. Second, there can be provision for a 'tag' system whereby an observer changes places with a goldfish.

Another option is to use this as a dialogical format, with an inner circle and an outer circle. This can be an alternative to a presentation. Those in the outer circle are attuned more to listening, and need to make a conscious decision to move in order to enter the dialogue. Those in the inner circle are typically less anxious about airing their questions, and can address concerns in a more conversational way. The facilitator can attend during the process to the needs of the limited number of participants in the inner circle. The metaphor of the goldfish bowl is somewhat cold, hard and wet for this process and at Surrey we call it a 'campfire'.

The imaginal

The imaginal world is 'the world we enter when we make up stories or see visions, or hear internal music, and so on' (Rowan, 1993, p53): it is a rich inner world of imagery, symbols and myths, and many modes of personal development (for example, Psychosynthesis) encourage it. The main distinction from the 'creativity' category is that the imaginal is concerned with people's inner worlds and often with the transpersonal dimension of development (Rowan, 1993). Such work typically has its roots in a combination of Eastern and Western mystical traditions, modern psychology, and psychic and spiritual development.

Affirmation is common in new age sources but is a long-established practice:

> There are many practical applications of the principle that what we affirm and program into the unconscious belief system, we tend in subtle ways to bring about... The basic principle has long been a core idea in the esoteric inner-core understandings of the world's spiritual traditions. (Harman, 1988, p77)

The process of affirming an image makes it stronger and more effective by activating the creative energies needed to achieve the outcome.

The history of visualization includes its use in early religions and philosophies as a tool for personal growth and transformation, while shamanic healers visualized going on a journey into a person's world in order to restore them to health (Samuels and Samuels, 1975). Guided fantasy is a method for enabling people to access their creative imagination and for enabling for inner experience to be brought to conscious awareness. It has been defined in various other ways, for example 'creative visualization' (Gawain, 1995), 'interactive daydreaming' or 'active imagination'. Guided fantasy can have many different applications. Its basic *modus operandi* is that the person is encouraged to become relaxed and is given some basic, fairly general information about a situation, place or journey; they are then encouraged to supply the detail from their own imagination. The guide or facilitator prompts them from time to time with further very open-ended suggestions or questions, and as the corresponding detail is added by the subject's imagination, or symbolic memory, the whole experience deepens. Subsequently the person may be encouraged to draw, paint, act, talk about or model the detail of their imaginative experience. This can bring fresh insight, altered mood or different perspective.

The notion of the heroic quest is that, rather than seeing each person as developing towards some standard idea of level or ideal state, we can see each person's life as a quest or journey. This idea is present in myths throughout the world (Campbell, 1985, p161) and focuses on the idea of gaining self-knowledge through journeying into the unknown and facing and overcoming ordeals. The outward journey of the hero myth is paralleled by the inward journey of psychic development. Several ancient symbol systems are thought to represent this journey; for example, the chakras (Myss, 1997), the tarot, and the tree of life. The tarot is one of many symbol systems that can be used in personal development as a symbolic representation of development, or as an aid to reflection and meditation (see Pollack, 1997, for a general introduction). The idea of the heroic quest has been applied to management development by Cairnes (1998).

Finally, the term 'vision quest' is from American First Nations' traditions (see for example Foster and Little, 1989). It or its equivalent is found in many cultures, and is a form of initiation ritual or search for self-discovery. Typically, individuals go out alone into some natural setting or wilderness and wait for, invite or seek an inspiring vision that helps them to connect with their core self and their purpose. Like many methods from spiritual disciplines, the concept of a vision quest is offered as a contemporary personal development training, is being made palatable for management training, and is even being used as a brand name.

Conclusion

The categories discussed above are not mutually exclusive and they can be, and are being used in a variety of educational and management contexts for personal development training.

References

Aronson, E (1994) Communication in sensitivity-training groups, in *Organization Development and Transformation,* 4th edn, eds W L French, C H Bell, and R A Zawacki, Irwin, Burr Ridge, IL

Assagioli, R (1975) *Psychosynthesis; A manual of principles and techniques,* Turnstone Press, Wellingborough

Back, K W (1972) *Beyond Words: The story of sensitivity training and the encounter movement,* Russell Sage Foundation, New York

Bandler, R and Grinder, J (1975*) The Structure of Magic: A book about language and therapy,* Science and Behaviour Books, Palo Alto, CA

Bion, W R (1961) *Experience in Groups,* Tavistock, London

Bodian, S (1999) *Meditation for Dummies,* Hungry Minds, New York

Bolton, G M, Bolton, G and Heathcote, D (1997) *So You Want to Use Role-Play?,* Trentham Books, London

Bozarth, J D (1986) The basic encounter group: an alternative view, *The Journal for Specialists in Group Work,* **11** (4), pp228–32, available online at http://personcentered.com/group1.htm, accessed 15.12.2000

Briggs-Myers, I and Myers, P B (1980) *Gifts Differing,* Davies-Black Publishing, Palo Alto, CA

Buber, M (1958) *I and Thou,* Charles Scribner's Sons, New York

Buzan, T (2000) *Use Your Head,* BBC Publications, London

Cairnes, M (1998) *Approaching the Corporate Heart,* Simon & Schuster, Sydney

Campbell, J (1985) *Myths to Live By,* Paladin, Granada, London

Clarkson, P (1989) *Gestalt Counselling in Action,* Sage, London

Davis, M, McKay, M and Eshelman, E R (2000) *The Relaxation and Stress Reduction Workbook,* 5th edn, New Harbinger Publications, Oakland, CA

de Bono, E (1990) *Lateral Thinking,* Penguin, Harmondsworth

Dilts, R (1998) *Harnessing the Imagination,* available online at: http://www.scruz.net/rdilts/Articles/artic16.htm, accessed 18.12.2000

Foster, S and Little, M (1989) *The Book of the Vision Quest,* Prentice-Hall, London

Gallwey, T (1999) *The Inner Game of Work,* Random House, New York

Gawain, S (1995) *Creative Visualization,* New World Library, CA

Gersie, A and King, N (1990) *Storymaking in Education and Therapy,* Jessica Kingsley, London

Glouberman, D (1989) *Life Choices and Life Changes Through Imagework: The art of developing personal vision,* Unwin Hyman, London

Goleman, D (1996) *Emotional Intelligence,* Bloomsbury, London

Gordon, W J J (1961) *Synectics; The development of creative capacity,* Harper & Row, New York

Gregory, J (1996) *The Psycho-Social Education of Nurses,* Avery, Aldershot

Harman, W (1988*) Global Mind Change,* Knowledge Systems, Indianapolis, IN

Hendricks, G (1995) *Conscious Breathing: Breathwork for health, stress release, and personal mastery,* Bantam Books, New York

Holmes, P and Karp, M (1991) (eds) *Psychodrama: Inspiration and technique,* Routledge, London

Hooper-Hensen, G (1992) Suggestopedia: a way of learning for the 21st century, in *Empowerment Through Experiential Learning: Exploration of good practice,* eds J Mulligan and C Griffin, Kogan Page, London, pp 197–207

Huczynski, A A (1983) *Encyclopaedia of Management Development Methods,* Gower, Aldershot

Hunt, C and Sampson, F (1998) (eds) *The Self on the Page: Theory and practice of creative writing in personal development,* Jessica Kingsley, London

Hycner, R (1993) *Between Person and Person: Towards a dialogical psychotherapy,* Gestalt Journal Press, New York

Jaques, D (2000) *Learning in Groups,* 3rd edn, Kogan Page, London

Jourard, S (1971) *The Transparent Self,* van Nostrand Reinhold, New York

Luft, J and Ingram, H (1967) *Of Human Interaction: The Johari model,* Mayfield, Palo Alto, CA

McCrone, J (1998) *Going Inside: A tour around a single moment of consciousness,* Faber, London

McCrone, J (1999) Left brain, right brain, *New Scientist,* 3 July, available online at: http://www.newscientist.com/ns/19990703/leftbrainr.html, accessed 2.1.2001

Meier, D (2000) *The Accelerated Learning Handbook,* Berrett-Koehler, San Francisco, CA

Myss, C (1997) *Anatomy of the Spirit,* Bantam Books, London

Nolan, V (1989) *The Innovator's Handbook: The skills of innovative management – problem solving, communication, and teamwork,* Penguin, Harmondsworth

Ornstein, R (1972) *The Psychology of Consciousness,* Penguin, Harmondsworth

Palmer, H (1995) *The Enneagram in Love and Work,* Harper and Row, San Francisco, CA

Peale, N (1953) *The Power of Positive Thinking,* Cedar Books, Heinemann, Oxford

Pollack, R (1997) *Seventy-Eight Degrees of Wisdom,* Thorsons, London

Postle, D (1988) *The Mind Gymnasium,* Macmillan/Papermac, London, digital edition available in 2001 at: http://www.mind-gymnasium.com

Rowan, J (1993) *The Transpersonal,* Routledge, London

Rowan, J (1998) *The Reality Game,* 2nd edn, Routledge, London

Samuels, M D and Samuels, N S (1975) *Seeing With the Mind's Eye: The history, techniques and uses of visualization,* Random House, New York

Schutz, W C (1971) *Joy: Expanding human awareness,* Souvenir Press, London

Shah, I (1973) *The Exploits of the Incredible Mulla Nasrudin,* Picador, London

Snow, H (1997) *Indoor/Outdoor Team Building Games for Trainers: Powerful activities from the world of adventure-based team building and ropes courses,* McGraw-Hill, Maidenhead

The Society for Effective Affective Learning (SEAL) Web site: http://www.seal.org.uk/

Sperry, R (1964) The great cerebral commissure, *Scientific American,* January, pp 142–52, offprint no. 174

Stevens, J O (1971) *Awareness: Exploring, Experimenting, Experiencing,* Real People Press, Moab, UT

Torbert, W R and Fisher, D (1992) Autobiographical awareness as a catalyst for managerial and organizational learning, *Management Education and Development,* **23** (3), pp 184–98

Tosey, P and Gregory, J (2001) *A Dictionary of Personal Development,* Whurr, London

Tosey, P and McNair, S (2000) Work-related learning, in *The Age of Learning,* ed P Jarvis, Kogan Page, London

Tuckman, B W and Jensen, M A C (1977) Stages of small group development revisited, *Group and Organizational Studies,* **2**, pp 419–27

Whitmore, J (1996) *Coaching for Performance,* Nicholas Brealey, London

Further reading

Hanson, P (1973) The Johari Window: A model for soliciting and giving feedback, in *Annual Handbook for Group Facilitators,* eds J W Pfeiffer and J E Jones, University Associates, La Jolla, San Diego, CA

Heron, J (1990) *Helping the Client,* Sage, London

Chapter 11

Practice-based and problem-based learning

Peter Jarvis

Despite their names, practice-based and problem-based learning are facilitative and experiential teaching methods which are becoming very popular in the professions; the former has always been undertaken in apprenticeship systems and through practice placements while in training, but the latter has perhaps gained its popularity as a result of the innovations introduced in health sciences education at McMaster University in Canada. The reasons for its growth lie with the fact that it is also practice-oriented and it is about integrated knowledge rather than the disciplines.

Underlying this chapter is the idea that the place of learning is a practice setting rather than a traditional classroom. Schon (1987, p37) called these practicums:

> a setting designed for the task of learning a practice. In a context that approximates the practice world, students learn by doing, although their doing usually falls short of real-world work... (it) is a virtual world, relatively free of pressures, distractions, and the risks of the real one to which, nevertheless, it refers.

Even so, a great deal of practice-based learning actually occurs in the real world, under slightly sheltered conditions.

This chapter, therefore, starts by examining the notion of practical knowledge and then looks at both practice-based and problem-based learning, concluding with a few critical comments.

Practical knowledge

Traditionally institutions of education taught the theory underlying practice and then students went out into their practice in order to apply theory to practice. However, the idea that 'there is nothing as practical as a good theory' is something that seems rather artificial nowadays. I well remember, when I was a teacher in a college of education preparing school teachers, how the bored students would return to college after their teaching practice quite excited about what they had been doing, but telling us that what we taught barely resembled the realities of their teaching experience. I can also remember an experienced teacher telling the students to forget what they had learnt in college because now was the time when they would start to learn to be a schoolteacher. So what was wrong with our understanding of what we were doing? Some claimed that either our theory was wrong, or else the students had not learnt it correctly.

But basically a number of things were wrong, and they revolved around the higher status of theory and the lower status of practice, but theory:

- tends to be abstract and general but practice is specific and unique;
- tends to assume that practice is static but practice changes with the passing of time, so that theory becomes historical;
- divided the knowledge into different disciplines but practice does not divide into a little bit of psychology and a little bit of ethics, and so on;
- tended to assume that things were not learnt in practice but were learnt in the classroom and applied;
- is cognitive but practice is both integrated and practical.

The students were implying all of these things although they did not articulate it quite so precisely. However, the idea that theory was applied to practice was quite destroyed with Schon's (1983) seminal study, *The Reflective Practitioner.* He suggests (p54) that professionals:

- know how to carry out actions spontaneously;
- are not always aware of having learned to do these things;
- are usually unable to describe the knowing which the action needs.

It was recognized widely that learning did occur in practice and that the idea of applying theory to practice was merely another formulation of instrumental rationality. The instrumentalism of modernity was really called into question and gradually it was recognized that the assumptions about knowledge itself had to be re-examined, which was something Lyotard (1984) and Foucault (1972) had already undertaken.

Indeed, this was a problem with which Ryle (1949) was wrestling long before this. He suggested (p50) that in practice individuals are both bodily and mentally active: that it was one activity that required more than one kind of explanatory description. In a sense, Ryle was still caught up with instrumental rationality and the discussion of knowledge rather than learning. Even so, his is an insightful and early analysis of these problems. He rightly discussed *knowing how* and *knowing that,* although knowing how might more usefully have been sub-divided into *knowing that this is how* and *having the skill to do.* But practical knowledge is actually more profound than this since *knowing that* might more usefully be called *content knowledge* in as much as it deals with the discipline(s) to be practised and *knowing that this is how* might be called *process knowledge,* which is integrated knowledge.

More than an element of subjectivity becomes apparent as we pursue this analysis and, indeed, the more frequently individuals practise a certain skill, procedure or behaviour the more likely they are to habitualize their processes and internalize their knowledge. This led Polanyi (1967) to discuss another dimension of subjective knowledge – tacit knowledge. Experts internalize their procedures and the knowledge that relates to these procedures so deeply that they take them for granted. This taken-for-grantedness of tacit knowledge is described by Nyiri (1988, pp20–21), quoting Feigenbaum and McCorduck (1984), thus:

> One becomes an expert not simply by absorbing explicit knowledge of the type found in textbooks, but through experience, that is, through repeated trials, 'failing, succeeding, wasting time and effort, getting a feel for a problem, learning when to go by the book and when to break the rules'. Human experts thereby gradually absorb 'a repertoire of working rules of thumb', or 'heuristics' that, combined with book knowledge, make them expert practitioners. This practical, heuristic knowledge, as attempts to simulate it on the machine have shown, is 'hardest to get at because experts – or anyone else – rarely have the self-awareness to recognize what it is'. So it must be mined out of their heads painstakingly, one jewel at a time.

Tacit knowledge is clearly a major dimension of practical knowledge, but practitioners are not automatons – they have their own beliefs and values and it is hard, nigh on impossible, to prevent these playing a significant role in practice and, therefore, they form a fourth dimension of practical knowledge.

We all learn in our everyday life and so we gain *everyday* knowledge (Heller, 1984), and we also use this in our practice of teaching. We acknowledge that sometimes we find it difficult to utilize all our learning in every teaching situation, but we do not deliberately neglect some aspects.

Finally, knowing *that this is how* is not the same as *having the skill to do* so that this element is also a major dimension of practical knowledge, which may be depicted in the manner shown in Figure 11.1. The double arrows between action and skills and the other dimensions illustrate the fact that we learn in all situations and, at the same time, our knowledge, attitudes, beliefs and values, etc affect our behaviour. However, we can only actually learn how to do things when we actually practise them. Consequently, we have seen the development of many forms of action learning. Practical knowledge, then, is:

- learnt in practice situations;
- practical, and not merely the application of some 'pure' academic discipline to practical situations;
- dynamic, in as much as it is only retained for as long as it works;
- integrated, rather than divided up by academic discipline;
- not an academic discipline in the same way as the sciences or the social sciences.

The problem confronting teachers now is how this complex formulation of practical knowledge can be taught and learnt.

Practice-based learning

In the preparation of individuals for a number of the professions the practical placement is quite crucial. We have to devise ways whereby students, whether full-time or part-time, may learn more from their practice than merely by doing it which, in turn, means that they need to have had preparation before

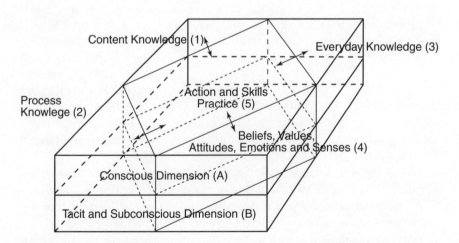

Figure 11.1 Knowledge and skills

they actually begin that practice – induction sessions, visits, discussions with other practitioners, and so on. As a result, we have to change our mode of teaching away from the didactic and towards the Socratic and the facilitative. Additionally, we have to recognize that those already in practice might act as mentors and so on for our students. In this way, teaching becomes a team exercise, with each member having specific expertise.

Through this approach, we need to encourage learners to generate their own data from practice, through writing learning journals and participating in peer learning communities. The students might never have experienced writing learning journals or participating in peer learning communities, so that it is important that, prior to their practice placement, they are taught the rudiments of journal writing and that peer learning communities are created. Journal writing is more than merely keeping a diary. It is useful in as much as it: 'may help adults break habitual modes of thinking and change life direction through reflective withdrawal and re-entry' (Lukinsky, 1990, p212).

Jasper (1999), however, did point out that some students keeping reflective learning journals found this a threatening process and consequently, the introduction of such teaching and learning methods should be undertaken with some degree of sensitivity.

The journal serves two reflective purposes. First, it helps students to become reflective learners, both on-action and in-action, recording data about reading, study habits and attitudes. Students are also invited to write about their own personal development – recording data about increasing knowledge, increasing ability to identify and articulate issues, reflecting upon important decisions that they have taken since they enrolled in the programme, and so on. Secondly, it is possible to get students to examine their own self-development and their own feelings of empowerment, and Morrison (1996) cites the work of Prawat (1991) to demonstrate this. Morrison (1996, p328) notes that when reflective practice prospers 'it is seen by many students as a major significant feature of their development in all spheres'.

Bush (1999) records how he kept a journal whilst teaching adult student nurses 'spirituality in nursing practice'. His entries, which were made within six hours of teaching and re-examined within two days, illustrate how he was grappling with both the teaching of the subject and the mature learners whom he was teaching. He recorded his thoughts about the teaching and the participation of students in this rather emotive but significant topic. He concluded (p26) that:

> The keeping of a journal provided the educator with an opportunity to connect thoughts, feeling and action and relate them to what was happening

now, as opposed to writing about what has already happened... It encouraged
the author to trace the development of any emerging interest and provided a
personal account of any growth with a factual reference that was repeatedly
examined in order to create some personal meaning.

As a result of his experiences Bush (1999, p25) has decided that in future
courses he will also ask students to keep their own journals of the
programme. Jasper (1999), using grounded theory, in a research project on
the use of journalling discovered that all the students who used it thought
that they changed and developed as people as a result. However, she also
discovered that it could not be assumed that students knew how to write a
reflective journal and that these skills had to be taught. Once acquired,
however, such skills led to journal writing as both a learning strategy and an
instrument for personal and professional growth. Thereafter, the teachers'
role becomes both Socratic, helping learners to interrogate their own journals, and facilitative in as much as we might facilitate the peer learning
community.

We, as teachers, may play a larger part in helping students to reflect on
their practice; this is not book knowledge but practical knowledge. However,
this is not a stand-alone method and students should still be encouraged to
continue their learning from theory and books, etc and integrate this into
their own personal theory, which is then tried out in practice again. In
another sense, we are encouraging students to become self-directed learners.

Practice-based learning can take a number of forms, as we shall see below,
but in each case the learner is involved in activity, so that another form is
action learning, which has been used in organizations and business since it
was designed to produce 'real-life' solutions (Reavens, 1982).

Finally, we have to devise new ways of assessing practical knowledge,
recognizing that this is pragmatic, generated in the practice setting and
always changing in the light of new experiences. Consequently, we cannot
test 'knowledge' in quite the same way – although we might want to retain
some of the more traditional ways of testing that knowledge which is taught
in the classroom. We may have to test the ability to analyse, to understand
why certain actions should be taken, the ability to reflect and evaluate, and so
on. This means that we need to get students to prepare reflective and evaluative assignments on their practice placement through which we endeavour
to understand what students have learnt and why they performed their roles
in the way that they did, which is more than just thinking on their feet but
also relating what they did to the teaching and reading that they have undertaken. In a sense, there is now no 'right' or 'wrong' answer, only reasoned
statements and it is these that we assess – in a sense we are preparing and
assessing reflective practitioners.

Problem-based learning

In 1969 the new Faculty of Health Sciences was established at McMaster University and its intention was to let the real issues of practice rather than the theoretical demands of the academic disciplines guide the curriculum. In a sense, learning rather than teaching was placed at the centre of the curriculum, although the teachers are still present as tutors rather than providers of new knowledge. Boud (1985, p14), quoting from Barrows and Tamblyn (1980) summarizes the principles underlying problem-based learning:

- The problem is encountered first in the learning sequence, before any preparation or study has occurred.
- The problem situation is presented to the student in the same way it would be presented in reality.
- The student works with the problem in a manner which permits his (*sic*) ability to reason and apply knowledge to be challenged and evaluated, appropriate to his level of learning.
- Need areas of learning are identified in the process of work with the problem used as a guide to individualized study.
- The skills and knowledge acquired by this study are applied back to the problem, to evaluate the effectiveness of the learning and to reinforce the learning.
- The learning that has occurred in the work with the problem and in individualized study is summarized and integrated into the student's existing knowledge and skill.

Kwan (2000, p137) summarizes problem-based learning in medical education in the following manner:

> In the traditional curriculum, preclinical disciplines, such as anatomy, biochemistry, physiology and pharmacology are a prerequisite for proceeding to paraclinical subjects and clinical specialities. They are mainly knowledge-based and usually taught didactically by experts in given disciplinary areas, often as large group classes in lecture theatres. In contrast, in PBL (problem-based learning) curriculum, health care problems (HCP) are used as a guide to direct learning from an integrative perspective. Knowledge... (from the disciplines)... will all come into place as long as they are of sufficient relevance to achieving the learning objectives of a given HCP as defined by the students.

Not only do the students define the problem, they control the pace and work out the solutions to the problems in their syndicate groups. This is a big jump from traditional teaching methods and several 'watered-down' variations have been developed, such as having the disciplines taught didactically before the problem-solving is undertaken, teaching *the knowledge that* and the *knowledge how* in parallel, teaching about the problem before it is discussed by the students, and so on. These versions of problem-based learning are quite familiar to many educators in the professions and can be classified as forms of practice-based education that we discussed above (see Boud and Feletti, 1991).

Many professions have now identified ways in which problem-based learning initiatives can be utilized in their professional preparation and even some of the more traditional disciplines, such as economics (Courvisanos, 1985). But it may be seen that any form of study that begins from a practice situation might start with practical problems rather than theoretical considerations. Such approaches are consistent with experiential learning theory (Jarvis *et al*, 1998, pp46–58).

In addition Hoon-Eng Khoo *et al* (2000, pp143–54) point out that the students regarded this approach to learning as fun and that their research skills had improved considerably and the library was also extremely well used. Even so, it takes a great deal of courage to move away from traditional approaches to such innovative ones and, whatever form these take, the innovators are usually confronted with varieties of objections, some more valid than others. Amongst those raised in this instance are that some student groups do not relate well with each other, that the whole of an academic discipline is not covered properly and that the 'big picture' is not fully understood (Leong, 2000). Leong actually practises problem-based learning, and agrees that the emphasis on student learning is commendable but she cannot accept that problem-based learning is a sufficient stand-alone technique. Instead, she has proposed a hybrid model with some problem-based and some problem solving in which the teachers, as facilitators, use their own expertise in working with the students as they examine the problems.

Conclusions

In the contemporary learning society, where education is becoming more vocationally oriented, more emphasis is placed on practical pragmatic knowledge, but what becomes clear from the experiences reported by some of those who have used these approaches, is that they are not sufficient in themselves. There is still a place for theoretical perspectives but the nature of theory has changed slightly – it is no longer to be applied to practice but tested out by the practitioners in practical situations to see whether it works. Theory can only be legitimated in practice situations if it is useful to the practitioners who use it and we can rephrase the old maxim, 'There is nothing as practical as good theory' thus: 'Theory is only good if it is practical'.

References

Barrows, H and Tamblyn, R (1980) *Problem-Based Learning: An approach to medical education,* Springer, New York

Boud, D (ed) (1985) *Problem-Based Learning in Education for the Professions,* Higher Education Research and Development Society of Australia, Sydney

Boud, D and Feletti, G (eds) (1991) *The Challenge of Problem-Based Learning,* Kogan Page, London

Bush, T (1999) Journalling and the teaching of spirituality, *Nurse Education Today,* **19** (1), pp 20–28

Courvisanos, J (1985) A problems approach to the study of economics, in *Problem-Based Learning in Education for the Professions,* ed D Boud, Higher Education Research and Development Society of Australia, Sydney

Feigenbaum, E and McCorduck, P (1984) *The Fifth Generation,* Signet, New York

Foucault, M (1972) *The Archaeology of Knowledge,* Tavistock, London

Heller, A (1984) *Everyday Life,* Routledge and Kegan Paul, London

Hoon-Eng Khoo *et al* (2000) Preliminary impressions of PBL: survey by medical students, in *Teaching and Learning in Higher Education Symposium,* eds C Wang *et al,* National University of Singapore, pp143–48

Jarvis, P, Holford, J and Griffin, C (1998) *The Theory and Practice of Learning,* Kogan Page, London

Jasper, M (1999) Nurses' perceptions of the value of written reflection, *Nurse Education Today,* **19** (6), pp 452–63

Kwan, C-Y (2000) Problem-based learning in medical education: from McMaster to Asia Pacific Region, in *Teaching and Learning in Higher Education Symposium,* eds C Wang *et al,* National University of Singapore, pp135–42

Leong, S K (2000) Problem-based learning – my critique, in *Teaching and Learning in Higher Education Symposium,* C Wang *et al,* National University of Singapore, pp173–78

Lukinsky, J (1990) Reflective withdrawal through journal writing, in *Fostering Critical Reflection in Adulthood,* J Mezirow and Associates, Jossey-Bass, San Francisco, CA

Lyotard, J-F (1984) *The Postmodern Condition,* University of Manchester Press, Manchester

Morrison, K (1996) Developing reflective practice in higher degree students through a learning journal, *Studies in Higher Education,* **31** (3), pp 317–32

Nyiri, J (1988) Tradition and practical knowledge, in *Practical Knowledge,* eds J Nyiri and B Smith, Croom Helm, Beckenham

Polanyi, M (1967) *The Tacit Dimension,* Routledge and Kegan Paul, London

Prawat, R S (1991) Conversations with self and conversations with settings: a framework for thinking about teacher empowerment, *American Educational Research Journal,* **28**, pp 737–57

Reavens, R (1982) *The Origin and Growth of Action Learning,* Chartwell-Bratt, Bickley, Kent

Ryle, G (1949) *The Concept of Mind,* Hutchinson, London

Schon, D A (1983) *The Reflective Practitioner,* Basic Books, New York

Schon, D A (1987) *Educating the Reflective Practitioner,* Jossey-Bass, San Francisco, CA

Chapter 12

Mentoring: the art of teaching and learning

Gill Nicholls

The particular focus of this chapter is on mentoring. The issues related to the role of mentoring are discussed followed by models of mentoring that can be used and adopted within the teaching and learning situation.

It is becoming increasingly clear that the quality of education, training and learning will depend crucially on the work of tutors and lecturers in the role of mentor both in the post-compulsory sector of education and in the world of work. Work-based learning has established itself as a means for organizational change and learning in the workforce. What the role is or should be, and what 'mentoring' means, are far less clear. One can go back to classical roots to appreciate what a mentor might be. Homer's wise mentor and his relationship with his protégé Telemachus offers an attractive and thought-provoking model of the teacher and educators of tomorrow. It highlights values such as role model, teacher, an approachable counsellor, a trusted adviser, a challenger, and an encourager, hence mythology suggests that a mentor would appear to need qualities of leadership and wisdom, as well as skills and knowledge.

The term 'mentor' has rapidly become used for a variety of roles and occupations in the last 10 years. Most recently in Britain it has been linked to the guidance given to students in their initial training, particularly in the field of teacher education and in the health service sector. The term has been imported to education from a diversity of other occupational contexts, changed to suit the educational contexts and as a result has caused some confusion as what a mentor is and the role they should play. Jacobi (1991, p169) gives a good account of the variety of context and uses literature to demonstrate her point. She states that:

Although many researchers have attempted to provide concise definitions of mentoring or mentors, definitional diversity continues to characterize the literature. A review of these varying definitions supports Merriam's (1983) contention that: 'The phenomenon of mentoring is not clearly conceptualized, leading to confusion as to just what is being measured or offered as an ingredient in success. Mentoring appears to mean one thing to developmental psychologists, another thing to business people, and a third thing to those in academic settings.'

Wrightsman (1981) also noted the diversity of definitions of mentoring within the psychological research literature and discussed the problems that resulted from the lack of consensus:

With respect to communication between researchers... there is a false sense of consensus, because at a superficial level everyone 'knows' what mentoring is. But closer examination indicates wide variation in operational definitions, leading to conclusions that are limited to the use of particular procedures... The result is that the concept is devalued, because everyone is using it loosely, without precision. (pp3–4; taken from Jacobi, 1991, pp506–08)

These statements make it clear that there is no consensus as to what mentoring or the role of the mentor are. It also begs the question about what mentors in the teaching learning situation can do best. What are the advantages and disadvantages of using a mentoring system? These questions form the basis of the discussion in the second section of this chapter.

Supervision on the other hand brings to mind other concepts and roles for those in educational settings. What do we mean by supervision, what is its role and how is it placed within the educational context?

Mentoring

Concepts and contexts of mentoring

In the introduction to this chapter mentoring was associated with Homer's epic poem, *The Odyssey*. The account given of the mentor suggests first and foremost that mentoring is an intentional process; second, that mentoring is a nurturing process that fosters the growth and development of an individual. Third, mentoring is an insightful process in which the wisdom of the mentor is acquired and applied by the protégé. Fourth, mentoring is a supportive, protective process and finally, mentoring is about being a role model. The above assumptions about the mentor and the role of the mentor need to be placed in the context of modern times and the expectations of mentors and their mentees. It would be very surprising if the classical mentoring relationship that existed between Mentor and Telemachus were readily found in modern organizations. With the passage of time and with the changing demands of the learning situations in which mentoring occurs, adaptation of the mentor–protégé has taken place. In order for a constructive discussion to take place a working definition of mentoring is needed – the type of definition that allows inquiry into the role of a mentor as well as giving insight into how the role of a mentor may be developed. Carmin (1993, pp10–11) gives such a definition:

> Mentoring is a complex, interactive process, occurring between individuals of differing levels of experience and expertise which incorporates interpersonal or psychosocial development, career and/or educational development, and socialization functions into the relationship... To the extent that the parameters of mutuality and comparability exist in the relationship, the potential outcomes of respect, professionalism, collegiality, and role fulfilment will result. Further, the mentoring process occurs in a dynamic relationship within a given milieu. (Cited from Carruthers, 1993)

This definition gives a context and concept of a mentor and the possible skills related to mentoring. The essential attributes of nurturing, role model, the focus on professional/personal development and a caring relationship underpin all aspects of mentoring. Nurturing implies a developmental process in which the mentor is able to recognize the ability, experience, strengths, weaknesses and psychological maturity of the individual that is being nurtured and can provide appropriate developmental and growth tasks that engage the individual. Nurturing also implies providing an environment in which the individual can grow and how best to choose that environment.

Anderson and Shannon (1995) concur with Camin but suggest that the five areas of mentoring need to be contextualized if they are to help in understanding what mentoring is. These include:

- teaching;
- sponsoring;
- encouraging;
- counselling;
- befriending.

For Anderson and Shannon *teaching* means the basic behaviours associated with teaching, including: modelling, informing, conforming/disconforming, prescribing and questioning. In the context of mentoring, these behaviours are guided by principles of adult education. *Sponsoring* means a kind of guarantor, and involves three essential behaviours: protecting, supporting and promoting. *Encouraging* is the process that includes the behaviours of affirming, inspiring and challenging. *Counselling* relates to the problem-solving process and includes behaviours such as listening, probing, clarifying and advising. *Befriending* involves two crucial elements: accepting and relating.

The five identified functions of a mentor should be seen as mutually inclusive, ie a mentor should be able to demonstrate and engage with all five aspects as and when required. A key function is that of an ongoing caring relationship, as Levison *et al* (1978) assert, the essence of mentoring may be found within the kind of relationship that exists between the mentor and protégé rather than in the various roles and functions denoted by the term, 'mentoring'. Figure 12.1 summarizes the elements of mentoring. It highlights that basic to mentoring is a relationship that views the mentor as a role model, who cares and nurtures.

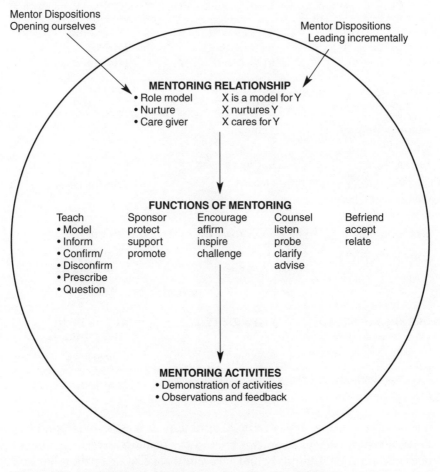

Figure 12.1 Mentoring model, Anderson and Shannon (1995)

Models of mentoring

Anderson's concept of mentoring is based on a caring/nurturing approach. Other models such as that put forward by Rothera *et al* (1995) suggest a process model. In such a model of mentoring the individual who is mentored will in due course, through experiential learning, internalize the values of the mentor, participate in problem solving and eventually become independent of the mentor. The process model identifies characteristics of mentors through considering professional competence, humanistic traits and functions. Table 12.1 shows the classification and ordering of attributes and roles as identified in a process model of mentoring.

Table 12.1 Classification and ordering of attributes and roles related to mentoring

	'Personal' ATTRIBUTES (qualities)	'Positional' ROLES (categories)
Professional Competence	**Humanistic traits**	**Functions**
Constructively critical comments	Approaches	Adviser
Knowledgeable	Encouragement	Object of trust
Conversant with requirements of the role of mentor	Helpful	Role model
Conscientious	Supportive	Assessor
Explaining subject	Gives time willingly Sympathetic Caring	Confidant Counsellor Friend
Gives praise		
INSTRUMENTAL	**EXPRESSIVE**	**REPERTOIRE OF ROLES**
(cognitive)	(affective)	(typology)

Taken from Rothera *et al* (1995)

The key areas of this model relate to attributes such as personal and positional qualities. Within these two broad areas mentors need to be able to demonstrate their legitimacy and credibility, quality of relationship and personality as well as being able to offer constructive criticisms.

The apprenticeship model

This model has its origins in Aristotle whereby some skills, including many that are difficult, complex, and of high moral and cultural value, are best learnt 'by the emulation of experienced practitioners and by supervised practice under guidance' (Hillgate Group, 1989). In the case of such skills they suggest that apprenticeship should take precedence over instruction. The role of the mentor in this model is one where the mentor gives first hand experience in real situations, eg trainee teachers need to experience real students, teaching situations, classroom strategies and subject matter. As Maynard and Furlong (1995, p79) suggest:

> In the early stages of teacher training the purpose of that practical experience is to allow them (trainees) to start from concepts, schemas or scripts of the process of teaching. But in order to begin to 'see', trainees need an interpreter. They need to work alongside a mentor who can explain the significance of what is happening.

In the apprenticeship model the trainee works alongside the mentor taking responsibility for a small part of the work, gradually gaining confidence and skill so that the reliance on the mentor becomes less as the mentee becomes more competent.

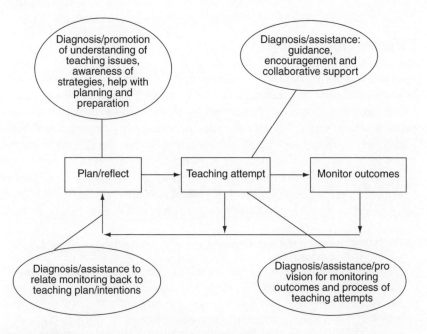

Figure 12.2 Functions of mentoring (Furlong, 1995)

The competency model

This model starts from the premise that the skills that have to be learnt for a given profession are a set of pre-defined competences that each individual has to master and show competence in. The mentor takes on the role of a systematic trainer, observing the trainee, with a predefined observation schedule and then provides feedback to the observed. The mentor can be considered as coaching the trainee on a list of agreed behaviours that form part of the list of competences specified by others, whether this is a professional body or an organization. Increasingly competency models are emerging in many of the professions including the training of nurse practitioners and teachers.

The reflective model

Supporting trainees in the reflective process of learning requires a shift in role by the mentor. To facilitate the process of reflection the mentor needs to be able to move from being a model and instructor to being a co-enquirer. Other aspects of their role as described in the other models may well continue, but in order to promote critical reflection a more equal and open relationship is required. Thinking critically about a process or a set of skills demands an open-mindedness and involves confronting beliefs and values.

Effective mentoring

Effective mentoring is a difficult and demanding task and those performing the role need time and training in order to perfect their mentoring skills. It may be seen as a complementary means to extend training through traditional roles, whether this is higher education, further education or work-based learning. It is increasingly being used as a support and development activity. Mentoring can be thought of as a multi-faceted concept incorporating personal support and the more rigorous notion of professional development leading to enhanced competence. It is possible to conceptualize mentoring in three successively more complex ways. McIntyre (1996, p147) suggests that:

> At its most basic, mentoring involves a personal relationship in which a relative novice is supported by a more experienced peer in coming to terms with a new role. At a second level, mentoring also involves active guidance, teaching and challenging of the protégé by the mentor, who accordingly needs to claim some expertise, wisdom and authority; and this may make it more difficult to maintain the necessary supportive personal relationship. At a third level, mentoring additionally involves the management and implementation of a planned curriculum, tailored to the needs of the individual.

Using mentoring as a form of professional learning

Educational institutions have for a long time been thought of as the place where students learn. It is only more recently however, that educational institutions have begun to be thought of as places where teachers' professional learning can also take place. Teaching is one of the loneliest professions, with teachers rarely having the opportunity to work with a colleague in a collaborative way so that they can learn more about the teaching–learning process. Mentoring in one form or another is a means by which teachers can break down their isolation and support professional learning in ways that focus on the daily work of teachers and teaching learning situations.

Professional learning about teaching is not simply a matter of propositional knowledge or knowing about a range of strategies. Information about new approaches to teaching may come from reading, workshops, conferences, etc, but for information to become understanding in a conscious way needs the individual to interpret and transform that knowledge into practice. Professional learning about teaching is a complex process that requires the putting of knowledge and understanding into practice. Part of the problem of translating teaching ideas into practice lies in the tacit nature of one's knowledge about what one is currently doing in their teaching. Mentoring can play a fundamental role in institutions and organizations that aim to be a professional learning community.

Knowledge about our teaching is in our actions, but the routines and habits of practice mean that in the complex decision-making world of the classroom we do not, as a rule, make our knowledge about teaching and learning explicit to ourselves (Carmin, 1988). In the busy world of teaching there appears no need to perform such a function. However, to make a new teaching approach understood in action terms requires individuals to make their current teaching practice, and the theories and beliefs that underpin such practice, explicit so that new approaches can connect with what the individual knows and holds tacitly.

Mentoring can greatly enhance the process of making tacit knowledge explicit. Through the mentoring process individuals are allowed to interrogate their practice, reflect and then reappraise the values, theories and aspirations attached to their individual theories of learning and teaching. What is interesting to understand here is that meaningful learning and development will not occur simply through being involved as a mentor or mentee in itself; this would not be enough. The kind of relationship individuals have with their own learning and the community in which the mentors perceive themselves to be mentoring for professional learning requires active contribution to knowledge and experience, respecting new and innovative approaches and recognizing as well as understanding how their contribution fits with their own purpose and the support that is expected of them.

The current interest in mentoring for professional development stems from the belief that mentoring, coaching and preceptorship are a way in which individuals and institutions can learn and develop. Mentoring can also be, and is often viewed as a means for assisting change in organizations. So what is it that mentorship offers teaching and learning? In an increasingly diverse and ever-changing educational setting, organizations look to see how change can be sustained from within. Mentoring is regarded as one such system to facilitate professional learning and thus create change.

The central premise of mentoring as a form of professional learning stems from the belief that individuals may best learn through observing, doing, commenting and questioning, rather than simply listening. The intern, initial teacher trainee, or student nurse can be described as someone who is 'initiated into the traditions, habits, rules, cultures and practices of the community they are to join' (Merriam, 1983: p37). Understanding these habits, rules, etc requires the learning of specific language, conventions, knowledge and patterns, the type of learning Schon (1983) calls 'knowing-in-action'. It is from this premise that mentoring of initial and post-service individuals is gaining ground as a significant method for professional learning.

Mentoring for professional learning emphasizes guidance, development and the use and enhancement of individual abilities. Preparation for the role of mentor is key in facilitating the learning of the mentee. The ultimate aim of training and development is to improve teaching and learning environments by adding the necessary value of competence and confidence to both the mentor and the mentee. Mentoring as professional learning can then be considered as a means of enhancing learning competence in such a way that the mentor, mentee and organization acquire specific competence and then apply them with confidence through performance in the workplace.

At the centre of this type of learning is the notion that professional learning requires systematic conversation and dialogue about the actions of teaching and learning, and being able to share experiences of the action. This is a crucial point for the development of understanding regarding the intellectual act of teaching and how this can be enhanced, and as a consequence of such enhancement improves student learning. When a mentor and mentee work in cooperative supportive and trusting environments it is possible to make values and beliefs about teaching and learning explicit, both for the mentor to themself and to their mentees. In this way learning is occurring through critical reflection by both mentor and mentee. The mentor starts to ask the important question, 'Why?'

Asking the 'why' questions allows the mentor to reflect, share practice and collaborate to improve the mentee's practice. Helping the mentee in a systematic way enables the mentee to develop processes by which they can interrogate their own practice through critical reflection and making explicit their tacit actions. Thinking systematically and analytically about what is taught and how it is taught requires commitment and understanding. Equally, understanding and acknowledging one's own abilities, strengths and weaknesses within the teaching–learning environment is a powerful form of professional learning. Through mentoring one can begin to identify and set one's own agenda for learning and development. Sharing practice is fundamental to professional learning.

Professional development through mentoring

Mentoring can be thought of in a variety of ways. Earlier in the chapter I showed how mentoring can be seen as a means of educating an individual through the concept of role model. Later I suggested that mentoring is an excellent tool for professional learning both for the mentor and the mentee through systematic critical reflection. Mentoring can also have a crucial role in staff development, particularly when used in the context of induction. The mentor's role in this context is one of support, normally offered by a more experienced member of staff, whether this is school, college or workplace. Mentoring within induction should be seen as a positive mechanism for developing management, communication and organizational skills. The mentoring process should move through a series of stages whereby the mentor helps to induct the new member of staff or trainee over a period of time, followed by the development of the individual and finally allowing the individual to move forward and taking on the role as friend.

Mentoring in this way is an active relationship built on negotiation and trust. It is not the mentor's role to dominate, judge and be overtly critical. Rather the mentor should develop a relationship built on constructive criticism, support and a relationship that allows for development. In short, mentoring is a process through which knowledge and understanding, skills and abilities, may be passed on to less experienced practitioners (Blandford, 2000).

Teaching and learning and the mentor

This chapter has focused on the variety of roles a mentor may have and the differing context in which those roles may be implemented. Increasingly today in a world where education and training are seen as key mechanisms for enhancing the quality of student learning, workforce skills and organizational change, mentoring has re-emerged as having a fundamental role in the enhancement of learning. Mentoring is seen as a tool by which an individual may learn and understand the ethics, rules and skills of a given community, whether this be teaching, nursing, medicine, or work-based skills. Mentoring is also seen as a powerful tool for professional development and learning for the mentor. It is seen as a means for encouraging systematic critical reflection. It is also a powerful tool to help mentors articulate the skills and knowledge they may have which are frequently tacit. Making explicit what one does and thus allowing someone else to learn from that knowledge is a powerful tool to have; mentoring facilitates the learning of such tools.

References

Anderson, E and Shannon, A (1995) Towards a conceptualization of mentoring, in *Issues in Mentoring,* T Kerry and A Shelton Mayes, Open University Press, Buckingham

Blandford, S (2000) *Managing Professional Development in Schools*, Routledge, London

Carmin, C N (1988) Issues on research on mentoring: definitional and methodological, *International Journal of Mentoring,* **2** (2), pp 9–13

Carmin, S (1993) Definitions of mentoring, in *The Return of the Mentor: Strategies for workplace learning,* Falmer Press, London

Carruthers, J (1993) The principles and practices of mentoring, in *The Return of the Mentor: Strategies for workplace learning,* ed B J Caldwell, Falmer Press, London

Furlong, J (1995) The limits of competence: a cautionary note on circular 9/92, in *Issues in Mentoring,* eds T Kerry and A Shelton Mayes, Routledge, London

Hillgate Group (1989) *Learning to Teach,* The Claridge Press, London

Jacobi, M (1991) Mentoring and undergraduate academic success: a literature review, *Review of Educational Research*, **61** (4), pp 505–32

Levinson, D, Darrow, C, Klein, E, Levinson, M and McKee, B (1978*) Seasons of a Man's Life,* Knopf, New York

Maynard, T and Furlong, J (1995) Learning to teach and models of mentoring, in *Issues in Mentoring,* T Kerry and A Shelton Mayes, Open University Press, Buckingham

McIntyre, D (1996) *Mentors in Schools: Developing the profession of teaching*, Fulton Press, London

Merriam, S (1983) Mentors and protégés: a critical review of the literature, *Adult Education Quarterly*, **33**, pp 161–73

Rothera, M, Hawkins, S and Hendry, J (1995) The role of subject mentor in further education, in *Issues in Mentoring,* T Kerry and A Shelton Mayes, Open University Press, Buckingham

Schon, D (1983) *The Reflective Practice*, Basic Books, New York

Wrightsman, L S (1981) Research methodologies for assessing mentoring, presented at the Annual Conference of the American Psychological Association, Los Angeles (*ERIC Document Reproduction Service No. ED 209 339*)

Chapter 13

The learning community: a design for teaching and learning

Paul Tosey

The term 'learning community' is in common usage but appears to mask significant variations in both theory and practice. This chapter considers how the nature of a learning community in an educational programme is shaped by the context and educational framework within which it operates. Rather than being a fortuitous or taken-for-granted aspect of a programme, such learning communities could, and perhaps should, be designed with as much intentionality as the curriculum itself.

I begin with a brief review of some relevant literature. Then I describe a particular model, that of the 'peer learning community' (Heron, 1974) as applied in the MSc in Change Agent Skills and Strategies at the University of Surrey. Six features characterize this model, and may help to differentiate applications in practice (Tosey and Gregory, 1998).

Finally I consider a number of critical questions about the peer learning community model, presenting these as four 'dilemmas' of learning community practice.

The concept of the learning community

By definition any group of participants on a course or learning programme could be said to constitute a 'learning community'. Thus the 'learning community is something of an umbrella term to describe learning situations where a group of people come together to meet specific and unique learning needs and to share resources and skills' (Burgoyne *et al*, 1978, p29, cited in Reynolds, 1998, p6).

An earlier paper (Tosey and Gregory, 1998) was prompted through discussion with participants on a postgraduate course elsewhere who came to discuss the notion of a learning community. The design and practices of the learning communities on our respective courses were widely and significantly different. Later, in a conference presentation on the theme of the peer learning community, an attendee offered an example of a workshop in which participants, who were unknown to each other, were instructed very early on to 'go and form yourselves into a learning community' – apparently on the assumption that everyone present was familiar with the term, and shared an understanding of what this meant.

There seems a significant difference between denoting a group of students or learners as a 'community' because of proximity alone; expressing a desire or normative intent that a group of learners should behave in a supportive fashion towards each other; and designing and facilitating the development of a community according to explicit principles.

There is relatively little literature specifically on the subject of learning communities in education. In developmental and educational settings, there are contributions from Pedler (1981), Fox (1994) and Critten (1996). There is a growing literature on collaborative and cooperative learning (Cooper and Robinson, 1997), but this is concerned principally with various interactive methods of learning within a given programme context and not with the learning community *per se*. Marsick and Kasl (1997) give a more collective emphasis and call for 'a pedagogy of group learning', which they define as 'when all members perceive themselves as having contributed to a group outcome, and all members of the group can individually explain what the group as a system knows' (p1).

The more recent concept of 'communities of practice' is related, but refers usually to groups defined by common problems or workplaces rather than to intentionally created educational groups. Bitterman (Marsick *et al*, 2000) considers this concept, as well as literature relating to several of the angles developed in this chapter, in a helpful review of literature relating to learning communities. Bitterman's survey relates to a more general concept of learning community, emphasizing a wide range of traditional communities and networks, and not concentrating principally upon formal education.

Peck's (1993) practice of 'Community Building' is a related idea. Reason, with Heron a co-developer of forms of collaborative inquiry, describes the development and functioning of the cooperative inquiry group (1988, pp18–39). This, together with work by the American educator Bill Torbert (Fisher and Torbert, 1995; Torbert, 1991), has influenced peer community practice on the MSc Change Agent Skills and Strategies at Surrey.

The peer learning community

The concept of the peer learning community originated in the work of the Human Potential Research Group (then the Human Potential Research Project). John Heron, the group's founder, intended the peer learning community as an experiential design for a living community. Heron does not offer a specific definition, nor does he attribute the concept to earlier sources, noting instead that this method was being developed through the work of the group at the time. He outlined key principles and implications of the peer learning community as follows (Heron, 1974):

- The notion of an educated person (emphasizing self-direction, self-monitoring and self-correction).
- Participative evaluation of course objectives ('In its basic educational procedures it cultivates the acquisition of self-directing competence in the student') (p2).
- Two fundamental principles of parity: equality of consideration (ie whatever each person brings is equally worthy of consideration) and equality of opportunity (it is equally open to anyone to contribute to or intervene in the course process at any time).

Equally significant principles are:

- Education of the whole person (particularly education of the affect, and the notion of emotional competence – for example, Heron, 1992a; Postle, 1993).
- Political modes of power sharing (particularly a progression from hierarchical to cooperative to autonomous modes of facilitating educative processes within the learning community – Heron, 1992b).
- The peer learning community is not a therapeutic community, yet there is a strong emphasis on personal growth and development. Much attention is given to group process and it is likely to involve a high degree of personal challenge for members, yet humanistic values reflected in ground rules and principles of power sharing distinguish it from, for example, an encounter group (Schutz, 1971) or other therapeutic formats.

The implications of these principles, for Heron, were that:

- The staff–student distinction is secondary to the fundamental parity between human beings.
- Course design is fully consultative.
- Participants are fully involved in evaluation through (a) monitoring of course process as it happens; (b) post-course evaluation which the group

designs, ie generating own criteria; and (c) evolution of methods for monitoring of participant's performance post-course – to give evidence not only of professional/practical competence, but also of self-monitoring.

- Participant resources are an important source of learning.
- Interpersonal learning is a key area (and important for self-awareness and self-monitoring).
- It is necessary to have one or more primary facilitators, especially to facilitate the adoption of the peer principle.

According to this concept a peer community is a process, a dynamic system and not an entity or 'product'. It is probably most accurate to emphasize the process of peer community learning, rather than to reify the notion of a community itself.

The MSc Change Agent Skills and Strategies began in 1992. It is an advanced, experiential course enabling participants to inquire about, and to develop their skills as facilitators of, human processes of change, learning and development in organizational and community contexts. Participants are postgraduates experienced in their field, which may be training, management development, organizational consultancy or a similar area. The course makes significant use of experiential learning and principles of action learning, for example through module by module tasks that involve drawing up learning contracts. There is also extensive, formalized usage of self and peer assessment.

It is a programme that is unusually challenging for both participants and staff. External examiners have attested to both the rarity and the excellence of the course learning community. Participants find the community a rich and diverse experience, bringing them, for example, 'love, support, anxiety, connections and family' (source: student evaluation); it can be intensely supportive and intensely challenging. There is much enthusiasm expressed in evaluations, but not universal satisfaction. When asked about the greatest strengths of the course it is usual for participants to cite, for example, 'The way in which the peer learning community developed', or 'the peer support'. Another participant, though, cited as a weakness, 'lack of emphasis up front on building a learning community where real interpersonal dynamics can be worked with'.

Six characteristics of peer community learning

On the basis of experience of the 10 year-group communities that have formed to date (involving some 200 student participants and with more than 600 days of community practice in face-to-face contact at the time of writing), together with data gathered through course evaluations and feedback sessions, Tosey and Gregory (1998) emphasized five characteristics of 'peer community learning'. To these I have reinstated Heron's dimension of power-sharing because I feel on reflection that it is not adequately covered by any of the other five. This is not to say that other characteristics could not be identified if a full description of peer community learning were attempted. Other factors too, especially critical thinking (eg Brookfield, 1987), would appear crucial to the quality of learning. However, the focus here is on variables relating directly rather indirectly to the learning community. The six characteristics are therefore:

1. personal development;
2. community interaction;
3. facilitation;
4. formal interdependence;
5. power sharing;
6. boundary management.

Personal development

The educational philosophy of the programme emphasizes the education of the whole person: mind, body and spirit. Of especial significance is the education of the affect, in order to develop emotional competence as well as spiritual, intellectual and behavioural competence. Emotional competence refers to:

> A person (who is) able to manage their emotions awarely in terms of the basic skills of control, expression, catharsis and transmutation... In everyday living, emotional competence means being able to spot the stimulation of old emotional pain and to interrupt its displacement into distorted behaviour. (Heron, 1992a, pp131–34)

Effective experiential learning, from this perspective, requires emotional competence. It is an explicit entry criterion for the programme that participants have undergone substantial personal development prior to entry, and it is expected that participants and staff intentionally continue their personal development throughout. (For example, I have been in some form of personal therapy throughout my involvement in the programme.) This, of course, is highly unusual for an academic programme.

Community interaction

A group of participants becomes a community through interaction. This may seem too obvious to state, but it is through interacting and experiencing common events that the community is created. There appear to be parallels between this aspect of the peer learning community and M. Scott Peck's practice of 'Community Building' (Peck, 1993; Sokolov, 1995). This is achieved through engaging in experiential learning together, participating in and being exposed to the group's dynamics, so that each person shows their vulnerability and opens themselves to receive the group's support. While there is focus on task, explicit attention is also given to group psychosocial processes. Group hygiene and blind spots need regular attention. Early on (ie in the initial attendance block) group 'ground rules' (about confidentiality, for example) are addressed explicitly and may be revisited any number of times.

An issue this raises is the extent to which community learning depends on face-to-face interaction. It is a matter for further debate of what a 'virtual' community, mediated by electronic communication, could achieve. While some course communities are of necessity distributed across vast geographical distances, it seems inevitable that the significant attenuation in sensing other's physical and energetic presence represents a limitation.

Facilitation

Skilled facilitation enables the resources individuals bring to be manifested through community interaction, and enables personal development to flourish within the community setting. For the purposes of this chapter, it is worth emphasizing that Heron sees the facilitator as 'an educationalist, not as a therapist', and a role which is relevant to 'experiential learning groups of all kinds... any group in which learning takes place through an active and aware involvement of the whole person – volitional, affective and cognitive – in the group process and its particular focus' (1977, pp1–2). The qualities and skills of facilitators are also emphasized by Bitterman (Marsick *et al*, 2000, p30). (Facilitation is addressed in more detail in Chapter 8 in this volume.)

Skilled facilitation is not the exclusive domain of appointed facilitators (ie the staff team). Every participant is in their own right a potential facilitator of the group's process. Nor is it necessary for an appointed facilitator to be present constantly. Arguably, facilitation can be seen as a function rather than necessarily a role to be occupied by an individual. Therefore an educational procedure, such as the programme's model of self and peer assessment, can provide a structure that is itself a form of facilitation. This relates to Torbert's (1991, p98) notion of a 'liberating structure', which he says is a structure that 'cultivate(s) members' development... while simultaneously generating continual quality improvement'.

Formal interdependence

There are structural aspects to the course design (structural in that they form some of its 'architecture') that support the development of peer community learning. These architectural features create a formal, required interdependence. Formal interdependence (Thompson, 1967) means that participants must rely on and work with each other in order to pass the course, rather than doing so only if they choose.

So, in addition to building a community that has cultural norms of peer support, students are required to participate in learning sets and in self and peer assessment processes. Here individual participants select and negotiate with peers acceptable learning goals and criteria by which their progress is to be judged. The assessment of these learning contracts (Knowles, 1986) is by the individual and a small group of peers. The role of staff in this process is as moderators or quality assurers of the process, not as assessors of the content.

These aspects are enshrined in course regulations, are non-negotiable and are used by peers in each module. The humanistic ground rule of voluntary participation, whereby a student can opt out of any of the learning activities, does not apply to this architecture. It is a hierarchical feature of the course, a contractual aspect that is a condition of joining. In this respect at least we do not claim to have met Heron's criteria for the course design to be fully consultative, or for participants to be fully involved as peers in evaluation.

Power sharing

This dimension relates directly to Heron's writing on political issues of facilitation (for example Heron, 1992b). Heron's view was that ideally a hierarchical mode of facilitation should shift towards cooperation – where negotiation largely replaces direction – and then towards autonomy, where the community becomes more self-sufficient and relinquishes dependence on those with hierarchical status. In the early phase of the peer learning community's life, trained staff facilitators help to keep the boundaries, to model the culture of a learning community, and to teach and coach key processes for interaction.

Heron also makes the point that the politics of facilitation are more complex than this; that what on the surface may appear to be a shift towards autonomy and peerhood may at another level be seen as a more subtle form of hierarchical control. Even if (with reference to Heron's principles), 'the staff-student distinction is secondary to the fundamental parity between human beings', it remains a persistent and figural feature of the programme. I feel I have shared power within face-to-face contact time, but not significantly outside that. The course design is by no means 'fully consultative'. There are feedback mechanisms, and there is consultation about course design and change. But control of the programme design and issues relating to accreditation remain largely the province of the department and institution in which the programme exists – hence my emphasis on the next characteristic, boundary management.

Boundary management

Heron's writing may give the impression that peer learning communities exist, if not in splendid isolation, then at least able to concentrate primarily on what goes on within the community. In higher education a peer learning community exists within an institutional context that does impinge on the life of the community, an aspect also acknowledged by Fox (1994, p251). Clearly the course also acquires its academic legitimacy from that context.

Merely setting up and supporting peer community learning requires a great deal of time and effort. It is unlikely to be effective unless it is integral to the philosophy and design of the course. Ideally the community needs a private space in which to meet where at least furniture can easily be rearranged, and noise can be made without disturbing others. Institutions' financial constraints, standard room booking systems and norms about course design and resources, can all militate against having the necessary inputs.

Miller (1993) identifies boundary management as a vital task in any system's functioning. The interface with the formal 'university system' feels at times like a clash of cultures, at others as a comfortable or necessary structure (perhaps a 'defence against anxiety' in Menzies', 1970, terminology). This in itself is an educative experience. It is a critical aspect of the learning community, and links directly to issues of power sharing. Programme staff necessarily occupy a key 'boundary management' role. The more power is shared with the learning community – including involving members of the community in boundary management – the more conflicts and tensions are likely to appear in that boundary management capacity, and the harder life may feel for staff caught between the community (who are in one sense customers) and the institution (which, for all its espousal of customer-orientation, may remain remarkably immune to customer influence on any matters regarded as 'academic'). But the consequence of staff retaining this role – which in one sense is the easier option for staff – is that participants gauge very easily the extent to which their choice and influence are real.

At Surrey there is also a clear community boundary in that all participants join each community group (ie one annual intake for the course) at its formation, and thereafter it remains a closed group. A closed course group is antithetical to contemporary trends towards fully modularized courses and the principle that students can define their own learning path through a menu of offerings. That this and other features (eg the high quantity of face-to-face contact time) have persisted may be attributed, at least in part, to the course's financial success.

The same issue of boundaries applies to the community's business. Tutors promote the principle of dealing with group issues within the group, as the more that is (or is thought to be) going on 'behind the scenes', or the more the community is disabled from handling community business, the more mystique and lack of safety may be experienced. As tutors we have taken some assessment issues back to the community that in more traditional course groups would be regarded as issues between an individual student and a tutor. A significant issue in community practice is therefore of where the boundaries between individual, community and institutional business lie.

This is not to suggest that strong, as in rigid, boundaries are good. On the contrary, this could result in a self-sealing group. It is a question more of attending to boundaries and their management.

The dimensions of community learning

Table 13.1 summarizes these characteristics and illustrates possible variations between 'high' and 'low' positions on each of them.

The six characteristics yield potentially useful design questions such as the following:

- How compatible is the level of development of participants with the aims and requirements of the programme?
- Where, when and how do participants interact?
- What provisions and resources exist to manage the affective life of the community?
- Through what mechanisms (if any) is there interdependence between participants?
- What is the nature of participants' contract with each other?
- How does the programme interface with its institutional or organizational setting? How is it resourced, sponsored and valued? How will the programme's outcomes be measured and rewarded?

I emphasize two particular consequences if the structure and dynamics of the learning community are not part of the educational agenda of the programme. First, it means that aspects of group process – conflicts, projections, transference and so on – 'go underground' or are dealt with incidentally rather than intentionally. At worst, especially if there is no educational contract to address and resolve such issues, the community's task and content can become significantly contaminated. This is not to say that the

Table 13.1 Dimensions of community learning

Characteristic	High	Low	Notes
Personal development	Interpersonal and group dynamics within the community are (a) more accessible and (b) a potential source of learning (community process integral to educational agenda)	The psychological life of the community is more obscure. More scope for unaddressed projection, transference, conflict etc. Community process separate from the educational agenda	'Education of the affect' is generally weak and under-emphasized in formal education
Community interaction	More human interaction and communication (quantity and channels) suggests eg more likely to enable group 'bonding'; progress through stages of group formation	Lower interaction (less quantity, fewer channels) means community 'field' may be weak or less likely to form; eg consequences of having no opportunity for 'storming'	Interaction limited by factors such as degree of face to face contact; eg attendance time, modularized programme, physical proximity
Facilitation	Skilled facilitation supports processing of dynamics	Absence of facilitation, or facilitator unfamiliar with group process, may increase collusion/blind spots, and focus on programme content not community process	Facilitation is not the exclusive role of programme staff
Formal interdependence	Creates collective tasks, shared interests	Rewards/success remain individual, thus co-operation left more to chance	Higher education has ethos of individual credit for individual effort
Power sharing	Greater degree of community autonomy	Greater degree of dependence, or power limited to hierarchically-defined tasks	'Autonomy' refers to capacity to 'act and influence', within an interdependent system, not to absolute independence
Boundary management	Community has clear identity, and relatively secure existence	Community identity is more diffuse, perhaps transitory, and existence more vulnerable to 'threat' from the environment	'High' boundary management does not imply that rigid or impermeable boundaries are preferable

community cannot or will not be healthy, but that it becomes more reliant on chance. One possible consequence is that the sense of community develops principally and informally among the student group, who come to support each other's 'survival' of the course.

The second consequence is that the enormously rich potential for learning that exists in the interactions and dynamics of the learning community is lost. Current enthusiasm for Goleman's (1996) concept of emotional intelligence might assist renewed interest in such potential. Sadly, however, this not only remains outside the 'comfort zone' of many educators, it is also quite absent, to my knowledge, from any stated set of professional competences for higher education.

In our practice I believe we inevitably trade-off between the risks and the perceived value of the learning community. Working towards the 'high' end of the six characteristics, as I perceive and experience it, increases the tensions involved in operating a formal educational programme. In order to sustain the particular form of learning community I have described, I am fortunate in having colleagues who are equally committed to this approach, and a programme that is successful in terms of public measures such as finance and student evaluations.

Four dilemmas of peer community learning

Since Heron's original paper, the intellectual context has changed from one of liberal education to one of postmodernity and lifelong learning (Jarvis *et al*, 1998). So, alongside discussion of the principles and mechanics of a learning community, there appears to be a need for critical reflection on the concept and practices.

Reynolds (2000), writing about management education, summarizes critiques of 'communitarianism', pertinent here because he identified Heron's notion of the peer learning community as perhaps the clearest application of communitarianism to be found in management education (Reynolds, 1998, p6). He argues that 'community' is a normative concept, and explores the 'darker side' of community, such as its dependence on individual conformity and its 'spurious homogeneity, the devaluing of those it excludes' (1998, p9).

Reynolds and others (eg Cervero and Wilson, 1999) raise more issues than can be addressed here in detail; however the following dilemmas are tentative formulations of implications for this type of educational practice. I do not see these as negating the value of peer community learning, nor do I see them as functional issues that can be resolved technologically or rationally – it would seem trite and dangerously arrogant to claim that such issues can be 'designed out'. They are more like moral and political questions that are present in any learning programme, which can be perceived as suitable for inquiry themselves, and thus further material for learning in any given context.

Authenticity vs social engineering?

One angle of critique challenges the notion that community is a context in which people can be 'authentic', or truly themselves. This risks blindness to the ways in which behaviour within a peer learning community can be seen as highly socialized, subject to norms, rewards and sanctions as in any other social context. For example, the notion of 'authenticity' itself is partial and value-laden (whose definition of authenticity has currency? Authenticity in relation to what?) and claims for its essentiality must be open to question.

People's ability and inclination to 'be authentic' (or perhaps to produce 'authenticity displays' congruent with a discourse of peer community) varies. It may be that those who are more adept find their behaviour rewarded, and perhaps find themselves more highly valued and influential members of the community. Those members who are less adept may experience themselves as disabled, and under pressure to conform. Therefore, acknowledging that I speak as someone who is more comfortable with one-to-one and small group than with large group formats, claims of achieving authenticity and personal growth within the community require critical examination.

Peerhood and pastoral idyll vs difference and conflict?

Another criticism of communitarianism is its idealization of consensus and harmony. Boot and Reynolds (1997, p99) say that:

> group methods can be used in management education and development to bring about cohesion and loyalty, rather than because the method is thought to be the best way to support learning. This is learning of a kind, but more as socialization into organizational values.

Reynolds points out that consensus is often unrealistic, and risks discounting important differences that exist in any social context. He proposes the 'bright lights' of the city as an alternative to the pastoral metaphor invoked by notions of harmony.

Boot and Reynolds (1997, p90) note the:

> disquiet among critical educators and more politicized professionals that the emphasis on openness, trust and self-disclosure in some versions of group-based training serves to obscure realities of power, difference and the conflicts of interest which characterize the workplace.

One risk here is that issues of power, particularly the power of the facilitator, become subsumed under a belief that the attainment of individual autonomy places all participants on an equal footing. In a course in which personal development is a significant strand, the power of facilitators who may be expert in psychotherapeutic as well as educational practices seems to be of great importance. To what extent, for example, are operational models of 'psychological health' made available for explicit critique, rather than being mobilized tacitly?

Reynolds (1998, p17) also highlights potential limitations of using the community itself as a method of critical reflection on community life:

> Another key aspect of the design is periodic reviews in which tutors and partic-
> ipants reflect on their experience of the learning community as it develops.
> The usual forum for this – evoking the 'pastoral' version of community – is a
> face-to-face meeting of all the students and tutors. This can work well as a
> forum for review, but it is undoubtedly vulnerable to pressures to conformity,
> inequality of opportunity to contribute and the risks of less powerful individ-
> uals or groups becoming marginalized.

Reading this is challenging as it describes well the 'community meeting format' used on the programme! This indicates a need both for scepticism towards the value of consensus, and also for reflexivity on the capability of the community to review and critique itself.

Voluntarism vs interdependence?

Another potential myth of communitarianism is that of individualism – that we are in principle independent human beings who participate voluntarily in social structures. Ironically, this seems more the case on traditional educational courses where assessment is of individual performance. The peer learning community, as noted above, has intentional interdependencies.

Another layer of this issue is the belief – perhaps it could be labelled a humanistic fallacy – that social behaviour is an aggregate of freely chosen individual behaviours. Individual behaviours may be psychologically distressed; therefore if people 'develop' by becoming distress free, there remain no further barriers to distress-free social interaction. This risks ignoring the ways in which our identities and behaviour are derived from social structures and settings.

Elitism vs universality

Is a peer learning community (as defined here) the exclusive province of elite groups of people who are committed to, and experienced in, their personal development? Writers such as Reason (1988) and Torbert (1991) argue that such a level of personal awareness and responsibility represents a significant capability of participants in a learning community or learning organization, and that the proportion of participants with well-developed skills is likely to be critical for the effectiveness of the community as a whole.

In principle, developmental, experiential learning can benefit any group of learners. Torbert (1991) gives the example of his use of liberating structures with business undergraduates in his own institution. To propose that peer community learning could only be achieved in a format comparable to that of our programme would ignore its extreme cultural peculiarity. The format is particular to its social and cultural context and would probably be less effective if transplanted elsewhere. Indeed both the characteristics and these four 'dilemmas' are contextual, not universal.

Conclusion

These dilemmas emphasize that learning communities, and the role of the facilitator, have political and moral dimensions. In negotiating these dilemmas I perceive a need to steer between the extremes of a romantic, politically naïve humanism (as may be represented by 'communitarianism'), and a more stark political intellectualism that neglects emotional competence and the human heart.

The six characteristics together with the four dilemmas may be used as criteria for self-assessment in any learning community. Thus participants could rate the community on the extent to which the characteristics are intended in the programme design, and represented in practice.

The four dilemmas provide a set of qualitative questions for inquiry, posing questions of, 'how do we as a community believe we should handle these dilemmas?' and, 'how do we handle these dilemmas in practice?'

Acknowledgements

I acknowledge the contribution of participants on the MSc Change Agent Skills and Strategies peer learning communities, and that of academic colleagues past and present, particularly Josie Gregory who co-authored an earlier paper on this subject.

Note

This chapter is a revised and extended version of a previously published paper, Tosey (1999).

References

Boot, R and Reynolds, M (1997) Groups, group work and beyond, in *Management Learning: Integrating perspectives in theory and practice,* eds J Burgoyne and M Reynolds, Sage, London

Brookfield, S (1987) *Developing Critical Thinkers,* Open University Press, Buckingham

Cervero, R and Wilson, A (1999) Beyond learner-centred practice: adult education, power and society, *Canadian Journal for the Study of Adult Education,* **13** (2), pp 27–38

Cooper, J and Robinson, P (1997) Small-group instruction: an annotated bibliography of science, mathematics, engineering and technology resources in higher education, Occasional Paper no 6, National Institute for Science Education, University of Wisconsin-Madison

Critten, P (1996) A learning community in the making: Middlesex University's new MA in personal and organizational development, *The Learning Organization,* **3** (5), pp 14–17

Fisher, D and Torbert, W R (1995) *Personal and Organizational Transformation,* McGraw-Hill, Maidenhead

Fox, S (1994) Towards a learning community model in graduate management education, *Management Learning,* **25** (2), pp 249–62

Goleman, D (1996) *Emotional Intelligence,* Bloomsbury, London

Heron, J (1974) *The Concept of a Peer Learning Community,* Human Potential Research Project, University of Surrey, Guildford

Heron, J (1977) *Dimensions of Facilitator Style,* Human Potential Research Project, University of Surrey, Guildford

Heron, J (1992a) *Feeling and Personhood: Psychology in another key,* Sage, London

Heron, J (1992b) The politics of facilitation, in *Empowerment Through Experiential Learning: Exploration of good practice,* eds J Mulligan and C Griffin, Kogan Page, London

Jarvis, P, Holford, J and Griffin, C (1998) *The Theory and Practice of Learning,* Kogan Page, London

Knowles, M S (1986) *Using Learning Contracts,* Jossey-Bass, San Francisco, CA

Marsick, V and Kasl, E (1997) Factors that affect the epistemology of group learning: a research-based analysis, paper presented at the 1997 AERC conference, available online at: http//:www.edst.educ.ubc.ca.aerc/1997/9/marsick.htm

Marsick, V, Bitterman, J and Van der Veen, R (2000) From the learning organization to learning communities toward a learning society, ERIC Clearinghouse on Adult, Career, and Vocational Education, Information Series no. 382, Ohio State University

Menzies, I (1970) *The Functioning of Social Systems as a Defence against Anxiety,* Paper of the Tavistock Institute of Public Relations, London

Miller, E (1993) *From Dependency to Autonomy: Studies in organization and change,* Free Association Books, London

Peck, M (1993) *A World Waiting to be Born,* Rider, London

Pedler, M (1981) Developing the learning community, in *Management Self-Development: Concepts and practices,* T Boydell and M Pedler, Gower, Aldershot

Postle, D (1993) Putting the heart back into learning, in *Using Experience for Learning,* D Boud, R Cohen and D Walker, The Society for Research into Higher Education and Open University Press, Buckingham

Reason, P (ed) (1988) *Human Inquiry In Action: Developments in new paradigm research,* Sage, London

Reynolds, M (1998) Bright lights and the pastoral idyll: social theories underlying management education methodologies, paper presented at conference on 'Emergent Fields in Management: Connecting Learning and Critique', University of Leeds, July

Reynolds, M (2000) Bright lights and the pastoral idyll: ideas of community underlying management education methodologies, *Management Learning*, **31** (1), pp 67–81

Schutz, W C (1971) *Joy: Expanding human awareness*, Souvenir Press, London

Sokolov, I (1995) Taking M Scott Peck's community building into organizations, *Organizations and People*, **2** (1), pp 12–16

Thompson, J D (1967) *Organizations in Action*, McGraw-Hill, New York

Torbert, W (1991) *The Power of Balance*, Sage, Newbury Park, CA

Tosey, P (1999) The peer learning community: a context for action learning, *Journal of Management Decision*, **37** (5), pp 403–10

Tosey, P and Gregory, J (1998) The peer learning community in higher education: reflections on practice, *Innovations in Education and Training International*, **35** (1), pp 74–81

Chapter 14

Assessment in post-compulsory education

Linda Merricks

Assessment is vital to any teaching and learning. Minimally, students and teachers need to know that a required standard has been reached for particular awards. More importantly, without adequate information about what has or has not been learnt, whether subject knowledge or skills, students cannot progress, teachers cannot assess their own teaching and institutions cannot have confidence in the awards they offer.

Assessment is also a moral activity. As Knight (1995, p14) claimed:

> What we choose to assess and how shows quite starkly what we value… Assessment systems advantage some learners and disadvantage others… effective assessment depends upon having a view of what it is that we are trying to do in a programme and hence of what we ought to assess.

This is echoed by Boud (1995, p35) who wrote, 'Assessment acts as a mechanism to control students that is far more pervasive and insidious than most staff would be prepared to acknowledge.' The ideological aspects of assessment are unavoidable. Therefore they should be recognized by all teachers and consideration of the effects of assessment made an element in the design of curricula.

Assessment is not simple. As the government's Lifelong Learning policies push towards a learning society, students in post-compulsory education are now diverse, of different ages and very different backgrounds. They also have different purposes for learning. Some study for interest, while skills and vocational learning is becoming more necessary in response to economic changes in the workplace. To achieve the new targets for employment in the various regions more people and different socio-economic and age groups will need to develop new skills or find new ways of using those they have. Modes of learning reflect this diversity of students and purpose. Full- or part-time, face-to-face or distance learning, the use of books, the Web, television and discussion are amongst the myriad ways of learning available to students. Courses too can be more complicated now. They cater for the range of students by offering different levels of award, different speed of progress and different kind of subjects, sometimes in new combinations. Combined, major/minor, interdisciplinary, and work-based learning are merely a selection. There is also an array of institutions to provide this learning. From sixth form colleges, adult education, continuing education, the WEA, FE colleges, universities, trade unions through to the University of the Third Age, there is an enormous choice. However, as a result of this multiplicity of provision and learners, assessing need and progress has become more complex.

Research and discussions during the last 10 years have led to an emphasis on assessment as an essential part of teaching and learning. In 1991/2 the Academic Audit Unit said very little about assessment in its reports of visits to universities and in a number of instances found nothing to report. Since then assessment has become more important as a measurement of the quality of provision in institutions. For example, the latest Quality Assurance Agency (QAA) Handbook, for 2001, contains a separate 'Code of Practice for the Assessment of Students', which will be one of the tools for the new academic review procedures. Issued in January 2001 is one of the three 'standard codes', together with 'Programme Approval, Monitoring and Review' and 'External Examining', which will be used by QAA to measure academic standards in the new methodology.

This degree of change in perceptions of the importance and role of assessment is not yet found in the FE sector where regular inspections and the verification role of GCSE or bodies like the City & Guilds have demanded particular modes of assessment, and will continue to do so for the near future at least. These have tended to concentrate on the achievement of specific learning as set out in the curriculum. However, some changes in vocational education now affecting the sector have been developed in the relatively new and fast growing work-based learning programmes. Because of the lack of tradition, these programmes have started almost from scratch and an important part of their progress has been a careful examination of the role and processes of assessment. They also work within an ethos of students' involvement in all aspects of their learning, and this naturally highlights assessment.

Why assess?

Assessment takes place for a number of reasons, for a number of different audiences – students, tutors, mentors, employers, and educational systems –

the management bodies of teaching institutions, government bodies and funding councils. Increasingly assessment is also seen as a vital part of the quality assurance processes. It has many different purposes, takes many different forms, has different levels of reliability and validity, takes place at different points in the learner's career and has findings communicated in different ways. These can be summarized as follows:

- students expect it and are motivated by it;
- to diagnose learning needs – especially important for mature students and adults, to select for next educational stage or work;
- to certificate learning;
- to provide feedback;
- to help remedy mistakes;
- to help with option choice and selection;
- to help diagnose faults;
- to provide a performance indicator for students and enable final award grading;
- to ensure that the learning outcomes for different awards and programmes are met;
- to provide a performance indicator for staff;
- to provide a performance indicator for course and institution;
- we have always done it.

Assessment is learning

Assessment is basic to learning: to students' learning; to academics learning about becoming better teachers and facilitators; to systems learning about what they are doing well and less well. However, as the QAA attempt shows, the difficulty lies in defining how this might be accomplished. Unless there are some principles for measuring what has been achieved by all teachers and learners, learning from the experience will be negligible.

The primary purpose of assessment is to ensure that the learning outcomes of any course or programme are achieved, and sometimes to measure the level of that achievement. In order to accomplish this deceptively simple aim, a number of stages are necessary:

- The learning outcomes, both in terms of subject knowledge and of skills and competences, must be clearly defined at the curriculum development stage.
- The methods of assessing *all* these should be established at this point and forms of assessment established and questions about whether self or peer assessment would be appropriate, or the need for formal examination should be asked and answered.

- The uses of the results of the assessment also need to be considered here. Formative assessment, designed to provide students with feedback on their work, can be used very differently from summative assessment, whose primary function is to measure achievement towards the award of grades.
- The contribution to learning should also be considered. Mere repetition of information from memory rarely encourages learning. More useful aims might be to encourage team-work, as well as developing specific skills in a subject.
- Finally, the students must be involved in the process. The teacher should explain the assessment processes early in the course to ensure students understand what is required of them and then explain the aims of each assessment task. Many research projects have shown that this stage is rarely completed and that students are left to guess the intentions of any task, hoping that they are right. Criteria for marking and grading should also be clear and comprehensible. The mystery of B+ + might amuse the teacher, but it can be totally obscure to the learner.

Assessment contributes to the learning process only when learners and teachers share an understanding of the purposes of the assessment and the criteria for marking and grading.

Teaching through assessment

One way in which understanding the processes of assessment can be clarified is through consideration of the purposes of the task. A convenient way of doing this is by using the summative/formative/ipsative forms.

Summative assessment, as its name suggests, is primarily designed to provide a description of what has been achieved and includes end of course assessment. It often results in grading of this achievement, which will indicate to learners, teachers, and outsiders, for example employers, the level of that achievement. Because of this, reliability of the process, including marking and communication of the results, is an essential feature. It is clearly desirable that there is parity between first class degrees awarded by different institutions and that this can be measured. To ensure the validity of the results, the marking should be criterion-referenced against pre-determined criteria. Comparison with other students' work is not necessary in this context, but in some forms of examination this is an essential part of the allocation of grades – the grades are norm-referenced, not criterion-referenced. Feedback to the learner beyond the grade awarded is not necessarily a part of this process.

The use of summative assessment in this unmediated form is coming under question. Students accustomed to public examination systems do not expect feedback on their examination papers, but new learners, especially perhaps adults, recognize that little learning can take place without comments on their practice. Teachers are now beginning to question the whole process, but the climate of rising student numbers makes any change that will increase workloads unlikely to be popular. Immediately, it is important that the process of assessment is transparent and clearly explained to all concerned. Students expecting a norm-referenced grade may be disappointed when another measurement is used.

The judgement of reliability depends on the purpose of the assessment. The purpose of formative assessment is to provide an estimate of achievement, which is principally designed to help in the learning process. It often takes the form of pieces of work in addition to those demanded by summative assessment, but can also be a part of continual assessment. As the primary purpose of formative assessment is to be a part of the learning process it does not necessarily measure achievement with the award of a grade, although 'informal' and unrecorded grades are often given to indicate the level of achievement. Thus, reliability is not an essential issue as the comparison is with earlier learning, not a grade that compares with other learners.

The essential part of the process is to identify strengths and weaknesses in the learner's work so that improvements can be made and gaps in knowledge or skills filled. In this case, feedback is essential and should identify the level of knowledge of the subject, the presentation of the work and the competences demonstrated in generic skills. The assessment of these areas may refer to both criteria-referenced and norm-referenced levels. The process here needs to be both valid and reliable, but as with all formative assessment, the process must reflect the learner's achievement and provide guidance for the future.

Ipsative assessment measures personal achievement and is designed to provide information for individual learners so they can check their own achievement. It must be criterion-referenced but need not be assessed by any outsider. The benchmark of achievement is oneself. It can be especially useful in some distance learning programmes where the learners can keep a note of their understanding and knowledge on a regular basis.

An additional complication is that formative and summative assessments are not necessarily mutually exclusive. One assessment can have a dual purpose and often does in continual assessment. The distinctions between the two are, in any case, not always clear. This is less important than ensuring that the assessment during the whole course of study achieves its prime purpose, which is to ensure that students achieve the outcomes of the course. To this end, and to overcome some of these difficulties of explanation, as Brown and Knight (1994, p15) have pointed out, 'the notion of reliability in HE assessment is being displaced by the concept of quality assurance in assessment'.

Who should assess?

Traditionally, teachers have assessed students. They have set the assessment tasks, explained what is required and then marked the results. Assessments have usually been defined in curricula but, especially in HE, have tended towards standard forms of 'the essay' or the 'seminar presentation'. As long as the majority of students came from traditional backgrounds this was adequate and tended to work well. However, with the increasing numbers of non-traditional learners there is the need for change towards more varied and more explicit forms of assessment. There has also been a difficulty with standardization and parity across courses and subjects. University lecturers have traditionally expected a degree of autonomy in their teaching and have relied on external examiners and examination boards for any regulation. This process has been changed within the HE sector by a number of Quality Assurance Agency initiatives including the publication of subject benchmark statements during the last year which describe the learning outcomes for individual subjects. The impact of these benchmarks has yet to be felt, but the intention is some standardization of learning outcomes.

The learners' role has been merely to complete the task and await a grade. With the new complex mix of learners, demands for more ownership of the process have been growing and this has coincided with the realization that students can learn more, and differently, from peer and self-assessment. It has also coincided with teachers finding they have less time for the marking of assessments, especially if formative assessment is developed as a coherent part of the curriculum.

Self-assessment and peer-assessment can lead to greater ownership of learning and to greater motivation by learners. It 'is fundamental to all aspects of learning. Learning is an active endeavour and thus it is only the learner who can learn and implement decisions about his or her own learning: all other forms of assessment are therefore subordinate to it (Brown and Knight, 1994: p51)'. When successfully implemented, it:

- allows sharing of learning;
- leads to autonomous learners;
- leads to more competent learners;

- promotes reflective students, who might become lifelong learners;
- develops skills – team work, group work leadership, problem solving.

Self and peer assessment can work with a number of different assessment methods. For example, a record of achievement or Personal Statement of Learning ask students to reflect on their learning through a course of study and to ask themselves to what extent they have achieved the learning outcomes of the course. They might also ask for an evaluation of the course itself and the teaching. Consideration of these questions demands reflection on the course itself and the learning that has taken place.

Questions about future study can also require consideration of the generic learning outcomes in addition to the subject-based achievement. Similarly, portfolios of work assembled during the course comprising learning journals and other materials demand careful assessing of what is being learnt. When the portfolio comprises an ongoing part of the whole course it can also help to reveal shortcomings in learning, which can be rectified before any summative assessment. Self-assessment forms require rather different skills for their completion. They are most useful when used in conjunction with clear criteria and examples of good and bad pieces of work so that learners can examine their own or their peer's practice and offer comments on the resulting assessment.

However, learners often find it difficult to grade their own work and can both under- and over-estimate their achievement. In view of this, self-grading should be used with caution, especially with returners to learning whose confidence in their abilities and understanding of what is required may need development. There are other limitations to the use of self and peer assessment which can be very useful as a means of persuading the group to ask who actually contributed what to the project, but it can be spoilt by strong personalities in the group. Friends can over-estimate each other's achievement while enemies can under-estimate. There may be caution about actually saying that one member did very little. Similar difficulties can arise with other forms of peer-assessment and versions of 'I'll scratch your back if you scratch mine' can arise so that grades are inflated.

There is also resistance to the process. Outside agencies can distrust it, arguing that only trained teachers can adequately assess the achievement of learners, thus ignoring the learning that takes place as a part of the assessment. Perhaps more surprisingly, learners themselves can react against it: they also argue that they are not able to assess their achievement. This can be overcome only by demonstration and persuasion and, as in all other kinds of assessment, making the process and its expected outcomes clear to all concerned. Confidence in self and peer assessment will normally grow once it is a usual apart of the assessment strategies.

Finally, it should be clear to everyone concerned that peer or self-assessment can only be a part of the whole. They are not normally used for summative assessments and almost never for graded examinations. They play a part, alongside teacher assessed work, in providing varied learning for self-confident reflective learners.

Forms of assessment

There are almost as many forms of assessment as there are teachers and learners. A number have already been mentioned. They vary from traditional, unseen, timed examinations whose grade contributes directly to a final award to self-assessed learning journals, from seminar papers or book reviews to formal essays with full academic references. They can be written, oral or pictorial. With the use of IT their range will increase. What the forms have in common is that they should be designed as a coherent part of the curriculum. They should each be designed to test specific learning outcomes, and all the learning outcomes of the course, subject-specific and generic, should be assessed. This full coverage may be ascertained by a curriculum map or less formally by some kind of checklist, but care should be taken that coverage of the outcomes can be demonstrated by teachers and learners. Finally, the kind of outcome of the assessment, grades or developmental, needs consideration in the context of the whole programme of learning.

Where there are progression routes, as through a three-year degree programme, there might be learning outcomes from the whole programme, as in definitions of graduateness. There is a need for the learning associated with these outcomes to be assessed as well as those of the individual modules.

There also might be demands from the awarding bodies for some kinds of assessment to measure the achievement of specific learning outcomes. As already described, HE institutions have specific outcomes associated with degrees. Further education and work-based learning programmes normally have clear vocational aims and objectives and lead to externally referenced awards. These might be NVQs with specific, already agreed learning outcomes in the form of competences which need to be achieved. The outcomes for work-based learning programmes are usually negotiated with employers and learners at the outset. Like vocational awards, GCSE students need to demonstrate that they have completed a national curriculum, which must be marked against nationally agreed criteria, with norm-referenced grades awarded on the basis of all students' achievement.

In contrast, HE tends to be largely autonomous with external examiners providing the external references. This form of peer review means that as a result assessment tends to be valid. Parity is achieved across an institution or subject, but it is not necessarily reliable across the sector. Subject benchmarks and the work of the QAA are attempts to address these issues without going so far as the FE/GCSE models.

Adult continuing education has traditionally been more flexible than any of these. However, the moves towards certification and accreditation since the changes in funding resulting from the 1992 Further and Higher Education Act mean that assessment here is coming under increasing scrutiny. The difficulty lies in retaining flexible processes designed to meet the needs of numbers of students with very different abilities and experiences while including summative assessments on which judgement of overall achievement can be made. In addition, these results must measure reliably against those of other HE institutions.

What is assessed?

The simple answer to this question should be learning – of the student, the teacher and the institution. The essential question to be asked of the process should be whether or not the learning outcomes of the course of study, which should be of two kinds, have been successfully achieved. Conventionally, assessment has concentrated on one part of the first, which is knowledge of a subject or discipline. This can be assessed as just a question of memory and the learner can be asked to rehearse that learning. While formative assessments during a course may be used to test memory in this way it is now more usual to also assess understanding of the subject through some kind of explanation of process either in written form, in essay or examination, or verbally in class presentation or discussion.

Generic competences and skills appropriate to the subject areas should also be assessed. As described above, this may be achieved through self-assessment, but the teacher as well as the student should record the achievement of an acceptable level. In some courses these skills are specifically assessed and the learning outcomes refer to them, for example, the ability to analyse and synthesize the results of some limited research. In others, the achievement of generic skills is assumed to be a part of the programme and there is an expectation that students who cannot adequately write an essay will fail. The latter procedure is tending to be phased out; as in many other instances, the changing student body demands more clarity and guidance.

However, as well as the learning of the students, the teaching of the course should also be assessed. If the majority of learners have not achieved the learning outcomes of the course then it is likely that there are problems with the teaching, either in the presentation of the materials or in the design of the course. In the most serious cases, some kind of institutional failure might be the cause. It is possible, but less likely to raise comment, that too high grades might lead to the same questions.

Quality assurance and verification of assessment

This is increasingly important and a number of external agencies are involved at course and institutional levels. At present, HE institutions are relatively autonomous with their own award-giving powers, but QAA does act as an assessor of the institution's teaching and learning procedures. The FE sector tends to be more regulated by outside stakeholders and other external agencies, most notably OFSTED and, from this year, the Adult Learning Inspectorate.

Increasing differences between learners and their needs results in the necessity for regulation by both internal and external bodies. All quality assurance agencies recognize the importance of this, but also the impossibility of standardization across institutions and sectors. The various level descriptors and subject benchmarks show the beginnings of attempts to provide a level of standardization, but although some progress has been made within the various sectors, there is little advancement across post-compulsory education as a whole. At present, there are different external agencies and methodologies within and across the various parts of the whole.

External verification of results takes place at course level primarily in further education. GCSE and GCE courses normally have appointed external examiners to mark examination scripts and to check samples of teacher-assessed work. For NVQ and GNVQ programmes external verifiers are appointed by the awarding body, RSA, Edexcel or City & Guilds, to confirm that assessment procedures are appropriate and that work is marked to national standards. The validating HE institution normally checks degrees taught in further education colleges.

Awards by higher education institutions are more autonomous. They have normally been subject to external scrutiny only by external examiners. There are exceptions to this, primarily in vocationally-based programmes where the professional body acts as an additional verifier of the course and the results; for example, psychology degrees are verified by the British Psychological Society. However, the external examiner system is becoming more difficult. As workloads increase there is a growing reluctance to fulfil this role by academics in the sector. Simultaneously, there is the development of auditing by external agencies that produce tools by which HE assessments can be measured.

In addition to these procedures, there is increasing scrutiny from the quality assurance bodies, although in HE this tends to concentrate on process not results of the process. The Quality Assurance Agency for higher education is responsible for auditing the quality of all HE teaching. It has also been responsible for the production of subject Benchmarks. OFSTED, with the Adult Learning Inspectorate, has increasing responsibility for much FE work and will be responsible for all non-higher education post-compulsory learning. In addition, the Further Education National Training Organization has set professional standards in education and teaching.

The Quality Assurance Agency code of practice for assessment sets out guidelines for all HE institutions. The attitude of the Agency is encapsulated in their *Precept 2:* 'The principles, procedures and processes of all assessment should be explicit, valid and reliable' (QAA, 2000). However, the effect of this publication may be disappointing. Despite a very positive introduction, the code itself emphasizes procedures and measurement. The Introduction describes assessment as 'a generic term for a set of processes that measure the outcomes of students' learning, in terms of knowledge acquired, under-standing developed, and skills gained'. Specifically, the many purposes of assessment include:

- the means by which students are graded, passed or failed;
- the basis for decisions on whether students are ready to proceed:
- the way students obtain feedback on their learning and help them improve their performance;
- enabling staff to evaluate the effectiveness of their teaching.

The Code continues, 'Assessment plays a significant role in the learning experience of students', and goes on to describe the different forms of assessment as diagnostic, formative or summative. At this point though, the Agency quietly demonstrates the difficulties of measuring the compli-cated view of assessment it has set out. The Introduction concludes, 'The code of practice assumes that these understandings of the nature and purpose of assessment are broadly accepted and implemented by higher education institutions.' The precepts that follow then concentrate on the 'measurable' aspects of assessment procedures and emphasize that assess-ment should demonstrate the achievement of learning outcomes. Even here, the Agency explains 'It is not the intention of the Agency to prescribe specific ways of implementing the precepts set out below.' An opportunity to examine the various possible methods of assessment and some kind of account of best practice in the sector seems to have been lost. The valuable work at a number of conferences, in books and the work of the Staff and Educational Development Association which have all contributed to changes in the view of assessment in HE seem to be judged too complicated to assess.

Implications

The implications of the changes now taking place are that the results of assessment are designed more closely to emphasize the learning that can be achieved. This learning is set out more clearly, in terms of learning outcomes of any course and how those outcomes will be assessed. However, there is a need for staff development if full advantage is to be taken of all the possibilities, and there is a demand for increased staff time, at least in the development phase. If these can be met, then assessment can become a truly useful part of learning and teaching, not just the bugbear of examinations.

References

Boud, D (1995) Assessment and learning: contradictory or complementary?, in *Assessment for Learning in Higher Education*, ed P Knight, Kogan Page, London

Brown, S and Knight, P (1994) *Assessing Learners in Higher Education*, Kogan Page, London

Knight, P (ed) (1995) *Assessment for Learning in Higher Education*, Kogan Page, London

QAA (2001) *Code of Practice for the Assurance of Academic Quality and Standards in Higher Education. Section 6: Assessment of Students,* The Quality Assurance Agency for Higher Education, London

Further reading

Boud, D (1990) *Implementing Student Self-Assessment*, Higher Education Research and Development Association of Australasia, Sydney

Chapter 15

Assessment of experiential learning in higher education

Josie Gregory

In this chapter I intend to illustrate some key educational processes involved in self and peer assessment and indicate some of the reasons why higher education has been slow to adopt this method of reflective learning for HE students. I consider the extent to which self and peer assessment, particularly of experiential learning can meet its developmental and emancipatory aims (Heron, 1974) within a formal academic structure. Thus the practice of self and peer assessment is compared to the philosophy of the education of adults (Knowles, 1990) and Torbert's (1991) concept of a 'liberating structure'. Self and peer assessment does possess the potential to operate as a liberating structure, and so contribute to emancipatory education (Habermas, 1972). At the same time there are various pressures within a higher education setting that may militate against this, and which may lead to self and peer assessment being operated in impoverished forms. I want to argue that this represents a failure to apply knowledge about adult learning within higher education, and an example of educational institutions as non-learning organizations.

Self and peer assessment: educational theory and intentions

The literature on self and peer assessment within professional education stretches back more than 30 years (Bond 1988; Heron, 1979; Kilty, 1978), yet only attracted serious study and application to learning and academic grading since the late 1980s (Boud, 1989, 1995; Ford, 1997). The form of self and peer group assessment discussed in this chapter was developed through experiential inquiry with groups of professionals in the medical, nursing and public service fields, before gradually extending to a formal Masters programme, where it is an integral part of the teaching and assessment processes (The MSc in Change Agent Skills and Strategies). As progressive liberal educators seeking congruence between our philosophical values of individual liberation and empowerment within social and hierarchical systems, we use educational methodologies aimed at keeping the power of 'knowing thyself' (Baume and Baume, 1986, p65) with the individual.

Heron (1974) stated that an educated person is one who is self-directing, self-monitoring and self-correcting. This premise continues to be used to benchmark what should constitute 'being educated' in higher education. The link between Heron's definition and Fisher and Torbert's (1995, p7) 'liberating structures' is not difficult to see, for:

> A liberating structure is a type of organizing that is productive and at the same time educates its members towards self-correcting awareness. Engaging in a process of mutual self-correction requires ongoing effort among participants to recognize and correct errors and incongruities in the midst of action, an effort we find to be the primary requirement for continual quality improvement.

'Mutual self-correcting' in Fisher and Torbert's statement is the linchpin of self and peer assessment. The values of self-direction, that is, believing that human beings have choice, and with that, responsibility, that they are intentional, aim at goals, and are aware that they cause future events and seek meaning, value and creativity (AHPP, 1998, p15) are all reflected in the self and peer assessment process. Heron (1994) writes that: 'Using self and peer assessment combines three strands: (1) it is a form of professional development, (2) it is an advanced continuing educational procedure; and (3) it is an action research inquiry into professional practice'. These three strands are essential in professional development and offer an educational rationale for the inclusion of this form of self and peer assessment on the MSc course. Self-assessment is therefore a teaching and learning activity as well as an assessment practice for accreditation purposes, a point confirmed by Boud (1995). He documents very clearly the conflicting purposes of assessment in higher education. One purpose is 'to improve the quality of learning' through formative feedback from the tutor, and 'the other concerns the accreditation of knowledge or performance' (p37), that is, summative assessment. Boud goes on to say that formative assessment is intended to facilitate the learner, helping him or her to improve performance, while the latter is 'for the record', that is, it serves the academic institution and the external world. It certifies competence to certain standards and provides for easier selection in the workplace.

The theoretical rationale for self and peer assessment has been suggested already through the philosophy of self-directed adult learners (Knowles,

1990), and under the principles of the Peer Learning Community (Heron, 1974; Tosey and Gregory, 1998; Chapter 13 in this volume) and on the notion of the educated person. Self and peer assessment in principle are supported by a number of educational theorists. The modern philosophical base, which gave rise to humanistic educational thinking during the 1950s and 1960s, has its origin in progressive education (Dewey, 1916). This link between Dewey's educational philosophy, humanistic psychology and the education of adults is discussed in an earlier chapter of this volume.

Dewey's educational philosophy, with the use of Kolb's (1984) and Heron's (1989) experiential learning cycles, provides the basis for a reflective self-assessment cycle used as part of the self and peer group assessment processes. Rogers' injunction that: 'The only man who is educated is the man who has learnt to learn' (Rogers, 1983, p120) forms the mandate for developing learning-to-learn skills, the most important of which is accurate self-assessment (Heron, 1974; Jarvis, 1995). This facilitation of learning has been the challenge of adult education for the past 30 years and philosophically has been the main change in professional educational thinking and direction over the same period (Jarvis, 1995).

Torbert (1991, p41) refers to a 'liberating structure' under the framework of a paradigm of 'just action'. This he states is an educational process. In summary, parts of these liberating structures include 'a cultivation of awareness that embraces the realms of the intuitive whole, the rational strategy, plan or rules, congruent action, and outcomes and that observes and corrects errors and incongruities in translations from one realm to another'. Torbert emphasizes that this should be part of raising children, and if done successfully then adults would be able to work within these premises in organizational work and, we believe, in education for professional and organizational work.

Much of traditional education is deemed to reinforce oppression. Inappropriate or oppressive pedagogy is considered to create imbalance in the psyche of the individual, causing unaware under-development of potentiality and distortion of self-identity and self-esteem (Boud, 1995; Freire, 1972; Heron, 1992; Knowles, 1990, *inter alia*). On the other hand liberating structures seek to empower, and empower in a way that Knowles (1990, p57) described under the term 'the psychological adult', that is, when individuals arrive at a self-concept of taking responsibility for their own lives, of being self-directed. Hence one particular intention in developing students' skills in self-assessing is to facilitate their liberation from oppressive self-perception to a more spontaneous, accurate and empowered view of their own knowledge and abilities, with the main emphasis being on learning from experience. This theme is developed in both Habermas's (1974) critical social science and Mezirow's (1981, 1999) transformation theory, where the two most important tenets are critical dialogue and the need to examine social and cultural environments as well as the subjective when assessing what needs to change and how to make prudent decisions.

Self and peer group assessment on the Master's programme

The introduction of the MSc in Change Agent Skills and Strategies in 1992 gave an ideal opportunity to review and adapt the model of self and peer group assessment for an award-bearing Masters programme. Previously the model had been used for a non-award-bearing Diploma course and other professional development short courses that had run for 12 years. The adaptation moved away from the ideals of the complete self-determined model to a more formally assessed and graded evaluation of learning outcomes.

The MSc provides a post-experience training for people such as management consultants, trainers and other professionals in the human resource field. The course group operates as a learning community (Tosey and Gregory, 1998; Chapter 13 in this volume) and the assessment process creates peer learning through its two main educational methodologies: to operate as an experiential learning group and foster learner participation in educational decision making. The course community works as a closed group over the two-year programme and fits the definition of peers as those who have shared knowledge and expertise in the subject matter, accessibility to the professional context and are accepted by each other as legitimate peers for the purpose of the educational process (adapted from Heron, 1974). This provided a rationale for the involvement of the peer group in the assessment of individual learning. For as Heron (1974, p1) stated: 'In all three stages, (of the educated person), as a self-directed, self-monitoring and self-correcting being, the opinions of his (*sic*) peers in the same domain of experience are an important source of influence'.

On the MSc, there are eight modules, seven of which are taught as experiential workshops where the module is assessed by four main criteria:

1. the diagnosing of learning needs, with the development and implementation of a learning contract within prescribed contract criteria;
2. satisfactory self assessment of the learning contract within the self and peer assessment format and submission of a portfolio summary in the form of reflections on learning and self accreditation of the module;
3. demonstration of advances in learning how to learn and change from modular activities;
4. the submission of a satisfactory theoretical assignment.

The first three criteria form part of the assessment for the experiential component of the programme and are the focus of this chapter. The theoretical assignment is also self, peer and tutor assessed using Masters' level learning descriptors and Masters' level marking criteria. Two internal examiners and one external examiner assess the dissertation in the traditional way. The theoretical assessments will not be discussed further.

Self-assessment as a procedure has embedded within it many processes and skills that need to be teased out and developed in the student. These skills include the students' ability to self-assess their learning needs, followed by other skills such as being able to set achievable learning goals or outcomes, being able to form a learning contract with peers' help to address the goals set, having the necessary resources and ability to make the changes or pursue the learning identified in the learning contract, and finally being able to self-assess their learning outcomes. Self-assessment in this case means being able to reflect on what one knows within the subject area of the module. It means knowing what one does not know but needs to know to meet academic learning criteria. The self-assessor needs to have the skills to determine the causes of success or failure, illuminating his or her practice in the light of theory and to make correct and realistic judgements about achievements. The individual and the whole group are able to self-audit in terms of academic and professional performance and standards to a rigorous degree with sufficient recourse to outside agencies, be that the programme tutor or professional auditors, to help them to decide for themselves whether they demonstrate sufficient knowledge or skills to succeed. According to Habermas (cited from Carr and Kemmis, 1986, p143):

> The structure of communication is free from constraint only when… all participants must have the same chance to initiate and perpetuate discourse, to put forward, call into question, and give reasons for or against statements, explanations, interpretations and justifications.

Such democratic discourse is part of the inquiry process on the programme generally and in the development of learning contracts in particular, and goes a long way towards facilitating its liberating and emancipatory aims.

Peer group assessment requires the same skills and knowledge of the process as for self-assessment. 'Mutual self-correcting' implies that only peers who have gone through the same training in the necessary skills and are able to self-assess to an equally good standard are eligible to peer assess others.

What makes self and peer group assessment liberating, in Knowles and Torbert's terms, is the shared knowledge and power of decision making. This is incorporated in the assessment process as shown in italics below:

- Self-directedness – *selection of personally and programme relevant learning goals, which is brought about through developing a learning contract (see example in Appendix A).*

- Recognition of the ability to develop self-criticism and to make valid judgements about performance, *demonstrated through the use of self assessment.*
- Competence to give and receive feedback directly and honestly, *actioned through the course group as a peer learning community feedback system and peer assessments (Appendix B).*
- Willingness to engage with and understand group dynamics, *through inter-personal and group skills development in working in learning sets and the course group as a whole.*

The learning contract

In our view as a course team, one of Knowles' (1986) greatest contribution to progressive adult education was in the formulation of learning contracts where many of the facets of self-directed learning come alive. Knowles observed in his studies of workers in part-time adult education, that provid-ing a learning contract was a powerful strategy for engaging students in their own learning. Within the MSc, the use of learning contracts forms the first phase on which self-assessment and peer group assessment are built. Following Knowles' model each learning contract has a description of indi-vidually identified learning needs and intended learning outcomes in rela-tion to some aspect of intentional change. The outcomes may be personal, interpersonal, or professional within the context of the module themes, and usually involve all three. The learning outcomes need to be developmental, usually based on experience of shortfalls or reduced competence in specific areas (Appendix A). The intended outcomes could range from minimum competency to standards of excellence. The various parts of the learning contract are:

- a description of the learning task;
- learning objectives and criteria of good practice;
- a list of resources and a plan of action;
- evidence of accomplishment, a specification of what evidence will be used and how learning is to be validated.

Learning sets (Hughes, 1983) are formed with four to five people per set who facilitate each other in creating the contracts in a peer helping relation-ship (Rogers, 1967). The importance of creating interdependence within the peer group is made very clear from the start of the process. They must explore each individual learning contract, looking for feasibility of the intended change, its scope and depth, significance for the individual and its relevance to the module objectives. This is followed with developing criteria for achievement, some minimum and other standards of excellence for the intended change. The module study guides offer guidelines on minimum criteria as well as a list of generic experiential criteria, which the learning set adapts to the particular themes of the module. Tutors act as resources to the learning sets while they learn the skills of creating realistic yet challenging learning contracts. The peer group also learns the interpersonal skills necessary to facilitate each other and play devil's advocate to the contract to test its robustness before the individual learner engages with the contract task. In that process the peer group is activating the first stages of the self and peer group assessment procedure.

The development of the learning contract and the self and peer group assessment procedure are interpersonally intense experiential learning encounters (Heron, 1989), and is an example of the learning and teaching strategy described earlier. Much of the professional development and action research inquiry mentioned by Heron (1994) is contained in the forming and refining of the learning contract. The dialectical process of inquiry by the learning set about personally perceived developmental needs and progress can and often is a challenge and includes degrees of personal disclosure and feedback as described in the Johari Window (Hanson, 1973). The challenges involve honesty on the part of all concerned, being transparent, trusting and non-collusive. It requires that the group is facilitative and supportive as well as being emotionally competent (Postle, 1993) – all valuable attributes of personal and professional development (Claxton *et al*, 1996).

In developing the learning contract, individuals are often confronted with self-reflective processes such as distortions in the person's self-formative processes, which prevent a correct understanding of themselves and their actions (after Habermas, 1974). Such insights are brought to conscious awareness, to facilitate a change in personal constructs. Equally, there is a need to examine frames of reference that are socially and culturally mediated, so that a valid diagnosis is made of what the subjective developmental needs are and what is socially constraining. Both may need attention. But to do the first without the second lends itself to the postmodern critique of individualism and psychologism, while to only attend to the latter negates the individuals' ability to construct their own reality, subjectively, and to take some responsibility for creating the social and cultural milieu they reside in. Much of the experiential learning on the modules offers students experiences to engage them with their belief systems, their interpretive frames of reference, and their actions, as students, peers in the learning community and as change agents in particular.

Following agreement with peers that the learning contract is ready for implementation, students work on the stated developmental task(s) outside the course contact time. Learners will also observe their own progress-in-action and reflect-on-action (Schon, 1991) using a (mandatory) personal journal to record progress and any significant aspect of their learning and intended change. A particular learning contract stays in operation from two to three months until the module is finished. In the final days of the module the self and peer group assessment procedure on the learning contract takes place.

The self and peer assessment procedure

The self and peer assessment procedure itself has a prescribed format (see Appendix B). Following completion of the learning contract the learner prepares an evaluative summary on each aspect of the task(s) and a reflexive account on the mode of engagement with the task and progress made. This will include developments/change in self-awareness, attitudes, values, behaviour, thinking, emotions and spiritual levels if appropriate and learning to learn as well as the degrees of completion and achievement acquired. The learning set come together for a three-hour period during which each person takes time as self-assessor, when he or she evaluates his or her accomplishments, celebrates achievements and acknowledges any underachievement. Individuals receive feedback on their self-assessment. A crucial principle within the programme philosophy is that the power and ownership of the learning stays with the learner, so that peers respond within the parameters set by the content delivered by the self-assessor, which they will all have been party to during the contract development. Peers will agree or disagree with the evaluation of learning against the criteria created in advance. They will state whether they accept the evidence to be as valid as promised. They will challenge under- or over-assessment of the individual, and any deprecating remarks as well as any grandiosity in the delivery of the self-assessment. They will finish by celebrating with the self-assessor what he or she has achieved, which may not always be the successful completion of the contract, but the value of the learning in the process of engaging with the task.

There is no doubt from our experience that this whole process serves all the students in the learning set and that the learning contract is a tool or channel through which self and professional development does occur. It is a teaching and learning strategy and its effectiveness lies in the development of prudent and sophisticated decision making. Our students have usually spent from five to 20 years in work situations assessing or auditing these businesses in the light of national, international and sometimes government criteria, hence the need for them to have diagnostic and assessment skills to a high level of competence. Yet the academic self and peer assessment processes experienced on this programme seem more personally challenging and equally more rewarding.

Being mindful to separate out the two aspects of assessment (improvement of learning and institutional requirements) the self and peer assessment of experiential learning is formative as well as summative, and is in the control of students as to whether they will pass self and peers in the learning set. The grading is a simple pass or fail grade. A fail grade, while seldom needed, is more like a referral with some requirement to complete parts of the learning contract if necessary.

In the nine years that the programme has run so far, the self and peer assessment process has for the most part been agreed with by peers with little unresolved conflict. There is often conflict in the sense of challenges by the group to the individual if the student does not seem to be stretching him or herself sufficiently. Equally the individual can challenge the group if the learning requirements seem unreasonable or the assessment criteria too demanding. Such conflicts are considered a vital energetic learning opportunity for all concerned as they ultimately challenge the whole learning set to work with achievable standards that they can all be confident to identify with.

The level and intensity of dialogue within the learning sets around the development and implementation of each learning contract and the assessment together form an action inquiry cycle.

Self and peer assessment – a liberating structure?

According to Broadfoot (1996, pp41–2), liberating assessment techniques are explicitly designed to promote rather than assess learning. In her review of assessment in mainstream education she states that: 'although the battle to liberate the learner though assessment has been temporarily lost to schools, the war continues with aspirations of a paradigm shift away from testing to learning'. Broadfoot also asserts that assessment drives learning, therefore the type of assessment will play a large part in determining the learning attitude and strategies that learners adopt. If we accept that assessment drives learning and our aim is to promote learning, then making assessment a teaching and learning strategy will allow these two aims to come together. The learning contract provides the optimal strategy for this alliance and provides a liberating structure while still aiming for valid academic standards.

The literature on the application of modified forms of self and peer assessment highlight the varying degrees of commitment to the process as a completely liberating one. The most obvious modifications of the original model are that while the assessment of educational tasks (be they scientific experiments or practical) and processes (such as team building or group involvement) are devolved to learners, the assessment and marking of theoretical work continues to be held by the 'professional' assessors (Boud, 1995; Brown and Dove, 1993; Burnett and Cavaye, 1980; Conway *et al*, 1993; Earl, 1986; Stenhouse, 1975). The percentage of grades allotted to self and peer assessment procedures also demonstrates a weakened commitment to the fundamental postulate of the educated person, as tutors hold on to an unequal allocation of grades, thus maintaining an imbalance in decision making (Boud, 1995).

For example, Earl (1986) reported that in the BSc in Mathematical Science, 10 per cent of the course marks were peer awarded for group communication skills as these were seen as an essential part of the group-based projects. However, students were not allowed to self-award and were neither given nor expected to set exacting assessment criteria. There appears to be a lack of trust in students' ability to set exacting standards for themselves and their peers or to accurately or honestly assess themselves, yet being able to do this for their peers.

Within a course that I know of for the training of adult educators, the course staff were content to allow self and peer award of 15 per cent of the total course marks based on self and peer group assessment of student competence in creating a positive learning environment among themselves. However, one of the course validation bodies (nursing in this case) reduced the proportion to 5 per cent of the total marks, making the acquisition of such a grade irrelevant to passing or failing the course. Students' motivation to engage in the exacting task of criterion setting and the self and peer group assessment process was seriously challenged.

As a final example, in Fineman's report (1980) on peer teaching and peer assessment as part of an undergraduate business administration course, a more self-determined strategy is described where students took complete charge of different parts of a module on organizational behaviour. Here the self and peer assessment were almost totally in the hands of the students. The tutor held the equivalent of one student vote and no more when dealing with content of subject, assessment criteria and the award of grades. This model fits the liberating structure as described by Heron (1994) and in higher education is closely aligned to Baume and Baume's (1986) self-determined self and peer assessment.

One of the key principles of a liberating structure is that of ownership of power and power sharing. On our Masters programme, while we remain mindful to work with the various combinations of power sharing as part of our facilitation style (see Chapter 8 in this volume), the module tutor holds hierarchical control of the module content to varying degrees depending on the module requirements. Part of this control is the setting of parameters for the learning contract within the context of the module themes. For example, the module on personal development prescribes that the learning contract must include an improvement of an interpersonal relationship, increased self-awareness and development of a (new) competence (Gregory, 2000). This degree of educational direction is intended to be an authoritative mode of facilitation, rather than autocratic (Heron, 1999), although purists of the self-determining, self-directed philosophy would dispute this. Indeed the prescription reveals the tutor's intention to comply with the modular aims and objectives, which they have hierarchically imposed as curriculum developers. The need here is for the curriculum designers to conform to the university's expectations to enable the course to be approved by the validation board before students ever join the programme.

Yet, just such an argument (or excuse in Freire's terms) makes for the deliberation of students when it comes to complete self-determining behaviour. As Freire (1972, p23) stated, 'Every prescription represents the imposition of one man's choice upon another, transforming the consciousness of the man prescribed to into one that conforms to the prescriber's consciousness.' Freire goes on to say that such prescriptions create fear of freedom particularly if the consequence of not following the prescription is punitive, 'as freedom would require them (the prescribed to) to reject this image (of oppression) and replace it with autonomy and responsibility (p23). Freire's argument is that oppressed people learn to fear freedom because they have not learnt to be autonomous and responsible. Our experience on the course would support this view, as students demonstrate discomfort and sometimes even disbelief when they realize that they really do have the power to self and peer assess and accredit each other on the programme.

This is experienced as a huge responsibility to group members, and not unlike Freire's studies, they show a fear of working with this freedom and look to see what punitive measures might be taken if they get it wrong. One student stated:

> I was quite struck last week to hear that there was no peer review/assessment for the dissertation and my immediate reactions was relief I suppose. In some ways I feel pressure with peer assessment and perhaps feel uncomfortable with it sometimes. That is my first reaction. That is about trust and confidence in the peer and it's also about the assessment process itself being assessed, leaving it in somebody else's hands, that feels uncomfortable, risky and difficult.

Another student said:

> I think the fear has subsided over time. I am not nearly as terrified as I was at the start. For reasons, which were, I suppose, about fair hearing or handling of the responsibility. I think what has happened is, as the peer community works

better, so does the peer assessment process. And it's something to do with giving people time and attention and getting an awareness of the work (to be assessed)... But I don't ever lose the terror of the assessment as such.

The programme tutors recognize such fears and allocate time during the workshops to discuss the assessment process and hear participants' fantasies and fears. The whole learning community is offered coaching until they feel confident with their knowledge and skills in criterion setting, the assessment process itself, managing the group dynamics in the learning set and managing emotionally and intellectually challenging situations as well. To tip the balance of power back to students in educational decision making, we encourage students to develop personal learning criteria, particularly standards of excellence in one or more areas of the contract that the individual has a particular passion to develop. So again, if we take the example of the personal development module, while a relationship is to be improved, the learner is the only one who will decide which relationship to improve and state how he or she will navigate through the complexities of that relationship.

The experiential learning assessment remains firmly in the hands of the learning sets who can award a module pass or fail grade to any one of the learning set members, including themselves. The tutor's role is that of moderator of the process, which they hold in cooperative mode (Heron, 1999) with the learning set. Therefore any collusion, scapegoating, 'dumping' of unfinished business or other biased or prejudicial behaviour will be flushed out as soon as identified, and corrective, reparative action taken.

Part of the learning process for students is the need to do some un-learning about how people learn, and who is best placed to assess learning. Most learners have only experienced unilateral power – hierarchical and sometimes oppressive (Boud, 1995), where people give over responsibility and accountability to 'higher' or expert authority. Through the action inquiry process of self and peer reflection and assessment the skill of learning how to learn is developed and practised. Learning how to learn embraces Bateson's (1973) levels of learning as the inquiry deepens and broadens to take in change at different levels of being and doing. It embraces Heron's (1989) four forms of knowledge, the experiential, imaginal, conceptual and practical as the learning contract is developed through these epistemological modes and assessed at a meta-level of analysis and critical reflection and evaluation. Learning how to learn is an emancipatory process. The educated person is one who has learnt how to learn, he or she is self-organizing, and can equilibrate his or her motivation, capacity to learn and transfer skills across contexts.

From the literature and in our experience it seems that critical compromises are often made for self and peer group assessment to be acceptable within the relevant institutional framework. We therefore argue that self and peer group assessment is a political structure, in that by its nature it will challenge institutionalized assumptions and practices. This political dimension is an inherent feature of liberating structures, an important theme that needs further exploration. The aim will be to consider how such political pressures could be managed by academics wishing to introduce self and peer assessment.

The compromise within our programme is that the theoretical assessment is less liberating as a structure because the tutor's assessment and grade takes precedence over those of the student and peer assessor. This has created some disillusionment and at times disagreement among tutors and students. The programme regulations allow for serious disagreement to form the basis for a meeting between all assessors concerned, self, peer and tutors where each explains and justifies their reasons for the grades against the stated criteria. Here all voices are equal and the tutors' decision is open to scrutiny by students. However, the grade is seldom changed even after such a discussion. This transparency mitigates a little against the hierarchical power held by the tutors.

Conclusion

There is a paradox that adult education remains, by and large, dominated by a hierarchical model of education. We know a very great deal about the learning preferences and needs of adults. Yet our education system has not only failed to implement these on any significant scale, but also the current trend is regressive in this respect.

Flexibility and accessibility do not, contrary to the popular view, enhance the 'adultness' of the learning experience. Primarily they facilitate the economics of education – enabling greater consumer access, and increasing the commercial opportunities of higher education institutions.

If the assessment strategy drives learning, then that strategy needs to mirror the values of the educated person in order to be a liberating structure (Torbert, 1991). The self and peer group assessment strategy for experiential learning we adopt aims to meet these criteria.

Acknowledgement

This chapter has been developed from an internal Human Potential Research Group (HPRG) publication co-authored with Paul Tosey.

Appendix A

A learning contract

> Learning contracts are based on the assumptions about how adults learn.
> (Knowles, 1986)

The learning contract is developed out of an assessment exercise where the student compares own present competence against externalized personal standards or other competences or standards (of professionals and peers).

A competency diagnostic list needs to be complied and agreed by peers who will support the individual and assess achievement of the learning contract. Use of inventories or other personality styles/learning styles can be used; however the choice of level of standards is negotiated in the learning set. By competence we mean appropriate standards of knowledge, skills, attitudes and values.

Questions to ask yourself are:

1. How important is the competence to my personal and professional life?
2. What is the level to which I have developed this competency to date?
3. What is its level of priority in my life now?
4. What is the level to which I want to develop this competency?

Below you will find a sample layout of a learning contract. All sections need to be completed for each new piece of learning.

Sample of learning contract layout

Name: Module:

Learning objectives	Resources and strategies	Targets date for completion	Evidence	Verification
No 1				
No 2				

(© Josie Gregory and Paul Tosey, October 1997)

Appendix B

Self and peer assessment (formal assessment)

STAGE	PURPOSE	ESSENTIAL CONTENT	OPTIONS/EXAMPLES	SUGGESTIONS
DISCLOSURE OF SELF-ASSESSMENT	Self-assessor gives assessment of performance in relation to the stated aims and criteria. The agenda throughout is what *has been* said or done, not what *could be* done in the future.	Have I (self-assessor) achieved the objectives in my contract to the standard agreed with my peers? What is my key evidence? What are the main strengths and weaknesses of what I have done?	What else have I learnt?	Begin by reminding peers of the learning contract. Then evaluate achievements, limitations and so on. Do not go into detail or 'story-telling' at the expense of a clear self-assessment.
CLARIFICATION QUESTIONS	Peers ask for clarification and further information. Self-assessor responds to questions by giving the minimum information needed.	What else do I (peer) need to know in order to (a) know what feedback I will give and (b) whether I accept the self-assessment?	What else do I need/want to understand/know? Eg 'Please expand on…?'; 'Tell me more about…'; 'What did you mean by…?'; 'How did you…?'	
NEGATIVE FEEDBACK	Peers respond to self-assessment with criticism, ie bases on which they disagree with or challenge the self-assessment. Deliver in a way that remains supportive of the person (however challenging to their actions or self-assessment).	*Self-assessor does not respond to any feedback.* In what respects do I (peer) disagree with the self-assessment? Is there any incongruity between the self-assessor's claims and their evidence?	Was the self-assessor congruent (eg did verbal and non-verbal messages match?) Eg 'I think/I don't think…'; 'I dislike/I like least…'. Eg rhetorical challenging questions; 'Do you really think …?'; 'Did you notice the contradiction…?'; 'Are you aware that…?'	It can be useful for the first peer responding to acknowledge the self-assessment (eg 'I'm delighted/surprised to hear…'). Ensure any challenges are challenges to the self-assessment (eg 'I challenge your claim that… on these grounds…'), *not*

continued overleaf

Self and peer assessment (formal assessment) *(continued)*

STAGE	PURPOSE	ESSENTIAL CONTENT	OPTIONS/EXAMPLES	SUGGESTIONS
NEGATIVE FEEDBACK *(continued)*				'dares' to the person (eg 'I challenge you to….). Ground feedback in concrete data, examples.
POSITIVE FEEDBACK	Peers respond to self-assessment with affirmation, ie bases on which they agree with or support the self-assessment. Deliver in a way that remains rigorous to the procedure/ educational aims of the process, and supportive of the person.	*Self-assessor does not respond to any feedback.* In what respects do I (peer) agree with the self-assessment?	Include appreciation, admiration, recognition etc. Eg 'I like…'; 'I value…'; 'I appreciate…'; 'I enjoyed…'	Ground feedback in concrete data, examples.
SELF-ASSESSOR RESPONDS	Self-assessor reflects on how they feel now, and how they experienced the self and peer assessment process – but *not* to respond to the content.	What am I (self-assessor) feeling now? How has the process impacted on me?	Eg 'I felt very anxious when I heard your feedback.'; 'Now I feel …'	It is for the self-assessor to decide whether or not they accept any item of feedback; not commenting on the content does not mean that the self-assessor agrees with the feedback.
QUALITY ASSURANCE	Group evaluates and 'quality assures' the self and peer assessment process, identifying modifications needed.	Have we kept to the principles and procedures? Has our process been degenerate? What do we need to improve next time around?		NB. Do not change principles. Avoid tinkering with the structure of process; maintain same timing structure; sequence; etc. unless important to change it.

References

AHPP (1998) Humanistic values. Self and society, *The European Journal of Humanistic Psychology,* **26** (3)

Bateson, G (1973) *Steps to an Ecology of Mind,* Paladin, London

Baume, D and Baume, C (1986) Learner, know thyself: self-assessment and self-determined assessment in education, *The New Era,* **67** (3)

Bond, M (1988) Self and peer assessment manual for nurse tutors, unpublished, The University of Surrey, The Human Potential Research Project, Department of Educational Studies, Guildford

Boud, D (1989) The role of self-assessment in student grading, *Assessment And Evaluation In Higher Education,* **14** (1), pp 20–30

Boud, D (1995) *Enhancing Learning Through Self Assessment,* Kogan Page, London

Broadfoot, P (1996) *Education, Assessment and Society,* Open University Press, Buckingham

Brown, S and Dove (ed) (1993) Self and peer assessment, Sced Paper 63, Society for Research into Higher Education, Birmingham

Burnett, W and Cavaye, G (1980) Peer assessment by fifth year students of surgery, *Assessment In Higher Education,* **5** (3), pp 273–87

Carr, W and Kemmis, S (1986) *Becoming Critical: Education, knowledge and action research,* Falmer Press, London

Claxton, G, Atkinson, T, Osborn, M and Wallace, M (eds) (1996) *Liberating The Learner: Lessons for professional development in education,* Routledge, London

Conway, R, Kember, D, Sivan, A and Wu, M (1993) Peer assessment of an individual's contribution to a group project, *Assessment and Evaluation in Higher Education,* **18** (1)

Dewey, J (1916) *Education and Democracy,* The Free Press, New York

Earl, S E (1986) Staff and peer assessment: measuring an individual's contribution to group performance, *Assessment and Evaluation in Higher Education,* **11** (1), pp 60–69

Fineman, S (1980) Reflections on peer teaching and peer assessment: an undergraduate experience, *Assessment and Evaluation in Higher Education,* **6** (1), pp 82–93.

Fisher, D and Torbert, W R (1995) *Personal and Organizational Transformation,* McGraw-Hill, Maidenhead

Ford, A (1997) Peer group assessment: its application to a vocational modular degree course, *Journal of Further and Higher Education,* **21** (3), pp 285–96

Freire, P (1972) *Pedagogy of the Oppressed,* Penguin, Harmondsworth

Gregory, J (2000) Understanding personal development, Study Guide, Module 2, MSc in Change Agent Skills and Strategies, School of Educational Studies, Human Potential Research Group. University of Surrey, Guildford

Habermas, J (1972) *Knowledge and Human Interests,* Heinemann, Oxford

Habermas, J (1974) *Theory and Practice,* Heinemann, Oxford

Hanson, P (1973) The Johari Window: A model for soliciting and giving feedback, cited in *The Annual Handbook For Group Facilitators,* USA

Heron, J (1974) The concept of the peer learning community, University of Surrey, Department of Educational Studies, The Human Potential Research Project, Guildford

Heron, J (1979) Peer review audit, University of London, British Postgraduate Medical Federation, University of Surrey, Human Potential Research Project, Guildford

Heron, J (1989) *The Facilitators Handbook,* Kogan Page, London

Heron, J (1992) The politics of facilitation, in *Empowerment Through Experiential Learning: Exploration of good practice,* eds J Mulligan and C Griffin, Kogan Page, London

Heron, J (1994) Self and peer assessment, in Boydell and Pedler, M, *Management Self Development,* 2nd edn, McGraw-Hill, Maidenhead

Heron, J (1999) *The Complete Facilitator's Handbook,* Kogan Page, London

Hughes, M (1983) Chapter 6 in *Action Learning in Practice,* ed M Pedler, Gower, Aldershot

Jarvis, P (1995) *Adult and Continuing Education,* 2nd edn, Routledge, London

Kilty, J (1978) Self and peer assessment and peer audit, University of Surrey, Department of Educational Studies, Human Potential Research Project, Guildford

Knowles, M (1986) *Using Learning Contracts: Practical approaches to individual and structured learning,* Jossey-Bass, San Francisco, CA

Knowles, M (1990) *The Adult Learner: A neglected species,* 4th edn, Gulf Publishing, Houston, TX

Kolb, D (1984) *Experiential Learning: Experience as the source of learning and development,* Prentice-Hall, London

Mezirow, J (1981) A critical theory of adult learning and education, *Adult Education,* **32** (1), pp 3–27

Mezirow, J (1999) *Transformation Theory – Postmodern Issues,* 1999 AERC Conference Proceedings

Postle, D (1993) Putting the heart back into learning, in *Using Experience for Learning,* eds D Boud, R Cohen and D Walker, SRHE and Open University Press, Buckingham

Rogers, C R (1967) *On Becoming a Person,* Constable, London

Rogers, C R (1983) *Freedom to Learn for the 80s,* C E Merrill, Columbus, OH

Schon, D (1991) *The Reflective Practitioner: How professionals think in action,* Ashgate, Aldershot

Stenhouse, L (1975) *An Introduction to Curriculum Development and Research*, Heinemann, Oxford

Torbert, W R (1991) *The Power of Balance: Transforming self, society, and scientific inquiry,* Sage, Newbury Park

Tosey, P and Gregory, J (1998) The peer learning community: reflections on practice, *Innovations in Education and Training International,* SEDA, **35** (1), pp 74–81

Chapter 16

Distance education in the learning society

Thomas Black and John Holford

Among the social and economic forces which have driven the creation of a learning society, two are commonly mentioned: globalization, drawing the peoples of the world into an international capitalist market, where goods, services and labour are bought and sold by multinational companies with little regard for borders, and national laws or geographical distance. Additionally, information and communications technology (ICT) makes many of these international movements and relationships possible. Both seem to offer real opportunities for distance education.

Traditionally, the face-to-face relationship between teacher and learners has been fundamental to education. The geographical extension of education was therefore a matter of carrying students to teachers, or teachers to students. Universities, colleges and schools – especially establishments where students are expected to 'board' or be 'in residence' – represent the former; for hundreds of years, young men travelled across continents to study at universities. In Victorian England, however, the new rail network created new opportunities, and university extension lecturers could travel from universities to far-flung towns and cities (Harrison, 1961). Distance learning therefore seems at once a way in which education is enabled to play a full role in a global society, and a mechanism that exploits the potential of developing information technologies to the benefit of learners.

Of course, distance learning is not new. Face-to-face relationships may loom large in our perceptions of what education has traditionally comprised, but there have been earlier attempts to utilize developments in communications technology. In mediaeval Europe, for example, writing and sending letters became a 'form of instruction' which ' solved the problem of conveying to a large public some of the results painfully arrived at in the schools' (Southern, 1953, p204). Correspondence courses were introduced in the 19th century, and became common in the 20th. But it was the establishment of open and distance universities in the late 1960s (Perry, 1976), in which the British Open University was the catalyst, which brought teaching at a distance towards acceptance as a normal, and effective, mode of educational provision.

This acceptance that degree-level qualifications could be taught and assessed on a distance basis proved to be the critical step. Over the last 30 years, distance learning has moved from the periphery to somewhere near the mainstream of educational and training methodologies. Many, if not most, British universities now offer some programmes on a distance learning basis. The last three decades have also, of course, seen unimaginable advances in ICT. Education has been affected, as much as any sector. With this background, the imagined potential of new distance learning technologies has become apparent and attractive to many.

At the same time, the radical changes taking place in the structures of education have particular salience in relation to distance learning. To take the example of universities, Middlehurst (2001) argues that the demands placed on public sector universities to widen access, demonstrate 'accountability', 'service' and 'value for money' to funders and students (as 'customers'), and establish new relationships ('partnerships', 'networks' and so forth) with other organizations are requiring universities to examine new ways of delivering their courses. New financial regimes are encouraging them to find ways of securing income from new markets, often distant from their campuses or even overseas. At the same time, public sector universities are challenged by a range of corporate universities, 'for-profit' educational providers, media and publishing businesses, and professional associations. These are invading the markets traditionally dominated by public sector universities, In response and in parallel, a range of educational services and brokers is emerging, selling specific services to universities (from administrative services to learning delivery platforms). At the same time, forms of collaboration between universities both nationally and internationally are growing and formalizing.

In all these developments, the ability to cooperate or compete through relating to learners over considerable distances is at a premium. The use of distance learning technologies is therefore key. Their promise is considerable, and much hope has been invested in them. (Whether the money invested is sufficient to justify the promise remains to be seen.) At the same time, however, learners now often expect teaching to be combined with forms of self-access learning support, often with online support. Thus even within campus-based universities, many learning materials are now available online as well as in printed form, and students are able to communicate with their tutors and fellow students in 'virtual classrooms'. For some universities, online materials are an important form of marketable intellectual property; it remains to be seen how many will follow the example of MIT in posting 'virtually all its course materials on the Web, free to everybody' (Goldberg, 2001, p1).

At the other extreme, one must consider the less technically developed countries striving to educate populations eager to learn and acquire qualifications. Perraton (1995) and Koul (1995) identify not only the problems of delivery, but also those more closely related to relevance and applicability to economically developing societies. The World Bank's contribution is the Africa Virtual University (http://www.avu.org/), which depends on the availability of computer hardware and Internet links to deliver lectures and materials. They even admit that 'The start-up costs for AVU Learning Centers with basic equipment are from US$20,000 to US$30,000, a not insignificant sum when considering the average annual income in most African countries is a fraction of this and that this is just the entry fee. Individual students are most likely to need to have access to such a centre, which places geographic restrictions on any audience.

Approaches to learning

With all these innovations in delivery methods, what is the state of play in terms of *what* and *how* students learn at a distance? Let us consider the background to changes with respect to educational theory and practice using Jarvis (2001) as a guide. He lists 12 changes, one of which is distance learning and four of which have specific relevance to the *delivery* of distance education:

- from teacher-centred to student-centred education;
- from rote learning to learning as experiential and reflection;
- from theoretical to practical;
- from education and training to learning.

As we will consider each of these trends from the view of the teacher/developer, the term 'knowledge' needs to be better defined. A distinction will be made in this section between information about (facts, principles, conventions, rules and procedures), understanding, and associated higher level intellectual skills to use this information (such as application of principles, problem solving, use of logical reasoning, critical analysis, creative development) in any discipline or subject of study (see Bloom, 1956; Gagné, 1985; Gagné *et al*, 1992). Hereafter, instead of referring to undifferentiated knowledge, the terms 'information', 'understanding', and 'intellectual skills' will be used.

While knowledge is no longer considered static it does often build on existing knowledge, the information, concepts, principles and skills that must be learnt in order to understand the new knowledge. Rarely is anything so radically new that it cancels the need to learn what went on before. Bearing these two caveats in mind, let us consider the four changes most relevant to distance learning.

From teacher-centred to student-centred education

One of the basic issues raised in discussions about any curriculum is what is meant by 'student-centred?' One concern is who chooses what is to be learnt? While some would support the learner in free choice of both content and means, particularly at the adult level, two practical concerns limit the degree of implementation.

First, the assumption that the professional role of the teacher can be completely replaced by a learner with limited knowledge of both content and learning resources is not realistic. This does not mean that the teacher is necessarily the only fount of knowledge or the only one who is able to determine what is 'best' to learn in terms of information, understanding or intellectual skills. It simply acknowledges the role of the teacher, as noted above, is changing from that of being the only source of learning to more that of a consultant to the learner, both in assisting in choices about content as well as delivery.

Second, the cost of development of effective and efficient learning materials. We have not yet reached the stage of having an endless menu of ready-made resources. At best, resources can be picked from what is available, at worst they have to be developed from scratch. While the menu grows, someone still has to put the dishes on the menu.

Those who focus on systematic design of learning materials and experiences (eg, Gagné et al, 1992) often focus on didactic approaches, but by no means have they excluded student-centred approaches, and in fact emphasize the appropriate match of objectives (learning outcomes) including those defined by the learners, with the most appropriate media or learning approach. In fact, one of the consequences of this has been to de-emphasize the teacher's role as the sole source of knowledge and replace it with one of manager of the learning environment. In other words, the teacher is not the only learning resource, not always (if ever) in front of the class, but is the one who serves as developer of materials and/or the consultant to the learner for selecting appropriate learning resources.

While in most classes this has meant group learning, either individualized, small group or large group, aiming to achieve a pre-determined set of objectives, as the cognitive emphasis rises, the flexibility increases as to what resources are needed and how the objectives are achieved. Thus out of necessity (and consistent with the desire to match objectives with resources) the approach becomes more student-centred as the emphasis shifts from gathering information and understanding of concepts to the acquisition of higher level intellectual skills. The greater availability of information (and increasingly activities to enhance skill development) on the Internet means the menu from which the learner can choose with the aid of the consultant teacher has increased enormously in recent years, but there is a need to plan encounters so they are not just visits to sites filled with information.

Distance learning almost by definition has to be student-centred from the viewpoint of delivery, simply because the learner will be trying to learn much of the time by him or herself. This places specific demands on students to be self-regulating, mature learners, people who (possibly with help) can govern their time and resources.

So what are some of the delivery styles possible that would reflect a learner-centred approach? Moore (1994) considers three types of interaction, to which one could add the following issues that need to be considered:

- Learner-content, what will the content be and who will decide?
- Learner-instructor, who is likely to be, or assumed to be, the initiator?
- Learner-learner, one that has been facilitated by conferencing software (in addition to e-mails), but raises issues of 'lurkers' who do not participate.

All three questions raise other issues about interactions based on the origins of the materials (Henri and Kay, 1994), whether the developer and tutor are one and the same, or if not, whether they share similar attitudes and views with respect to the nature of support for facilitating the achievement of the objectives. Outcomes at higher cognitive levels require different support from those that are lower: prompting, coaching and assistance as opposed to answers. Providing support for higher level skills requires different skills on the part of the tutor than those for facilitating acquisition of information and concept learning.

From this we can see that a shift to student-centred learning is more than a change in attitudes: it requires considerable skill on the part of developers and tutors to make it happen. This in turn may have implications for staff development for developers and tutors new to distance learning.

From rote learning to learning as experiential and reflection

One of the tools used by developers is the description of learning outcomes in terms of objectives. This is not behaviourist in the traditional sense of being concerned only with the behaviour itself, but stems from an interest in behaviours from which one can infer the possession of information, understanding and intellectual skills. The limitation of objectives is not with the tool but the users and the skill with which they defined learning outcomes.

We do not let children play with chainsaws; maybe we ought to restrict those who write objectives to those who are intellectually skilled enough to do so. The trivial outcomes that focus on lower cognitive skills described with some learning materials demonstrate the misuse of a valuable tool for developers, and should not be taken as indicative of what can be done. It is quite possible to describe higher level learning outcomes that by necessity would require the demonstration of skills within the realm and employment domain of the learner.

In addition, objectives written at a sufficiently high enough level emphasizing problem solving, critical analysis and creativity, should be able to accommodate unanticipated intellectually honest learning outcomes that could be encouraged. Thus objectives do not have to place a limit on learning, but should define a minimum.

Teaching is better defined as not only the delivery, but also all the planning of learning that precedes the learning and the supplying of feedback on progress during and after the event. Thus experiential and reflective learning have to be planned if they are to occur. This can be accomplished in a wide variety of ways:

- by focusing on higher level skills, learning about disciplines and how they develop knowledge and understanding;
- developing new skills, including those necessary to gain new knowledge as well as using existing knowledge to solve immediate problems;
- employing Socratic-type approaches with questions for students to address to stimulate reflection, instead of consolidating thoughts only at the end (Chapter 7, this volume).

In general this is an issue of how one delivers the materials and not something that is an intrinsic characteristic of distance learning. A conscious effort has to be made on the part of the developer to encourage reflection on experience, to foster critical analysis of applying generalities and principles to specific situations.

From theoretical to practical

This is most frequently reflected in the nature of the application of principles learnt to the place of work as part of activities and assignments. The real value in higher intellectual skills often comes when they are transferable to a variety of situations and applications. How one provides opportunities to accomplish this as part of a course structure can vary, and includes such approaches as problem solving and problem-based curricula.

Such a tendency towards practical aspects of a subject does not have to lose sight of the theoretical underpinnings. While tasks tend to be at higher cognitive levels, they can require not only reflection on practice, but application (with critical view) of new principles and procedures. Practical problems can be evaluative, in other words provide the learners with opportunities to judge which approach is best, for example of two equally valid choices, for the situation at hand. Considering much of real life has few right–wrong choices, and many require the identification of the best solution considering the reality of the situation, this could provide a sound preparation for the world after the course.

From education and training to learning

The discussion of delivery styles often assumes (possibly rightly so in some cases) that teachers tend to have only one, or a limited repertoire. The focus of educational technology has been on widening this to accommodate a greater variety of learning needs.

While there has been some tendency towards learner-centred, self-directed and experiential learning in some areas, many learners would still prefer to have the experiences and materials structured for them. The assumption is that this is a more efficient way to learn, entrusting the subject expert/teacher to provide optimum choice of materials, resources, media and sequence of learning experiences in a new subject area in which the learner has little or no expertise. Even those of us who tend to learn on our own will search for a well-structured textbook to guide us in our learning. Thus the study guide in a distance learning course will tend to give this organization, providing the links and integration across the various other resources, a bit like lectures in a traditional classroom. They may also provide the motivation, rationale and links with reality for the subject matter. The main difference lies in the possibilities for interrupting the lecture and introducing other activities and exercises to allow for reflection, practice, questioning, etc. In this way, the study guide tends to differ from the traditional textbook with all the questions at the end of the chapter.

The need for certification of qualifications by organizations and the underlying validation procedures with and by external bodies has necessitated that lecturers provide structured and well-documented materials, particularly for distance learning courses for which students may not ever be physically present.

To focus successfully on learning, it is necessary to face the needs of students for support and communication, which will include access to tutors for questions, formative feedback on work, ideas or reflections, and even the opportunity for communication among learners. The careful crafting of objectives to guide the development of materials will reflect the need of the learner to relate the new skills and information to reality and his or her own situation.

Implications for teachers and developers

The trends that have been discussed to this point all have implications for those who are responsible for the development of learning materials and tutors on distance learning courses. If the trends are to continue, then appropriate skills will have to be developed. For example:

- Writing for learners at a distance is more than just giving a lecture, therefore transcribed lecture notes will inevitably result in some pretty boring prose. Effective study guides tend to create a dialogue with the learner, and sometimes you the tutor actually hear their responses. If learners are going to reflect on their own experiences and learning, then communication is necessary and this must be stimulated (Hawkridge, 1995).
- The teachers need to have the teaching/planning skills to impart their discipline's skills and knowledge, and to have mastered the teaching skills such that they will do so with sufficient flexibility that when their discipline's skills and knowledge change, they are able to transmit them to their students. In reality, the effective lecturer developing distance learning materials will not be de-skilled, but will have to develop even more skills than those needed for the traditional classroom, face-to-face lecture/tutorial environments.
- It is assumed that the developers actually have the intellectual skills associated with their discipline and not just the information and concepts. They have also learnt how to learn so that when their discipline grows, they are able to acquire new skills and concepts. In higher education, this is the basis for the argument for lecturers carrying out first-hand research and not just recycling the work of others. This may seem contradictory in some disciplines where the theoretician is seen as the leader. For example, the theoretical physicist is seen as the initiator of research based upon his or her theories, a view not shared by many physicists who pursue research in more applied areas. What is important is that the teachers and developers share the aim to impart information, concepts and higher level skills to students.
- The developers are discerning, critical and able to choose appropriate media and approaches for facilitating the acquisition of information, concepts and higher level skills, and do not just jump on bandwagons as they pass.

Smaller departments or institutions face problems with the above because of the skill demands made of staff. To ensure quality of delivery as well as validity of content, the Open University in the UK employs teams of subject experts and educational technologists, with appropriate technical support (video, computer aided learning, graphics, etc) to design study guides and support materials for their courses. The question arises, how can smaller institutions achieve the same quality when the size of the programmes does not justify the expenditure for such a diverse team of experts?

ICT and distance education

Is the use of new ICT essential to creating a learning society, or is it just another technological aid? The learning society literature has a strongly 'futuristic' dimension, and few authors have been able to resist the attractions of what new technologies can offer. This section explores some of the potential and limitations of ICT in teaching and learning.

The promise of new learning technologies

The attractions of the new ICT for the development of learning are acclaimed internationally (Dimitropoulos, 2000, p34). Hawkridge (1995), in his vision of the future, saw full implementation for distance learning of remote library access, instant document delivery, electronic journals and interactive browsing no later than 2010, and many of these are already available on-campus today. The first Fryer Report argued that:

> Harnessing their use will provide additional means to open up access, overcome barriers to learning associated with distance and timing, give new opportunities for both individual and groups learning and constitute mechanisms through which to create and disseminate new learning materials. Properly related to arrangements to give students reliable information and guidance and linked to facilities for interaction with other learners and tutorial support, the new technologies can also offer opportunities to widen participation and bring high quality learning schemes to learners at an affordable cost. (NAGCELL, 1997, p 86)

Flexibility

A key perception is that new technologies will permit the widespread individualization of learning. We can, it is suggested, learn what, when and where we want. We can purchase the units of learning we want (eg 'modules'), so ICT permits an 'individual learning revolution' (Cm 3790, p17). Individuals, suitably guided, will purchase units of learning for themselves, negotiating 'learning contracts' in a learning market. The assumption is that all the learning will occur using the technology, but begs the question of what medium is best for the learning task required.

Cheapness

It is commonly assumed that ICT will make education cheaper. This belief is founded on the belief that new learning technologies will enable institutions to:

- increase productivity – individual teachers will teach more students at the same time;
- reduce costs – eg by buying CD ROMs and Web-based resources, rather than books and journals;
- operate in distant markets;
- form 'partnerships' – reducing development costs and finding new market niches.

Unfortunately, promise is not always matched by reality when development and delivery are properly costed.

Technology and innovation

Many people believe ICT must provide great opportunities – their fervour can be almost religious. Organizations sometimes seek innovative uses of ICT, instead of good or effective ones. As with any new market opportunity, there is the fear of losing out.

Profit

If educational institutions win new markets then, perhaps, they will need less public subsidy. Some do succeed in 'making money' from marketing courses (though more do not), and do so by using new learning technologies.

Realities

ICT, outreach and partnership

ICT has the potential to enhance a learning society. It can, for instance, facilitate learning in the workplace, carry education into remote geographical areas, or into specialist areas. The opportunities which ICT offers for collaboration – 'partnership' – are also substantial, as the UfI's attempt to establish a 'network' of 'learning centres', in colleges, libraries, community centres, employers' premises, shopping malls and so forth shows (Cm 4392 1999, p.40).

Variety and choice

Offering learning at a distance changes the relationship between teachers and learners in various ways:

- *Recruiting students internationally*. Many educational institutions – universities and private schools – now recruit students from across the world. This has real potential for increasing international and cross-cultural understanding, as well as generating income.
- *Widening choice*. Expertise in one institution can be transmitted to others. For example, a module can be offered from another institution, and lectures and teaching materials can be stored for use by learners at a later date. Costs of development can be shared with other organizations, and spread over more learners.
- *Flexibility in timing*. ICT allows learners to study when it is relevant, and at convenient times. This does, of course, assume that the learner has highly-developed self-regulatory skills.

Problems

The promise of theory is often let down by practical reality.

Cost of development

Producing learning materials using ICT – transforming the intellectual expertise into written (or audio-visual) form, suitable for individual learners to engage with successfully – is substantially more costly than teaching the same material in a classroom. As a rule, these costs call for large numbers of students. Some, such as the Open University in the UK, have sufficient students of their own; others with lower numbers resort to purchasing materials written elsewhere.

Too few students

High origination costs require relatively high and stable student numbers. Without buoyant recruitment and income, the ability to reinvest is limited, and the 'ideal' of offering the course to a few students in scattered locations is impossible.

Materials production and revision

Development and revision of learning materials is logistically complex as well as expensive. Subject expertise must be combined with skills in instructional and graphic design, publishing and printing. Many organizations have underestimated the challenges of maintaining a system of materials production and revision. ICT brings additional costs, depending on the nature of the learning task. Computer assisted learning (structured learning, simulations) can cost £50,000 per hour of student learning, or more. Quality video is expensive; animations and graphics require skilled and expensive personnel.

Transience

The 'shelf-life' of materials is increasingly short, so the ideal of materials being a 'store' of knowledge for small numbers of later students is seldom achieved. ICT presents its own problems. For example, Web sites can disappear without notice, so learning materials with Web links must be continually updated.

Interactive learning and learner support

Interactive online support for learners, whether simple e-mail systems or more sophisticated online discussion forums or 'virtual classrooms' are also expensive. Software systems such as Learning Space or First Class require personnel to monitor student–student interactions and to respond to queries. Other demands on tutors include telephone, video or online conferencing, face-to-face workshops or tutorials at study centres, student counselling, marking and returning student assignments. Advantages for the learner must be balanced against additional costs, which vary in proportion to the number of students. Interactions with learners through e-mail can be more demanding of staff and resources than meeting face-to-face.

Curriculum and focus

There is a balance to be struck between establishing a curriculum – an educational or intellectual logic to study – and learner choice. The coherence, identity and marketing of programmes often require a strong focus. Programmes with extensive freedom of choice can lose in the marketplace.

Learner progression and assessment

Learners need to be aware of what they know, and of how their learning is advancing. Progression implies a structured approach, with the learner moving in some kind of sequence. The random selection of learning opportunities makes this very difficult to achieve. Most subjects build from simple to complex, require the refinement of skill development, and are more than a huge collection of facts that can be acquired in any order.

Bureaucracy

In any system of learning, the tracking of individuals and their progression is a substantial task. Systems for tracking learners in a learning society, where study can be lifelong, nation-wide (and even international) presents considerable challenge. Policies and schemes such as assessment of prior learning (APL) and progress files (NAGCELL, 1997, p84) are attempts to begin to address this problem. However, maintaining an effective record-keeping system for students aged over 20 remains a major challenge.

Competition

Educational entrepreneurs are involved in a process of doing 'better' than the competition. Markets can actively discourage cooperation, reducing the potential benefits of drawing on expertise on a worldwide basis. In recent years strong competition has generated calls for stronger regulation, to the extent that regulatory frameworks can often seem stultifying – as well as very costly – to the professional educator.

Learner needs

What do learners need? What are the essential or desirable features of any system of learning support?

- *Communication.* A few people study quite happily in isolation, but for most a system of learning should incorporate mechanisms for interaction with other learners who are at roughly comparable points in their studies.
- *Interaction with teachers.* Learners need meaningful interaction with tutors, and opportunities for feedback. Many learners will also want personal support.
- *Confidence and regularity.* We learn from change and from the unexpected, of course. But much more profoundly we require regularity to provide confidence that what we learn is valuable, and will continue to be so. Educational institutions should establish secure patterns of study and progress, and ensure that the currency of qualifications is not debased.
- *Learning resources.* Students need learning resources commensurate with the cognitive emphasis of the learning outcomes and consistent with their learning situation. This means clear learning outcomes and intents, and arrangements for resource allocation.
- *Administration and records.* Reliable and effective monitoring of student progress, and a fair system of assessment of prior learning and credit transfer among institutions, are required.

- *Learning materials.* Effective systems for the development, review and updating of learning materials, and for their quality assurance, are essential. To be competitive, an institution has to invest in its courses in order to maintain its competitive advantage.
- *Staff.* In practice, staff – teachers, trainers, instructional designers, educational technologists – are key. They must maintain a common purpose and team spirit, and do this in the context of a more fragmented working environment, for they may be working in different parts of an organization, or even in different companies.

Conclusions

The use of ICT in the delivery of learning, particularly with the aim of facilitating the expansion of the learning society, offers advantages but has limitations. It places a greater decision-making burden on the teacher-developer. The choices are numerous, the options often expensive. Fashion is no justification for using a medium. The teacher or developer should match the medium to the learning task, taking into account cognitive emphasis, learner situation and background, and the availability of the medium. ICT does not solve all the problems, but it does add to the 'toolbox' from which wise choices can be made.

Issues outstanding

In the spirit of critical analysis, there should be an opportunity to consider where the future could take us and how we should be led. While a number of specific issues have been raised above, a few general ones underlie them all, such as:

- Should technology drive learning styles? There is the danger of technology driving learning needs instead of *vice versa* and the present initiatives are seen as a panacea. But as Hawkridge (1995) notes, 'academic objectives must be seen to lead rather than follow the technology'.
- Competency-based skills versus breadth and diversity: is there a conflict?
- How can what we have learnt from distance learning be applied to support more traditional classroom teaching, and even the generation of hybrids?
- What might be the impact of 'study guides' on the writing of textbooks? Could they have an influence on the writing of textbooks?
- Jarvis's 'charismatic teacher' must have writing skills that reflect this trait.

The future of distance learning is bright: not only will the resources available probably increase in diversity, but in availability. On the other hand, the potential for distance learning to influence more traditional classroom practices is there as well.

References

Bloom, B S (ed) (1956) *Taxonomy of Educational Objectives: The classification of educational goals. Handbook 1: The cognitive domain,* McKay, New York

Cm 3790 (1998) *The Learning Age: A renaissance for a new Britain,* The Stationery Office, Norwich

Cm 4392 (1999) *Learning to Succeed: A new framework for post-16 learning,* The Stationery Office, Norwich

Dimitropoulos, A (2000) *International Educational Research in the 1990s: A survey,* Office of Official Publications of the European Communities, Luxembourg

Gagné, R M (1985) *The Conditions of Learning and Theory of Instruction,* Holt, Rinehart and Winston, New York

Gagné, R M, Briggs, L J and Wager, W W (1992) *Principles of Instructional Design,* 4th edn, Harcourt Brace Jovanovich, Fort Worth, TX

Goldberg, C (2001) No net profit: MIT courses are going online (free!), *International Herald Tribune,* 5 April, pp 1, 6

Harrison, J F C (1961) *Learning and Living 1790–1960,* Routledge & Kegan Paul, London

Hawkridge, D (1995) The big bang theory in distance education, in *Open and Distance Learning Today,* ed F Lockwood, Routledge, London

Henri, F and Kay, A (1994) Problems of distance education, in *Distance Education: New perspectives,* eds K Harry, D Keegan and M John, Routledge, London

Jarvis, P (2001) The changing educational scene, in *The Age of Learning: Education and the knowledge society,* ed P Jarvis, Kogan Page, London

Koul, B N (1995) Trends, directions and needs: a view from developing countries, in *Open and Distance Learning Today,* ed F Lockwood, Routledge, London

Middlehurst, R (2001) University challenges: borderless higher education, today and tomorrow, *Minerva,* **39,** pp 3–26

Moore, M G (1994) Three types of interaction, in *Distance Education: New perspectives,* eds K Harry, D Keegan and M John, Routledge, London

National Advisory Group on Continuing Education and Lifelong Learning (NAGCELL) (1997) *Learning for the Twenty-First Century,* first report of the National Advisory Group, Chair: Professor R H Fryer, NAGCELL

Perraton, H (1995) A practical agenda for theorists of distance education, *Open and Distance Learning Today,* in ed F Lockwood, Routledge, London

Perry, W (1976) *Open University,* Open University Press, Buckingham

Southern, R W (1953) *The Making of the Middle Ages,* Hutchinson, London

Chapter 17

Further developments in teaching

Peter Jarvis

The traditional image of the practice of teaching as 'chalk and talk' has long been destroyed. If distance education has done nothing else, it has demonstrated to a wider public new ways of teaching. This book has also shown that even the old ways are undergoing tremendous change and, in a sense, rediscovering some of the techniques used in adult education for many years. The changing nature of teaching reflects the changing nature of society itself. For instance, there is a sense in which distance education began with letter writing but now, through the wonders of technology, the Internet provides instant communication to masses of people worldwide. Even in face-to-face teaching there were wandering scholars, individual students travelling to the seats of learning, and then the generation of the 'knowledge factory' with hundreds of students all assembled in one place to receive the pearls of wisdom that would drop from the lips of one scholar. Now they do not need to travel. But even more so, as the learners are often older and more experienced, they are participants in the teaching and learning process. Teaching has not dropped the old in the face of the new, it has merely incorporated the new into the old, and adapted to all the changes that are occurring. There are now a multitude of ways by which teaching is performed. It will continue to change in the future and we will briefly examine a few of the ways that teaching is changing and might continue to do so. We will do this in four sections:

- the continuing division of labour in teaching;
- the changing nature of what is taught;
- the changing nature of the learners;
- the preparation of teachers.

The continuing division of labour in teaching

Society has seen many forms of division of labour since Durkheim (1893;1933 edition) first wrote his classic study on the subject. Teaching has also seen a division of labour, for traditionally a single teacher taught a course. However, in recent years a variety of different approaches to team teaching have occurred for a variety of reasons, including:

- the recognition that a great deal of teaching is about practice, which is not divided by academic disciplines, and practical knowledge is integrated. Hence it needs different subject specialists to combine to produce a practical course, including practice-based teachers;
- the fact that academic courses are being modularized – in a sense this is a Taylor-type means of production, with specialists concentrating on their own specialisms in the production of a course;
- the growing emphasis on modularization, since it is also a useful approach to marketing with small pieces of a course being marketed for lower cost, and so on;
- the need to update material very rapidly in a world where knowledge is changing very fast indeed;
- the growing complexity of knowledge production, especially in such approaches as distance education – where there are not only subject experts but also process and production experts;
- the increasing need for practice-based teachers, such as coaches and mentors.

In common with many production processes, teaching is become a team activity – groups rather than individuals prepare the teaching material. Once this process begins, it is possible to envisage its expansion so that the production is not only by members of one institution of teaching and learning. Programmes will be prepared by teams spanning different educational institutions, and even from different countries, each using the expertise of members of these departments. Now students might not know who their teachers actually are since one has prepared and another has delivered the learning material. The traditional teacher-student relationship is disappearing and with it the interpersonal ethic (Jarvis, 1997). Now students are clients purchasing a quality product.

However, this impersonality has given rise to other roles in teaching: the personal tutor, the academic counsellor and the adviser. If one wanted to be cynical and pursue the metaphor to its logical conclusion – this is becoming customer services. A major significance of the personal tutor role is that students still have a sense of continuity throughout a whole programme and there is still somebody who knows them. Nevertheless, the economics of teaching are such that there are fewer personal tutors as a counselling and guidance role becomes a specialist occupation in its own right. This role is less personal than that of the personal tutor since counsellors are not so closely associated with individual students and advise more students from a variety of different disciplines. American universities have for a long while now employed academic advisers.

However, in contrast to this division of labour in teaching, another approach is also possible: one well-known academic – a guru – can put together a single course for an academic institution and it can be marketed throughout the world, thereby putting at risk the jobs of many not quite so well-known subject specialists. If global capitalism continues to invade education, this will begin to occur. Already some commercial companies are employing well-known academics to produce lecture series that they can transmit over the Internet. 'Star models' of teaching have already been considered and not rejected by educational institutions and consortia. Indeed, we can expect to see teaching develop in the same way as other manufacturing industries, as Peters (1984) has already shown for distance education.

Traditionally in universities, academic specialization was related to subjects being researched and taught by the same scholar but, as we pointed out in the opening chapter, there is a growing division between research, which is the discovery, and teaching, which is the production and marketing of knowledge about these new discoveries. However, many of the discoveries are now no longer made in the traditional seats of learning, so the material taught does not necessarily contain any that has been discovered by the teacher, or in fact by any teacher, since, as Lyotard (1984) showed, knowledge is now often produced commercially, is of commercial worth and used in a knowledge economy.

The changing nature of what is taught

Teaching used to be concerned with disseminating knowledge that was regarded as the truth. Truth, however, is a difficult phenomenon to envisage when knowledge changes daily and what was up-to-date one day becomes obsolete the next. Knowledge in many areas does change almost daily, which means that the 'shelf-life' of many courses is very short indeed. Consequently, if teaching material is to be regularly updated, it can only be produced in small pieces that allow for the substitution of new knowledge in a course between each time it is taught. Teachers, therefore, become more removed from the source of the knowledge as they seek to incorporate findings from diverse sources into their courses.

Knowledge is not necessarily truth. It is personal and subjective, as constructivism has shown us. Indeed, there may be competing interpretations of a single phenomenon and now teaching may assume a role of offering interpretations and evaluations of these competing perspectives (Bauman, 1987). This means that students have to be taught to understand that teachers no longer teach the truth and that they, the learners, have to be critically aware of what is occurring. Indeed, learners do have to be taught to learn in a critical and analytical manner (Barry and Rudinow, 1990). Consequently, the status of teaching is changing since it no longer legislates on what is true. Consequently, despite its high reputation in the past, even Dearing (1997) can suggest that university teaching needs to professionalize.

It is now widely recognized that a great deal of what is taken-for-granted knowledge is actually discourse (Foucault, 1972) and that the more powerful the propagators of the discourse, the more likely it will be taken as true. Curriculum specialists have always recognized this in as much as they have written about the 'hidden curriculum'. Hence, the interpretative nature of teaching must also assume a critical function, helping students to deconstruct the interpretations and the taken-for-granted and reach decisions for themselves. However, this creates its own problems with many teachers of adults since, if they work within a commercial enterprise, they may be required to assist employees acquire a company culture and learn company knowledge (Meister, 1998). We are becoming increasing aware that the discourses of corporate capitalism relate far more to company interest than to truth, as Monbiot (2000) has clearly demonstrated. Teachers in such organizations may be refrained from teaching 'truth' and be required to teach company policy. The ethical nature of teaching is thus reinforced in the knowledge economy, especially as students are of all ages and from all walks of life, bringing varying levels of experience with them to the teaching and learning situation.

The changing nature of the learners

Adult educators have always endeavoured to recognize the differences and the experiences of their students. In continental Europe, andragogics has always been separated from pedagogics, although in the USA Knowles (1980) used the term 'andragogy' in a different way from continental Europe. For him, it was about responding to the experiences of older learners and the new teaching and learning techniques this demanded. Knowles' formulation has subsequently shown to be flawed in a number of ways (Hartree, 1984, *inter alia*) but the substance of what he expressed – the different approaches to teaching that experienced learners require – is standing the test of time. But then this was not a new discovery when he popularized the term 'andragogy'. Increasingly, education is becoming a lifelong process and so Knowles' argument, which was specifically about adult education, remains significant, as various chapters in this book have illustrated.

Learners do come to education with a great deal of knowledge and expertise. They should not be treated as empty containers to be filled, what Freire (1972) called 'banking education'. Education should now both seek to use the learners' expertise and build on their knowledge, which can be done through a variety of teaching techniques, including a mutual sharing of expertise amongst the learners (and the teachers) – hence the development of peer learning communities. At the same time, there is new knowledge and there are new interpretations to learn, which calls for a skilled use of the different styles and methods of teaching. Lifelong education not only makes this demand, it is also a basis for generating new teaching and learning methods. Consequently, all the methods in face-to-face teaching are not exhausted by those contained in this book. There are others and there will be even more new ones in the future. Clearly this calls for some form of teacher preparation, as Dearing (1997) suggested, but the approach in that Report was narrow and, perhaps, slightly uninformed.

The preparation of teachers

Until about the 1960s school teachers were the only teachers who were expected to receive formal training before they could enter the teaching profession: those in all forms of post-compulsory education did not need to be trained. However, in the latter part of the 20th century a concern for professional preparation among teachers of adults emerged. In the UK, Eldson (1975, 1984) was amongst the foremost agitators for the introduction of such training. The Haycocks Committee (Haycocks, 1975, 1978, 1980) reported between 1975 and 1980, recommending that there should be a phased part-time training programme for adult and further education teaching. Significantly, the Committee also recommended training in management skills – something that will also occur in higher education, as universities and colleges are becoming increasingly run like corporations. Early in the 1980s the Department of Adult Education at the University of Surrey introduced a postgraduate certificate in the education of adults, which was immediately seized upon by nursing as a qualification for nurse educators. At that time nursing was the only occupation, apart from school teaching, that insisted on professional preparation before teaching.

At the same time, professional preparation was an issue for educators of adults throughout Europe, as Jarvis and Chadwick (1991) showed. As the years have passed many courses in this professional preparation have emerged, but now the field of practice has also developed into a field of study: there are a multitude of Masters degrees and a considerable amount of doctoral research on the topic. Much of this is actually occurring in institutions of higher education.

Now Dearing (1997) is asking the same of post-compulsory education – this is not surprising considering the complexity of the teaching and learning process. Some might marvel at the lateness of this demand, while others might wonder why it has occurred at all. Nevertheless, its emphasis is to be welcomed, even if its understanding of the complexities of teaching was a little limited and the emphasis on professionalization misplaced. Surprisingly, universities have been slow to utilize the expertise that their departments of adult and continuing education have acquired, probably because these departments always occupied a marginal position in the academic hierarchy of universities. At the same time it will almost certainly foster the growth of professional preparation of teachers in higher education, which will no doubt lead to more accredited courses emerging, including higher degrees, and the amount of doctoral research will no doubt grow. Paradoxically this further separates teaching from research since the teachers are expected to become increasingly aware of the process while the content may almost certainly be the research of others. Education is a process subject and its emphasis is on the knowledge of the process; it is a form of practical knowledge. Indeed, this is another indication of the division of labour in academia and the generation of new specialisms. Now the specialism is the process of teaching and performativity, as Lyotard (1984) argued, is a major basis for the legitimation of knowledge in this postmodern world. In this case, it may be claimed, this emphasis on the teaching process is a sign of the times, or a product of the learning society, and the university teacher becomes separated from the university researcher.

Other professional groups have agonized over the extent to which professional preparation and continuing education should be compulsory. In the early days of professionalization, the licence to practise was only granted after professional preparation and then the debate shifted to whether practitioners should be allowed to continue to practise without continuing education. Houle (1980) records some of this debate in the professions in the United States, but it reflects a similar debate in the UK. Dearing also suggests that continuing education might be introduced for educators in higher education. Naturally, this emphasis on teaching in higher and further education is to be welcomed, but the extent to which it separates teaching from research is to be questioned. Research institutes are already separated from teaching and this will no doubt continue, and so the debate about teaching and research universities might well be resurrected.

Conclusion

This book has endeavoured to examine both the theory and practice of teaching and it implicitly recognizes that practice might well lead theory in teaching innovation. Naturally, debates about the efficiency, the philosophy and the moral issues in teaching will continue. While our emphasis has been on post-compulsory education, many of the points raised are relevant to compulsory education as well. The practice of teaching has changed and has become more complex, so teachers need to be trained for the complexities of their occupation, especially in the learning society.

References

Barry, V and Rudinow, J (1990) *Invitation to Critical Thinking,* 2nd edn, Holt, Rinehart and Winston, Forth Worth, TX

Bauman, Z (1987) *Legislators to Interpreters,* Polity, Cambridge

Dearing, R (Chair) (1997) *Higher Education in the Learning Society,* Department for Education and Employment, London

Durkheim, E (1933) *The Division of Labour in Society,* The Free Press, New York

Eldson, K (1975) *Training for Adult Education,* Department of Adult Education, University of Nottingham in association with the National Institute of Adult Education, Nottingham

Eldson, K (1984) *The Training of Trainers,* Huntington Publishers in association with Department of Adult Education, University of Nottingham

Foucault, M (1972) *Archaeology of Knowledge,* Routledge, London

Freire, P (1972) *Pedagogy of the Oppressed,* Penguin, Harmondsworth

Hartree, A (1984) Malcolm Knowles' theory of andragogy: a critique, *International Journal of Lifelong Education,* **3** (3), pp 203–10

Haycocks, J (Chair) (1975) *The Training of Teachers for Further Education,* Advisory Council for the Supply and Training of Teachers, London

Haycocks, J (Chair) (1978) *The Training of Adult Education and Part-time Further Education Teachers,* Advisory Council for the Supply and Training of Teachers, London

Haycocks J, (Chair) (1980) *Training Teachers in Education Management in Further and Adult Education,* Advisory Council for the Supply and Training of Teachers, London

Houle, C O (1980) *Continuing Learning in the Professions,* Jossey-Bass, San Francisco, CA

Jarvis, P (1997) *Ethics and the Education of Adults in Late Modern Society,* National Institute for Adult Continuing Education, Leicester

Jarvis, P and Chadwick, A (eds) (1991) *Training Adult Educators in Western Europe,* Routledge, London

Knowles, M (1980) *The Modern Practice of Adult Education,* 2nd edn, Academic Press, Chicago, IL

Lyotard, J-F (1984) *The Postmodern Condition,* University of Manchester Press, Manchester

Meister, J (1998) *Corporate Universities,* revised and updated edition, McGraw-Hill, New York

Monbiot, G (2000) *Captive State: The corporate takeover of Britain,* Macmillan, London

Peters, O (1984) Distance teaching and industrial production: a comparative interpretation in outline, in *Distance Education – International perspectives,* D Sewart, D Keegan and G Holmberg, Routledge, London

Index